THEATRE AND THE STATE IN TWENTIETH-CENTURY IRELAND

This major new study presents a political and cultural history of some of Ireland's key national theatre projects from the 1890s to the 1990s. Impressively wide-ranging in coverage, *Theatre and the State in Twentieth-Century Ireland: Cultivating the People* includes discussions on:

- the politics of the Irish literary movement at the Abbey Theatre before and after political independence;
- the role of a state-sponsored theatre for the post-1922 unionist government in Northern Ireland;
- the convulsive effects of the Northern Ireland conflict on Irish theatre.

Lionel Pilkington draws on a combination of archival research and critical readings of individual plays, covering works by J. M. Synge, Sean O'Casey, Lennox Robinson, T. C. Murray, George Shiels, Brian Friel, and Frank McGuinness. In its insistence on the details of history, this is a book important to anyone interested in Irish culture and politics in the twentieth century.

Lionel Pilkington teaches drama and theatre studies, Irish writing and cultural politics in the Department of English at the National University of Ireland, Galway.

THEATRE AND THE STATE IN TWENTIETH-CENTURY IRELAND

Cultivating the People

Lionel Pilkington

London and New York

First published 2001
by Routledge
11 New Fetter Lane, London EC4P 4EE

Simultaneously published in the USA and Canada
by Routledge
29 West 35th Street, New York, NY 10001

Routledge is an imprint of the Taylor & Francis Group

© 2001 Lionel Pilkington

Typeset in Garamond by Steven Gardiner Ltd
Printed and bound in Great Britain by TJ International, Padstow, Cornwall

British Library Cataloguing in Publication Data
A catalogue record for this book is available from the British Library

Library of Congress Cataloging in Publication Data
Pilkington, Lionel, 1956–
Theatre and the state in twentieth-century Ireland: cultivating the people /
Lionel Pilkington.
p.   cm.
Includes bibliographical references and index.
1. Theater – Political Aspects – Ireland – History – 20th century.
2. Irish drama – 20th century – History and criticism.
3. Unionism (Irish politics). I. Title.
PN2601.P55 2001
792'.09417'0904 – dc21
2001019647

ISBN 0–415–06938–6 (hbk)
ISBN 0–415–06939–4 (pbk)

This publication was grant-aided by the
Publications Fund of **National University of Ireland, Galway**.

FOR ELIZABETH AND COLIN

CONTENTS

ACKNOWLEDGEMENTS

It is a pleasure to acknowledge the many debts incurred in the course of writing and researching this book. By far the greatest of these – for solidarity, support and daily sustaining happiness – is due to my wife Elizabeth and to our son Colin. This book is for Elizabeth and Colin, without whom it could not have been written.

Barra Ó Seaghdha and Gearóid Ó Tuathaigh devoted much time (and, I suspect, even more patience) to the reading of an entire early version of the book. Both have been unfailingly generous in providing helpful support and advice over a long period. More recently, I am indebted to my colleague Adrian Frazier and to my dear friend Patricia Palmer. In both cases, their detailed readings of individual chapters have been perceptive and very helpful.

I would like to thank a great many archivists and librarians for their courtesy and professionalism during my research. My thanks, in particular, to Marie Boran, Bernie Finan, Kieran Hoare, Pauline Nic Chonaonaigh, Marie Reddan, and to all the staff of the James Hardiman Library at NUI, Galway; to Mairead Delaney of the Abbey Theatre; to Robert Bell, Ophelia Byrne and Yvonne Murphy of the Linenhall Library, Belfast, to Caitriona Crowe and Tom Quinlan of the National Archives, Dublin; to Elizabeth Kirwan and Colette O'Daly of the National Library of Ireland; to David Sheehy of the Dublin Diocesan Archives in Drumcondra, Dublin; to Jane Maxwell of the Manuscripts Room, Trinity College, Dublin; to David Lammey, Trevor Parkhill and Oonagh Warke of the Public Record Office of Northern Ireland (PRONI); to Séamus Helferty of the Archives Department, University College Dublin; to Helen Davis of the Special Collections Department at University College Cork; to Bríd Loan of the Northern Ireland Arts Council in Belfast; to Kate Targett of the Plunkett Foundation in Long Hanborough, Oxford; to David and Loretto Koch of the Morris Library, Southern Illinois University at Carbondale, Illinois; to the librarians of the Berg Collection at the New York Public Library. In addition, I am especially grateful to Mary and Pearse O'Malley, and to their son Conor, for hospitality, information and many days of excellent conversation in Booterstown.

I am also grateful to the following individuals for their generous and varied assistance: Dan Baron Cohen, Kevin Barry, Kathleen Burke, Caitriona Clear, Mary Clark, Síle de Cléir, John Devitt, Roger Dixon, Tony Doherty, Ann Dooley, Angela Eborall, James Ellis, Charles Fanning, Peter V. Farrelly, Brian Ferran, Garrett FitzGerald, Tadhg Foley, Roy Foster, Andrew Gailey, Luke Gibbons, John Gray, Barbara Harlow, Mary Harris, Seán Kennedy, John Killen, Su-ming Khoo, Padraic Lenihan, David Lloyd, Eoghan MacCormaic, Mícheál MacCraith, Hubert McDermott, Kathryn Mullen, Caoilfhionn Ní Bheacháin, Margaret O'Callaghan, Niall Ó Cíosáin, Niall Ó Dochartaigh, Philip O'Leary, Tom O'Malley, Christopher Morash, Catherine Morris, Tom Moylan, Ray Murphy, Trevor Parkhill, James Pethica, Michael Sidnell, Elizabeth Solterer, Seán Ryder, Elizabeth Tilley, Roma Tomelty, Karen Vandevelde, Tony Varley, Gauri Viswanathan, Oonagh Warke and Des Wilson.

Parts of Chapter 2 are adapted from 'Every Crossing Sweeper Thinks Himself a Moralist: the Critical Role of Audiences in Irish Theatrical History; in *Irish University Review* 27(1) (1997) 152–65, parts of Chapter 7 are adapted from 'Theatre and Cultural Politics in Northern Ireland: the *Over the Bridge* Controversy, 1959' in *Éire-Ireland* 30(4) (1996) 76–93 and parts of Chapter 8 are adapted from 'Language and Politics in Brian Friel's *Translations*' in *Irish University Review* 20(2) (1990) 282–96. I am grateful to Christopher Murray of the *Irish University Review* and to Philip O'Leary of *Éire-Ireland* for permission to republish.

I wish to record my gratitude to the Arts Council of Northern Ireland and to its former Chief Executive, Mr Brian Ferran, for permission to quote from ACNI documents and to the Deputy Keeper of the Records of the Public Record Office of Northern Ireland for permission to cite from selected PRONI files. I am grateful to the Trustees of the National Library of Ireland for permission to reproduce for the book's front cover a copy of the 1931–2 Cumann na nGaedheal election poster, 'The Shadow of the Gunman'.

Finally, I would like to pay special tribute to Talia Rodgers of Routledge for commissioning this book in the first place, for soliciting such outstandingly helpful readers' reports, and for waiting – so very patiently – for the manuscript to arrive. To Talia, and to her assistant, Rosie Waters, my sincere thanks.

INTRODUCTION

This book examines the relationship between theatre and the state in twentieth-century Ireland before and after political independence. Its particular focus is the Irish literary theatre movement at the Abbey Theatre and, to a lesser extent, the history of theatre and national theatre initiatives for successive unionist governments in post-1922 Northern Ireland. This study is, therefore, a selective treatment of an extensive and complex topic. Much has been omitted from its ambit, including consideration of the state-supported Irish-language theatre, Taibhdhearc na Gaillimhe (1928–) and alternative national theatre projects such as Theatre of Ireland (1906–12) and the Ulster Literary Theatre (1904–15). Instead I concentrate on tracking in detail an evolving theatre history in relation to the politics of the British, Irish and Northern Irish states. This task was undertaken in the first place as an attempt to counteract the long-standing assumption that Irish theatre exists outside politics and apart altogether from the determining power of the state.

For Lady Gregory, as for the poet W. B. Yeats who frequently reiterated the same point, Ireland's principal national theatre movement was thought of as a sublimation of a failed nationalist politics into a higher and more liberating form of cultural energy. 'Parnell's death. That was the unloosing of forces, the disbanding of an army. In the quarrels that followed and the breaking of hopes, the imagination of Ireland had been set free, and it looked for a homing place' (Gregory 1912: 189). Here the death of the nationalist leader Charles Stewart Parnell in 1891 and the subsequent splits in the Irish Parliamentary Party in the 1890s constitute the vital catalyst for theatrical regeneration in Ireland. It is this late nineteenth-century 'unloosing of forces', 'disbanding of an army' and 'breaking of hopes' that releases the Irish imagination from political servitude and propels it forward to its ultimate 'homing place': Dublin's Abbey

1

Theatre, formally established as the Irish National Theatre Society in December 1904. For Gregory and Yeats (and many later theatre historians and critics) the Abbey Theatre is seen as a haven for Ireland's longed-for modernity: a place in which the impromptu dramas of political militancy are now transformed, felicitously, into a theatre of national citizenship.

Lady Gregory's account emphasizes the collapse of an Irish nationalist politics, but there is silence concerning any other kind. There is no mention, for example, of two other major political events that also contributed to the breaking of nationalist hopes in the 1890s: the overwhelming rejection by the House of Lords of the second Home Rule Bill in 1893, and the landslide victory of the Conservative and Unionist party in the general election of 1895. If the object of Gregory's essay is to suggest that an Irish national theatre sublimates nationalist militancy, the essay's own effect in relation to the role of the British state in Ireland, and to Irish unionist politics in particular, is remarkably similar. Both are wholly irrelevant, or at least so it would appear, to Irish theatre history. Gregory's formulation, elaborated at more length in her seminal *Our Irish Theatre* (1913a), still serves as the historiographical template: the Irish national theatre movement tends to be viewed as an essentially nationalist cultural initiative, and as belonging to a sphere relatively uninfluenced by the politics of the British or Irish states.

Theatre and the State in Twentieth-Century Ireland: Cultivating the People sets out to challenge both of these assumptions. I argue that the Irish Literary Theatre (1899–1902), the Irish National Dramatic Society (1902–4), the Irish National Theatre Society (1904–6) and the National Theatre Society, Limited (1906–) owe as much, if not more, to the imaginative energies associated with 'constructive' unionism as they do to those energies associated with the struggle for Irish political independence. Conservative and ameliorative in its objectives, constructive unionism engaged with the increasing prospect of some form of Irish home rule through a range of legislative reforms and conciliatory social measures. It was a political phenomenon chiefly associated with southern Irish politicians and intellectuals such as Sir Horace Plunkett, W. E. H. Lecky, and the Earl of Dunraven, and with the British Chief Secretaryships of Gerald Balfour (1895–1900) and George Wyndham (1900–5). Although it suffered a serious upset in 1904 when a mooted scheme for limited political devolution outraged more traditional unionists (and led to the collapse of the Wyndham administration), it remained for over a decade the favoured British government approach to 'the Irish problem'. Arguably, however, constructive unionism was designed not so much to undermine the threat posed by home rule (the so-called policy of 'killing home rule by kindness'), but to defeat the threat of socialism and agrarian insurgency. In this respect it was spectacularly successful. Plunkett's agricultural co-operative movement, Arthur Balfour's Congested Districts Board (1890), Gerald Balfour's Local Government Act (1898), George Wyndham's Land Act (1903), and even Dunraven's (failed) attempt to secure devolution helped to put into place much of the administrative and legislative basis for independent Ireland. In the words of historian Andrew Gailey, constructive unionism helped to establish 'a fiercely parochial and conservative society which would have little interest in social revolution' (Gailey 1987: 314). In the same way, it also contributed to the relatively smooth transition from British rule to the political independence of the Irish Free State.

Ireland's celebrated national theatre movement owes more to this (albeit maverick) Irish unionist tradition, than it does to any of the wide variety of political nationalisms represented by Arthur Griffith, Patrick Pearse, John Redmond, Michael Collins or Eamon de Valera. As a specifically literary movement, what emerged as the National Theatre Society, Limited (the word 'Irish' was dropped in 1906 and never reinstated) set out to establish a cultural arena free of party politics. It would be a 'Celtic or Irish school of dramatic literature', claimed the Irish Literary Theatre's 1897 statement, 'a work that is outside all the political questions that divide us' (quoted in Yeats 1997: 124). But, in the context of the struggle for Irish political independence, the literary philosophy of the Irish Literary Theatre and the National Theatre Society was itself profoundly political. Some nationalist intellectuals (such as Thomas Kettle and Arthur Griffith) felt that a national theatre should serve as a forum for the expression of the views of the majority, at least until the ending of British rule in Ireland. But not so Yeats and Gregory. For them, a national theatre was not a forum for the expression of majority orthodoxies, but rather a means to critique dominant, widely held opinions from a critically sceptical perspective. In this, Gregory and Yeats were, of course, articulating the core element of a commonly accepted literary aesthetic. What may be less obvious, however, is that they were also expressing a distinctive cultural response to Ireland's envisaged political future, a response that has its roots in *fin de siècle* southern Irish unionism. As writers closely associated with a once-Ascendancy élite, and within the context of the virtual certainty of some form of home rule or at least limited devolution, the idea of a nationally accepted aesthetic based on the critical importance of a minority perspective constituted an important reassurance. To this extent, the defiantly literary impulse of Ireland's early national theatre movement arises, at least in part, from a desire to anticipate and moderate the traumatic prospects of majority rule.

That this southern unionist contribution to the beginnings of the Irish literary theatre movement has received little scholarly attention is due less to nationalist intolerance than to a more extensive critical reluctance to concede the politically conservative and class-based character of Irish cultural institutions. Indeed, the most striking feature that emerges from a detailed history of Ireland's national theatre movement at the Abbey Theatre is the continuity that exists between its function under British rule – asserting the existence of an Irish public sphere while simultaneously criticizing nationalist militancy – and its role as a state-subsidized national institution, articulating national consensus and yet engaging in frequent scabrous critiques of republican militancy. Criticizing majority orthodoxies may well have been the credo of the Abbey Theatre in its early years, but such critical abrasiveness is only rarely in evidence in the decades after independence. From the 1920s, the aesthetic agenda of the National Theatre Society tends to be dominated instead by a newly invigorated thematics of modernization: in particular, the idea that a national theatre institution has an important role in educating its nation's citizenry by consolidating and extending the authority of the state. Political elements deemed recalcitrant to that authority, such as the legacies of anti-colonial militancy, are portrayed either as dangerously recidivist or as urgently requiring reassessment and revision. The Abbey Theatre's overt support for the post-independence Irish state, as evident, for example, in plays such as Sean O'Casey's *The Shadow of a Gunman* (1923) and *Juno and the Paycock* (1924), may well have prompted the then Cumann na nGaedheal government to award the National Theatre Society an annual subsidy in 1925. Theatre-going and political militancy were regularly presented as naturally opposed, the former as evidence of a mature civility and the latter as pre-modern and intemperate. In this context, maintaining the stability of the Irish state and supporting the national prestige of the Abbey Theatre were also about protecting Ireland from a menacing 'shadow of a gunman'.

And yet, despite the undoubtedly strong *parti-pris* element to the Abbey Theatre repertoire (and the failed attempt to establish a 'national' theatre in Northern Ireland), the actual productions that occurred are frequently surprising and sometimes disturbing and controversial. Accelerated modernization has indeed remained the dominant cultural objective in twentieth-century Ireland, but it is also a notoriously wayward and contradictory project. Politics and cultural practice never fully coincide and in the theatre, where there always exists a particularly volatile tension between the tendentious urges of the state and the libidinous physicality of performance, this is especially the case. To this extent, Irish theatre history offers a fascinating understanding of the country's complex political and cultural life.

1

HOME RULE AND THE IRISH LITERARY THEATRE, 1893–1902

> I believe that in about a year or perhaps two years we will find that Irish Unionists will begin to read Irish things greedily. . . . It is very curious how the dying out of party fealing [sic] has nationalized the more thoughtful Unionists. Parnellism has greatly help[ed] also, & the expectation of Balfours threatened emmense [sic] local Government scheme.
>
> (W. B. Yeats to Katherine Tynan Hinkson,
> 25 March 1895; Yeats 1986: 455)

Among the May 1899 inaugural performances of the Irish Literary Theatre was a scene from W. B. Yeats's *The Countess Cathleen* that involved the breaking of a statue of the Virgin Mary by a starving Irish peasant.[1] It was a strange start to a complicated history. Two months before, Irish Roman Catholics (then 84 per cent of Dublin's population (O'Brien 1982: 282–3)) had experienced a major setback when unionist pressure forced the British government to abandon its plans to establish a separate Catholic university (Gailey 1987: 125–31). For Ireland's middle-class Catholic élite (precisely those who strongly supported the notion of a national theatre) the absence of a separate university related directly to their lack of higher educational opportunities and their consequent disadvantage, relative to Irish Protestants, in terms of entry to the professions (Morrissey 1983: 168–70; Gailey 1987: 130–1; Paseta 1999: 5–16). And yet, apart from a small group of students from the Royal University, the Catholic Primate, Cardinal Logue, and a well-known polemicist, Frank 'Crank' Hugh O'Donnell, Yeats's play did not provoke any serious public objection. Those protests that were made were isolated and unsupported – derided not only, and most famously, by James Joyce in his essay 'The Day of the Rabblement' –

but by the well-known nationalist advocate and later founder of Sinn Féin, Arthur Griffith.

And yet from a nationalist point of view the beginning of the Irish Literary Theatre was hardly promising. The amended sub-clause of the Local Government Act, under which the Irish Literary Theatre had been established, emphasized the Irish Literary Theatre's indebtedness to the British Lord-Lieutenant. The opening programme published in *Beltaine* gave prominent feature to the theatre's high proportion of titled guarantors, and the acting troupe employed for the theatre's first performances was brought directly from London. Moreover, the first performance of Yeats's *The Countess Cathleen* (billed along with Edward Martyn's *The Heather Field* as the theatre's opening production) took place not, strictly speaking, for the Irish Literary Theatre at all, but five months earlier, as a kind of command performance for a select group from the upper echelons of Ireland's British administration. Produced by Lady Betty Balfour, wife of the Chief Secretary, *The Countess Cathleen* was first presented as a series of fashionable *tableaux vivants* in January 1899 at the Chief Secretary's Lodge in the Phoenix Park.[2] While Yeats made it clear that he could not possibly participate in or attend the Phoenix Park performance because doing so would compromise him politically (Yeats 1972: 117–18), he was careful nonetheless to facilitate and assist Lady Balfour's production in whatever way he could (Yeats 1997: 326–7). Like the enthusiasm of Lady Cadogan (wife of the Lord-Lieutenant) for the Irish Literary Society, Lady Balfour's interest in Yeats's play and the author's reciprocal co-operation with her production briefly foregrounds the extent to which the Irish literary theatre movement of the late 1890s was intellectually, culturally and socially aligned not so much to Irish nationalism, but to the British administration in Ireland and its policies of reform and conciliation. That the première of *The Countess Cathleen* – a play that Yeats described as 'in all things Celtic and Irish' (Yeats 1997: 165) – took place as a *tableau vivant* at the home of Britain's chief administrator in Ireland was not an oddity, therefore, but the playing out of an important alliance between the 'constructive' section of landlord interests in Ireland and a British administration enthusiastically pursuing a policy of Irish national development. Had the Unionist MP and Trinity College historian, W. E. H. Lecky, accepted Edward Martyn's invitation to appear on stage at the May 1899 inauguration of the Irish Literary Theatre (Yeats 1997: 403) then this link between constructive unionism and the literary theatre movement would have been even more conspicuous. Indeed,

Yeats's and Gregory's problem was not so much finding sufficient aristocratic and influential patronage so as to ensure that the Irish Literary Theatre would be financially, legally and socially viable, but rather making sure that such support could be kept reasonably discreet.[3]

Nevertheless, the opening of the Irish Literary Theatre on 8 May 1899 received extensive nationalist support. Newspaper editorials and reviews in the *Irish Daily Independent* (9 May 1899: 6), the *Freeman's Journal* (9 May 1899: 5) and the *United Irishman* (13 May 1899: 2) offer varying degrees of enthusiastic endorsement. In the case of Arthur Griffith's *United Irishman*, this is especially notable. As a weekly national review commenting on political, economic, cultural and literary affairs, the *United Irishman* was forthright in attacking what it termed the 'Union of Hearts dung heap' of conciliatory unionism (*United Irishman*, 26 March 1899: 2), and the 'pseudo nationality' of 'an Irish cult in art and literature' (*United Irishman*, 4 March 1899: 2). Despite such criticisms, however, the *United Irishman* supported the Irish Literary Theatre initiative and Yeats's and Gregory's idea that a national theatre should be educational, literary and subsidized. In a weekly newspaper that sparkles with polemical remarks and sometimes hair-splitting critiques of compromised nationalism, Griffith's only reservation about the Irish Literary Theatre is that a national theatre should be popular, and that Yeats's penchant for mysticism and Celticism ('mystery-mongering or speculative philosophy' (*United Irishman*, 8 April 1899: 1)) is esoteric. Its main criticism is reserved for the harmful effects of English commercial theatre on Irish life (whether in the form of feminist-oriented 'problem plays', sensationalist melodrama or music hall) which, the paper claimed, had made 'the task of revolutionising taste in matters dramatic . . . stupendous' (*United Irishman*, 6 May 1899: 1). An urgent need had arisen for 'a healthy national drama [that] would educate the people far quicker, far easier, and more permanently than any number of histories or lectures' (*United Irishman*, 11 March 1899: 1). But alongside the *United Irishman*'s robust opposition to Celticist opportunism and Balfourian 'kindness', Griffith's support for the Irish Literary Theatre as an idealistic contrast to philistine English commercialism appears oddly naïve. His enthusiasm for an Irish theatre as a prestigious, literary institution simply overrides any political criticism of the manifestly unrepresentative class origins and political alignments of its initiators. What, then, are the reasons for the relatively muted protests against Yeats's *The Countess Cathleen* and for the extensive nationalist support for the Irish Literary Theatre?

Part of the answer lies in the complex attractions of a prestigious national theatre for a country without statehood. In a period in which the lack of a nationally responsive state power dominated the political debate, unionists and nationalists alike looked to an Irish or Celtic theatre as proof that Ireland ought no longer to be thought of as a colony. As well as combating the colonial slur of the stage Irishman, its existence as a social and cultural institution was seen as a demonstration that Dublin was no colonial or provincial outpost, but a civilized, European metropolis. Along with other existing or planned national institutions, such as the newly expanded National Library of Ireland (1890), an indigenous theatre institution would reveal that which the Act of Union of 1800 had set out so cruelly to deny: Ireland's independent public sphere and civilized national character. By proclaiming both, an Irish national theatre would underline the conspicuous and therefore quite unjustifiable absence of a more devolved Irish administration. Unionists and nationalists agreed that an Irish national theatre was a highly desirable sign of modernization.

This is not to say that nationalists and unionists concurred on the degree of political devolution that Ireland required, or on the strategies necessary for achieving it. But what they did agree, at least initially, was that a national theatre was a wholly beneficial sign of a desired political and social consensus. In the 1895 issues of the moderate nationalist monthly *New Ireland Review*, for example, several articles campaign for an Irish literary drama that would reject the 'battering ram effects' of melodrama, as in the work of popular dramatists like Dion Boucicault, J. W. Whitbread and Hubert O'Grady, and substitute in their place a less partisan approach to Irish history. William Barrett remonstrates that 'the real dramas' of Irish political instability have led to a dearth of an Irish literary or 'respectable' drama ('We have been living through real dramas and have no time for dramas of the imagination' (Barrett 1895: 40)), but hopes that the situation will soon change. A symposium on Irish drama in the August issue is equally forthright. Rejecting the notion that political conflict between landlords and peasants may be suitable material for an Irish national drama, and portraying nationalist patriotic melodramas as tending to the hackneyed and conventional, the symposium argues in favour of 'an elevated historical Irish drama . . . free from the narrow environments of a Land League struggle' (Barrett 1895: 106). Several years later, a series of articles in what was then Dublin's foremost unionist newspaper, the *Daily Express*, reiterate exactly the same point. A national drama may serve as a benchmark of nationality – 'a test of what nationality really amounts to in Ireland' (*Daily Express*, 10 September 1899: 3) – to the same extent that it rejects 'any plea of a narrow nationalism . . . the patriotism which looks back for the patriotism that looks forward' (*Daily Express*, 17 September 1898: 4).

Yeats's and Gregory's views on the setting up of the Irish Literary Theatre (1899–1901) were closely similar. While many of Yeats's early thoughts concerning the establishment of an Irish national drama are formulated as plans for a 'Celtic theatre' that could be based as easily in London as in Dublin, what is so noticeable in the case of Yeats's comments about an Irish theatre *in Ireland* is his emphasis on what he sees as its proselytizing, anti-separatist mission. And for Yeats, at least in this early period, the practice of literary theatre in Ireland was, inescapably, an act of quasi-Ascendancy philanthropy. It was, that is, a matter of promulgating literary values to an Irish *populus* whose cultural history appeared notoriously partisan and tendentious. Conceived initially as an adjunct to his National Library Scheme in 1892, Yeats's earliest ideas for an Irish theatre was for a travelling company that would bring theatre to outlying rural areas. To this end he had hoped to organize a tour of his play *The Countess Cathleen* as well as to write a history play dealing with the life and death of the Irish patriot Robert Emmet (Yeats 1955: 200). Gregory also maintained that her initial vision of an Irish theatre had been one of bringing historical plays 'through all the counties of Ireland' since, she reasoned, 'to have a real success and to come into the life of the country, one must touch a real and eternal emotion, and history comes only next to religion in our country' (Gregory 1913a: 91). For both writers, therefore, the assumption that literature and tendentiousness were opposites was crucial to their perception of the theatre's beneficial national effects. Yeats remarked later that the national literary theatre movement might never have existed at all had it not first been preceded by its decisive rejection of separatist nationalism.

> All the past had been turned into a melodrama with Ireland for blameless hero and poet; novelist and historian had but one object, that we should hiss the villain, and only a minority doubted that the greater the talent the greater the hiss. It was all the harder to substitute for that melodrama a nobler form of art, because there really had been, however

different in their form, villain and victim; yet fight that rancour I must, and if I had not made some head against it in 1892 and 1893 it might have silenced in 1907 John Synge, the greatest dramatic genius of Ireland.

(Yeats 1955: 205–6)

On this occasion, as in his other later published writings, Yeats attributes the beginning of the national theatre movement to a crucial shift in attitude in the years that followed the death of Parnell in 1891. But Yeats's contemporary letters and articles suggest that this change of attitude coincides far more exactly with the defeat of the second Home Rule Bill in 1893, and with the subsequent landslide Tory victory of 1895. For Yeats, this shift from a Liberal to a Conservative and Unionist administration in Dublin heralded a major cultural opportunity. In an optimistic letter to his friend Katherine Tynan in March 1895 (four months prior to the general election in July), Yeats remarks that Parnellism and 'the expectation of Balfours threatened emmense local Government scheme' [sic] has 'nationalised the more thoughtful Unionists' and that there would soon emerge an Irish unionist audience for Irish literary culture (Yeats 1986: 455). Seven months later, Yeats's review of John Todhunter's *The Life of Patrick Sarsfield* celebrates what he regards as a *fait accompli*: a 'transformation' in Irish historical attitude in which 'the mystery play of devils and angels we call our national history' is replaced by what he considers to be a more scholarly and critical approach (Yeats 1975: 388). That Yeats should refer to a separatist Irish history as a melodrama and a mystery play – both dramatic genres positioned low on the ladder of literary achievement – indicates the extent to which didacticism was seen as contaminating literary success. Such ideas were widely supported. Even for the Parnellite weekly, *United Ireland,* Yeats's view of an Irish national literature was exemplary. Yeats had rescued Irish poetry from 'the ruck of Young Ireland rhetoric', enthused a sub-editor [so as to] 'place it . . . on the floor of English and international literature' (quoted in Yeats 1997: 14).

There is, of course, nothing especially unusual about the perception of theatre and literary culture as a site of conciliation. In the late nineteenth century and early twentieth century, such ideas were normative (see Doyle 1986; Viswanathan 1987). But in Ireland in the mid-1890s conciliation had the added significance that it was both the new orthodoxy of British government policy in relation to Ireland and a key feature of southern Irish unionist strategy. One of its principal advocates was the unionist MP for South Dublin, Sir Horace Plunkett. Plunkett was a friend of Yeats and Gregory, a keen supporter of the Irish literary revival, and a regular and illuminating commentator on Irish social life. In August 1895, within weeks of the new Tory administration arriving in Dublin to take up office under the Chief Secretaryship of Gerald Balfour, Plunkett announced a new political opportunity by arguing that it was now time for nationalists and unionists to sink their party differences and concentrate on an agreed future. As the prospects of obtaining home rule were now 'extremely improbable', Plunkett reasoned, the moment had arrived for the setting up of a committee of politicians and 'men of vision' capable of advising the government on measures beneficial to national reconciliation (*Irish Times*, 28 August 1895: 10). The subsequent Recess Committee (so called because its meetings took place during the 1896 Parliamentary recess) underlined the general need for education in Ireland, and, more specifically, advocated the setting up of a Department of Agriculture and Technical Instruction. As his 1898 lecture, 'The Economic Movement in Ireland' makes clear, Plunkett's primary concern was establishing an effective Irish administration. He believed that the deficiency of previous attempts to govern Ireland was that they were either too coercive, as in the Cromwellian invasions in the seventeenth century, or, as in the case of the Act of Union, that English government had been founded mistakenly on a policy of political assimilation without any matching effort to educate the individual (*Daily Express*, 1 November 1898: 6). Apart from the north-east of Ireland 'where English individualism succeeds', Plunkett claimed that there was an urgent need to transform the country's 'economic thought . . . until the people come to see that they must work for their own economic salvation' (*Daily Express*, 1 November 1898: 6). Education, therefore, was the key to Ireland's political amelioration. What was being attempted by the co-operative movement as embodied in the Irish Agricultural Organization Society, by the Recess Committee initiative, and by the Department of Agriculture and Technical Instruction (established by Act of Parliament in 1899) was the development of that which the Irish – and Irish Roman Catholics in particular – were thought to be singularly most lacking: individuality and self-reliance.[4] Modernization, with a particular emphasis on developing individuality, was the key to resolving the hitherto intractable Irish question: the establishment of '*modern* relations between the government and the people', Plunkett assured Lady Betty Balfour in 1896, would constitute the 'coup of the century' (quoted in Gailey 1987: 17). As we shall see, Yeats's and Gregory's plans for an Irish literary theatre were fundamentally imbricated with this ambitious project of cultural modernization.

Unsurprisingly, Plunkett's initiatives also had a direct political objective. They functioned as a means by which the southern Irish landlord class could find expression as champions of modernization rather than stand out as colonial anachronisms and remain vulnerable to the vagaries of the now much expanded, increasingly confident, and predominantly Roman Catholic, Irish electorate. Following the extension of the franchise brought about by the 1884–5 Reform Act, the frightening sense of embattled isolation experienced by Irish landlords during the Land War, and the dismal failure of the Irish Unionist Alliance to galvanize support in the 1885 general election (Bowen 1983: 18), the key political issue for Irish unionism in the 1890s was how, if indeed at all, its traditional leadership position might be reconciled to this recently enfranchised nationalist majority. Arguably, this had always been a feature of unionist thinking in Ireland. In 1886, for example, W. E. H. Lecky insisted that the government of Ireland could not be 'safely entrusted to the National League – to priests and Fenians and professional agitators, supported by the votes of the ignorant peasantry', but then later added that 'national feeling, instead of being repressed, should in every safe way be encouraged in Ireland' (quoted in McCartney 1994: 129). But while unionist and Protestant involvement in national initiatives was by no means unprecedented in the nineteenth century (Isaac Butt's Home Government Association had campaigned for a nationally responsive government as recently as the 1870s (see Foster 1993: 62)) the aftermath of the Land War of the 1880s and the realization that peasant proprietorship and land reform were now inevitable gave special and urgent momentum to Plunkett's initiatives. That unionist MPs like Lecky and Plunkett should campaign in 1896 for the release of Fenian prisoners in England (West 1986: 50) and even for the abolition of the Dublin vice-royalty (Plunkett Foundation: Diary, 7 May 1896),[5] was an indication not of eccentric gentry quixoticism, but of an acute sense of political expediency.[6] Quite simply, if Irish unionism outside of the north-eastern part of the island was to survive at all in an age of mass democracy, it had no alternative but to develop 'constructive' policies that were conspicuously directed towards Ireland's amelioration.

The main strategy of constructive unionism in the 1890s, then, was a determined attempt at self-nationalization. Colonial associations with England were repudiated either as economically unjust (as in the case of the overtaxation of Ireland as indicated by the Financial Relations Committee in 1896), or as politically inappropriate to a sister nation that had once (albeit briefly) possessed a parliament of her own. Thus, Ireland was considered less as an object of colonialism than as a producer of colonies in her own right. In terms of policy, there was a general acceptance of the need for increased peasant proprietorship and land reform, and recognition of the inevitability of some measure of Irish self-government or devolution. Gerald Balfour's 1895 proposal of a Local Government Bill (implemented in 1898) was welcomed as a positive step towards political reform and homogenizing Irish and English local government (see Gailey 1987: 47), while at the same time introducing reforms that might dilute support for what was regarded as the common scourge of unionist and constitutional nationalist alike: socialism and agrarian insurgency. Social conciliation was encouraged, a range of informal alliances was established with the Irish Parliamentary Party (IPP), and Anglo-Irish relations were idealized as a 'union of hearts'. A lot had changed since the coruscating anti-home rule polemics of the 1880s; southern Irish unionism had become eirenic.

It was in the cultural sphere that constructive unionists were especially successful in cultivating an image of themselves as belonging to a broadly Irish nationalist, rather than to a garrison English, social and cultural identity. Oxymorons proliferated. A conservative and imperialist like the author Standish James O'Grady was described by Yeats as 'the first Fenian unionist on record' (Yeats 1994: 147), Lord Castletown, leader of the New Unionist Party in Ireland, held the post of President of the Pan Celtic Association, and T. P. Gill was described by Plunkett as the propagator of 'National Unionism'.[7] Descriptions like these may have sounded contradictory, but they also bore witness to the ideological overlapping of constructive unionism and Parnellite or constitutional nationalism. For example, the notion that Ireland needed to be educated away from a state of colonial subjecthood and political insurgency and towards a state of national autonomy and modern citizenship was one that was widely shared by many nationalist, Catholic intellectuals. For this reason alone constitutional nationalism readily engaged with the new mood of reconciliation. Moderate nationalists such as John Redmond, leader of the Irish Parliamentary Party, and nationalist publications such as the *New Ireland Review*, the *Irish Independent Weekly*, and the *United Irishman* celebrated the advent of a post-Land League political climate and its attendant opportunities for class conciliation. Just as in 1897 the *Irish Independent Weekly* claimed that the local elections promised by the local government bill need not necessarily be seen as threatening to landlords (Bew 1987: 32), an article in an 1898 issue of *New Ireland Review* argued strongly against an exclusively political definition of nationalism. Belief in political autonomy as the supreme goal of nationalism is 'vastly and deplorably mistaken', the writer insists, and many who are now hostile to nationalism would join the movement if only the term could be made more inclusive (Hickey 1898: 129–30). Thus, the *New Ireland Review* describes its targeted audience as a new and responsible citizenry 'recently admitted to their share in the duties and responsibilities of government' and declares that its objective is to encourage that readership to speak 'their deliberate opinion in the ordered discussion of public affairs' (Editorial, 1894: 2). Increasingly from the mid-1890s, therefore, constructive unionists and constitutional nationalists alike were concerned with establishing and controlling the means by which Irish devolution, or possible statehood, might eventually be achieved and exercised. Newspapers and literary journals, educational and cultural institutions, even public monuments (Hill 1998: 134–6), were all regarded as vitally important ways of contesting, maintaining, or achieving this objective.

This, then, was the broad context for the establishment of the Irish Literary Theatre in the summer of 1897. It was a context that included constructive unionism's anxious desire to hibernicize itself, bourgeois nationalism's intent on modernization, and Yeats's and Gregory's quasi-evangelical belief in the educative value of a literary culture for Ireland. But by far the most crucial aspect of the Irish Literary Theatre initiative was its Ascendancy beginnings. It was not just that this was a theatre fortuitously dreamt up in the course of a leisurely afternoon's conversation in an aristocratic summer residence in the west of Ireland – the house of Lady Gregory's neighbour, the Count de Basterot, at Kinvarra in County Galway (see Yeats 1955: 397–8). Nor was it that this project entailed a group of people immediately involved or closely associated with Irish landlordism, nor even that this was a venture that depended on the patronage of wealthy and influential guarantors such as Lord Ardilaun or the Marquess of Dufferin and Ava. Far more importantly, the proposal to establish a 'Celtic theatre' was formulated in a way that addresses two key ideological concerns of Ireland's rapidly declining landlord class. On the one hand, the conventional association of 'imaginative', 'respectable' or 'literary' drama in the 1890s with a leisured contemplation of existence insulated from the crude exigencies of the marketplace ensured an apparently natural connection between the establishment of a prestigious national theatre and its instigation, support and direction by representatives of Ireland's own traditional leisured class. On the other hand, this theatre's nationalist objective – that of presenting Irish character in a newly favourable and anti-colonial perspective – offered the initiators of the theatre the prospect of a popular support that was now conspicuously lacking in nearly all other spheres of Irish social life. In a circular letter soliciting financial support, Yeats and Gregory formulated the objectives of the Irish Literary Theatre as follows:

> We hope to find in Ireland an uncorrupted and imaginative audience trained to listen by its passion for oratory, and believe that our desire to bring upon the stage the deeper thoughts and emotions of Ireland will ensure for us a tolerant welcome, and that freedom to experiment which is not found in theatres of England, and without which no new movement in art or literature can succeed. We will show that Ireland is not the home of buffoonery and of easy sentiment, as it has been represented, but the home of an ancient idealism, and we are confident of the support of all Irish people, who are weary of misrepresentation, in carrying out a work that is outside all the political questions that divide us.
>
> (quoted in Yeats 1997: 124)

On the eve of local government legislation which was to axe the last formal means by which Irish landlords were able to exercise direct and massively disproportionate political authority in Ireland,[8] the Irish Literary Theatre proposal may be read as an attempt at ideological counterbalance. True, the familiar Arnoldian contrast between Celtic imagination and English philistinism evokes a popular nationalist sentiment, but it does so in a manner that is formulated according to anxieties that are specific to Ireland's beleaguered landlord class. Celticism of this kind, to use Marjorie Howes's apt phrase, is 'an Ascendancy nationalism' (Howes 1996: 49): an 'enlisting [of] the Irish peasantry . . . in a shared national project while continuing to dominate them politically and economically' (Howes 1996: 45). By means of a national theatre, that is, Irish native culture (in landlord eyes more notorious indeed for its 'passion for oratory' rather than any reputed simplicity and imagination) is now felicitously reconceptualized ('trained to listen') as an audience. To this extent, proposing a 'Celtic Theatre' 'outside all of the political questions that divide us', was an underwriting rather than an under-cutting of the national importance of an aristocracy.

For the Ascendancy promoters of the Irish Literary Theatre, then, no less than for the Parnellite contributors to the *New Ireland Review*, a national theatre both evoked and demonstrated the enticing prospect of social consensus. In the theatre, nationalists and unionists were agreed, spectators would behave not like a crowd but like individual citizens – maturely suspending their personal circumstances and vested interests within the context of an over-arching national ideal.[9] Or as Michael Hickey's article puts it, the 'real dramas' of militant rebellion (actions that were regarded as 'dramatic' to the extent that they appeared unpredictable) could now be replaced by a theatre of political citizenship. Like the apparatus of the nation state to which some constructive unionists and all constitutional nationalists were variously committed, a national theatre is thought of as an ideal body, dissipating political conflict, shaping social behaviour, and reinforcing traditional structures of authority. 'In the theatre', as Yeats pithily declared in his famous misquotation from Victor Hugo, 'the mob becomes a people' (Yeats 1975: 141).

With the idea of a national literary theatre, in other words, Irish unionists and Irish nationalists shared a broad cultural agenda. A similar situation existed in relation to the Kilkenny Theatre which was similarly dedicated to 'producing plays on Irish lines with Irish ideas' (*Kilkenny Journal*, 1 November 1902: 1). Established in October 1902, it was also associated with the local Ascendancy and yet supported by nationalists. Built and operated by the Hon. Otway Cuffe and owned and funded by Ellen, Countess of Desart, the Kilkenny Theatre was initiated partly to commemorate the centenary of the establishment of a local institution, the Private Theatre of Kilkenny, which had been associated almost exclusively with Irish gentry and unionist 'society' culture.[10] Notwithstanding these associations the Kilkenny Theatre received extensive nationalist approval with Cuffe and Lady Desart cheered on the opening night and the local branch of the Gaelic League declaring itself as the Theatre's strong supporter. As is the case with the Irish Literary Theatre, the establishment of the Kilkenny Theatre suggests the theatre's enduring function as a traditional site for the display of social and political prestige. To this extent, an Irish theatre (and the Irish Literary Theatre in particular) was especially amenable to bourgeois nationalist demonstrations of an envisaged social and political hegemony, and to Ascendancy projections of social consensus.

Broadly speaking, the Irish theatre movement of the 1890s was a project of recuperation. Its themes portrayed the traditional sites and themes of popular insurgency and political tension in Ireland (such as landlord–tenant conflict, the 1798 rebellion and famine) as consistent with a contemporary scheme of national modernization. Thus, acts of political insurgency that often had been organized according to logics that were local and sporadic were represented instead in terms that were homogeneous and instantly recognizable. In all cases, political action was seen as motivated by a heightened sense of individual conscience and directed towards some form of constitutional autonomy. In the period 1890–1910 this trend is almost universal. In plays such as J. W. Whitbread's *Lord Edward, or '98* and *Wolfe Tone* (1898) W. B. Yeats's *Cathleen Ni Houlihan* (1902) and Gregory's *The Rising of the Moon* (1907), insurgency is presented exclusively in terms of individual volition. In much the same way, the notion of a national drama itself sought to replace what were regarded as pre-modern cultural forms (such as wakes, mumming and other 'folk' practices) with theatre, a cultural practice fully consistent with the idea of the state as a community of individual subjects or citizens.[11] To this extent, the Irish theatre initiative of the late 1890s also coincides with widespread attempts in England and in Ireland to curb the extent to which theatre was perceived as a site for unruly social behaviour (see Davis 1992: 111–32). Although often portrayed as opposites, Yeats's calls for a reform of the theatre and nationalist attacks on music hall and melodrama in Dublin were, in fact, part of the same movement. Both were motivated not merely by an antipathy to English commercial interests, but by distaste for these theatres' disruptive social reputation. Hence, the actor Frank Fay condemns as anti-national what he regards as the noisy, ill-behaved, and boorish conduct of audiences at the Theatre Royal (Fay 1970: 20), while the diarist Joseph Holloway writes disapprovingly of a typical audience at the Queen's Royal Theatre as 'noisy and full of suggestions' (quoted in Hogan and Kilroy 1975: 19). Just as in England the Salvation Army and the National Vigilance Association purchased music halls for conversion to evangelical use, so the same policy was advocated in Dublin by the journalist D. P. Moran in relation to transforming music halls for nationalist purposes (Moran 1901: 139).

This helps to explain why the dramatic narratives of the Irish

Literary Theatre were sometimes concerned explicitly with Ascendancy preoccupations and yet still enjoyed considerable nationalist popularity. Edward Martyn's sympathetic treatment of the leadership tribulations of reforming Irish landlords in *The Heather Field* was judged a particular success. An Ibsenite study of a landlord in the west of Ireland, the play's protagonist, Carden Tyrell, is crippled by debt, but clings fervently to his dream of reforming the Irish landscape from its unproductive native state. Although Tyrell's Sisyphean task – reforming an intractable Irish nature by ridding his estate of heather – is strikingly colonial, it is presented by the play as simply quixotic: doomed to failure, that is, not so much because of any intrinsic lack of merit, but because the task is pursued too dogmatically. As Tyrell's neighbouring landlord, Barry Usher, reminds him, such a scheme must be 'generous and loving' (Moore and Martyn 1995: 220) otherwise the land's wild nature will be bound to avenge itself.

USHER: I do not know whether his treatment was sufficiently kind, as farmers say here in West Ireland. . . . He was hardly considerate enough, perhaps, in the accomplishment of his will.

(Moore and Martyn 1995: 221)

The play ends with Tyrrell virtually imprisoned in his house ('like Moltke fighting battles from his study' (Moore and Martyn 1995: 225)) as a result of the evictions that he has effected as a way of making money. Tyrrell is presented as a landlord myopically unable to recognize the benefits of the constructive unionist policy of 'kindness', but he is, nevertheless, meant to come across as a sadly tragic figure for whom the audience has the most sympathy. Despite the restricted social parameters of the play and its portrayal of the Irish landowning class within a perspective of tragic decline, the May 1899 production of *The Heather Field* was described in superlatives by nationalist organs such as the *Freeman's Journal, Independent* (see Hogan and Kilroy 1975: 45–6) and the *United Irishman*. Nationalist audiences displayed no objection to the play's unrepresentative characters or Ascendancy preoccupations. Indeed, the only negative comments about the play emanate from the unionist-oriented *Irish Times* which disliked Martyn's application of Ibsenite naturalism to Ireland's landlord class: 'the cold methods of the Norwegian dramatists can never be applied with any truth to even the Irish landlord . . . without parodying the very essences of Irish life' (*Irish Times*, 10 May 1899: 5).

In Moore and Martyn's *The Bending of the Bough*, for example, there is a similar thematic emphasis. Yeats described the play as 'a splendid and intricate gospel of nationality' with the potential to 'make our theatre a national power' (Yeats 1997: 480, 464), and Gregory claimed that *The Bending of the Bough* (first performed for the Irish Literary Theatre on 20 February 1900)[12] was chosen because the financial question that it dealt with was something upon which 'all parties are united . . . the cause nearest to each of our hearts' (Gregory 1913a: 26). But the ideas of *The Bending of the Bough* seem to be organized much more according to a southern unionist political perspective. It focuses on what it considers to be the perennial difficulty of Irish nationalist politics: its failure to find an appropriate leader. As the play's landlord and Ascendancy representative, Jasper Dean is an Oxford-educated Irishman (or, in the play's parlance, a Norththavener), who comes under the influence of a brilliant nationalist politician, Alderman Ralf Kirwan. Kirwan's difficulty is that despite his perspicacity and political acumen, he is too familiar to 'the mob' to become its leader.

KIRWAN: . . . I cannot lead. My opinions are too well known, and when I write them or speak them people merely say 'There is Alderman Kirwan again, how many years has he been saying that now?' and they yawn and talk about something else.

(Moore and Martyn 1995: 106)

Kirwan's difficulty turns out to be Dean's opportunity. With his fortuitous discovery of Celtic literature and folklore complementing the inbred eloquence and composure of his class, Dean commands immediate respect. He is a leader from the ranks of the Irish gentry, one not only steeled to resist the bribes of England (or Southhaven) and prepared to press home Ireland's claim against unjust taxation, but also familiar with and appreciative of the culture of the native. Dean is both a Parnell redivivus, and a simulacrum of progressive unionist figures like Horace Plunkett, Lord Castletown and T. P. Gill (for these identifications, see Yeats 1997: 497; Frazier 2000: 280).

The play's crisis and Dean's moral dilemma reflects the leadership quandary of southern Irish unionism: an awareness that assuming the role as a leader within the context of Irish nationalism threatens the regeneration and prosperity of a class which depends precisely on *maintaining* the union with England. Forcing England's (Southhaven's) repayment of the loan will, Dean learns, necessarily entail a reduction in his prospective wife's income. How is Jasper Dean (or

Plunkett or Castletown or, for that matter, Moore or Martyn) to take up his rightful place as an Irish national leader without at the same time undermining his identity as a member of a loyal and imperial élite? In all of this *The Bending of the Bough* frankly articulates the dilemma of an Irish leadership cadre in the throes of a crisis. Torn between a new constructivist policy of reform (Jasper Dean is described as having written an article on conciliation) and a more traditional unionist hostility to all shades of Irish nationalism, Dean ends up like Carden Tyrell in *The Heather Field*, tragically unable to act. Can a 'National Unionism' exist as a viable political phenomenon, as anything other than the 'pale and delicate flower' of George Russell's (AE) sketch caricature of Plunkett? For many of the Irish landlord class such questions were neither far-fetched nor rhetorical. A few months later (in April 1900) George Moore wrote to the *Freeman's Journal* arguing that Irish landlords should become Irish nationalists and abandon, once and for all, the British government that was bankrupting them and, in May 1900, Edward Martyn wrote to the *Tuam Herald* urging the formation of a 'National' landlord party (Frazier 2000: 291). This Ascendancy orientation to *The Bending of the Bough* is not an issue for nationalist reviews of the play. Instead, they praise the play's satire on contemporary politics and its patriotic emphasis on the need for nationalist politicians to resist English bribes (*Irish Daily Independent*, 21 February 1900: 5; *Freeman's Journal*, 21 February 1900: 5).

But nationalist enthusiasm for the early years of the Irish literary theatre movement in spite of, or in some cases because of, its explicitly Ascendancy associations still does not illuminate the (relatively muted) controversy that arose following the May 1899 performance of Yeats's *The Countess Cathleen*. This controversy began following a complaint, published in the *Freeman's Journal* on 1 April 1899, concerning the play's portrayal of Irish Catholic peasant life. Written by the polemicist and former nationalist MP, F. Hugh O'Donnell, the complaint was subsequently published, along with the second instalment of O'Donnell's attack, as the pamphlet *Souls for Gold*. This in turn was followed by a protest that involved a group of students from the Royal University on the night of the play's first performance, and by a letter of protest from the Royal University students published in the *Freeman's Journal* on 10 May 1899. The protesters claimed that on the basis of *The Countess Cathleen's* portrayal of Irish Catholic peasants selling their souls for gold at a time of famine, Yeats's play contradicted the Irish Literary Theatre's role as a national institution. In Yeats's play, a community of Irish peasants is starving in the midst of a famine with the wholesale selling of their souls to merchant devils as their only remaining resource. This resource the peasants freely expend until the local magnate, Countess Cathleen herself, saves the community by bartering her far higher valued soul in return for food for the tenantry. But if national representativeness was not a difficulty for nationalist audiences and commentators in relation to the conspicuous Ascendancy origins of the Irish Literary Theatre, nor a problem in relation to the landlord setting and thematics of Martyn's *The Heather Field*, why on this occasion should the question of national representativeness become so sensitive an issue?

Lady Gregory's theatre history places the blame squarely in the court of Irish Catholicism and O'Donnell's personal vindictiveness. In her *Our Irish Theatre* the overall impression of the controversy is that the protests directed against *The Countess Cathleen* were motivated by a critical illiteracy that emanated from O'Donnell's long-standing and curmudgeonly animosity towards Yeats, and from a wider and more serious cultural ailment: Roman Catholic cultural paranoia.

> The pamphlet, *Souls for Gold*, had been sent about, and sentences spoken by the demons in the play and given detached from it were quoted as Mr. Yeats' own unholy beliefs. A Cardinal who confessed he had read none of the play outside these sentences condemned it. Young men from the Catholic University were roused to come and make a protest against this 'insult to their faith'. There was hooting and booing in the gallery.
>
> . . . But that battle was not a very real one. We have put on Countess Cathleen a good many times of late with no one speaking against it at all. And some of the young men who hissed it then are our good supporters now.
>
> (Gregory 1913: 24–5)

Gregory's phrase, 'young men from the Catholic University' (Gregory 1913a: 24) is anachronistic. Ireland's 'Catholic' University was not, in fact, established until the formation of the National University of Ireland in 1908, and then only after a long-running and bitterly fought campaign which, as has been mentioned, had suffered a serious setback in the months immediately prior to the first performance of Yeats's play (see Morrisey 1983: 168–70). As one of the most divisive controversies of the period, this was not a point that Gregory – or anyone else in Ireland for that matter – would be unlikely to forget. But whether Gregory's anachronism was disingenuous or not, her placing of inverted commas on 'insult to their faith' and her concluding dismissal of the controversy as a triviality ('that battle was not a very real one' (Gregory 1913a: 25)) undermines the possibility that the protesters' objections may have had a political or cultural validity, and it removes the controversy altogether from the context of contemporary history. That O'Donnell's tirades in print and the objections of the Royal University students are viewed as strident and extremist, tends to subordinate the critical meaning of these protests, and of *The Countess Cathleen*'s own relationship to anti-Catholicism.

O'Donnell's first letter to the *Freeman's Journal* (written prior to the play's performance) begins by identifying the kicking to pieces of the shrine of the Blessed Virgin as especially objectionable. That Yeats omitted the statue-kicking incident in performance and replaced it by a scene that had the icon falling from its wall did not change things. O'Donnell argues that, on the basis of the broken statue, and the play's 'faith for gold' theme, *The Countess Cathleen* would be more appropriate to a 'souper meeting at Exeter Hall' than 'to the applause of an Irish Literary Association' (O'Donnell 1899: 3). Similar associations between Yeats's play and Protestant proselytism were made by O'Neill and Gill, and by the Royal University students in their letter of 10 May. The implication in both cases is that there are particular difficulties involved in establishing an Irish public sphere within the context of the legacy and continuing existence of anti-Catholic rhetoric and of legislative discrimination against Catholics in the area of university education. Indeed, all of the play's protesters agree that what was most objectionable about *The Countess Cathleen* is not any flouting of religious orthodoxies as such, but the play's contribution to an already existing discourse of anti-Catholic prejudice and legislation. For O'Donnell, and the Royal University students in particular, anti-Catholicism and anti-Irishness are inextricable. If the Irish peasant is a 'mere crooning barbarian' filled with superstition and/or a Catholicism barely distinguishable from superstition, then, argue the University students, anti-Catholic and anti-Irish legislation is encouraged automatically: '[I]f this be a true portrait of Irish Catholic character, every effort of England to stamp out our religion, and incidentally our nationality, is not merely to be justified but to be applauded' (*Freeman's Journal*, 10 May 1899: 6). It is this point in particular – the sense that *The*

Countess Cathleen endorses a view that Catholic Ireland is, by definition, not fully modern and therefore not ready for political or administrative independence – that may well explain the depth of irritation that Yeats's play generated among some intellectuals like Fr. George O'Neill, T. P. Gill, and C. P. Curran (Curran 1970: 103–4).[13] And while anti-Catholic prejudice was commonplace among the utterances of even the most liberal of Irish unionists of the period, the special offensiveness of *The Countess Cathleen* was that this was a play performed under the auspices of an institution which declared itself as 'national'.

O'Donnell's more florid denunciations, mainly contained in his second letter of objection which the *Freeman's Journal* refused to print belong to this broader context of offence. Attacking Yeats's Celticism as 'an agreeable diversification' from the stage Irishman and political Irishman of London, O'Donnell claims that *The Countess Cathleen* should be seen *not* as a replacement of anti-Irish stereotypes (the declared aim of the 1897 Irish Literary Theatre prospectus), but as the means for their development.

> Instead of Donnybrook and Ballyhooley, or rather by the side of these types, and, as it were, suggesting their development, the genial Anglo-Saxon is asked to regard the fine old Celtic peasant of Ireland's Golden Age, sunk in animal savagery, destitute of animal courage, mixing up in loathsome promiscuity the holiest homes of the Christian Sanctuary with the gibbering ghoul-and-fetish worship of a Congo negro, selling his soul for a bellyful, yelling alternate invocations to the Prince of Darkness and the Virgin Mary. Surely this is a dainty dish to set before our sister England!
>
> (O'Donnell 1899: 9)

O'Donnell's juxtaposition of Irish Catholicism with what he regards as the savage primitivism of the African Congo implies a world whose values have been cataclysmically inverted. The extremity of O'Donnell's language conveys outrage at an inversion of what he considers to be a fundamental distinction: between an Irish civility demanding political independence in the form of equality with other European nation states and the barbarism of an indigenous African culture that justifies Belgian (Catholic) colonialism. If the Irish can be inferred to be anti-modern largely on account of their Catholicism, then the clear implication of such a logic is that they are indeed little more than colonial natives, transparently undeserving of autonomous state institutions. But this, O'Donnell infers, is as absurd as the claim that the Catholic colonial enterprise in Africa is a travesty. Grossly overstated, O'Donnell's complaints also reveal (albeit inadvertently) the degree to which anti-Catholicism is linked to the overarching discourse of anti-Irish racism. That *Souls for Gold* is itself racist merely underlines that point. To this extent, O'Donnell's stridently rancorous remarks are symptomatic of the sectarian disputes then underlying the nature, definition, and purpose of Irish national institutions. That, as John Kelly puts it, 'Irish Catholics had to have the heterodoxy of the play forced upon their attention' (Yeats 1997: 669) indicates not the obtuseness of the protesters' motivation, but the degree of tension that existed between the longed-for national public sphere that the Irish Literary Theatre appeared to herald and the continuing reality of anti-Catholic discrimination that made the realization of that public sphere an impossibility, and of which *The Countess Cathleen* was a mordant reminder. The play was considered objectionable because within the context of British-dominated Ireland at the turn of the century, the ideology of anti-Catholicism was inextricably connected to the view that an indigenous Irish social and political life was itself *inherently* incapable of autonomy.

Some measure of the tensions experienced by the first audiences to *The Countess Cathleen* can be gauged by the insistence of Revd O'Neill and the Royal University students that while they objected to *The Countess Cathleen*, they also fully supported the aims of the Irish Literary Theatre in establishing a prestigious national theatre. But as one letter writer to the Dublin *Daily Express* put it, even the applause that followed the play was complicated by reservations:

> In their, no doubt, praiseworthy efforts to uphold the Irish Literary Theatre, many drowned alike their national pride, their religious scruples, and their profound disgust. The Irish Literary Theatre (the outcome of a noble and disinterested national endeavour) triumphed, but oh! what a sacrifice.
>
> (*Daily Express*, 16 May 1899: 7)

There is a similar strain in Griffith's discussion of Yeats's play in the *United Irishman*. Despite his description of *The Countess Cathleen* as 'a startling misconception of the character of his countrymen', Griffith defended Yeats's play from attack for its alleged anti-nationalism, and described the protesters from the Royal University as motivated by 'narrow-mindedness and prejudice' (*United Irishman*, 13 May 1899: 2). In language that closely resembled Yeats's own, Griffith rejected the view that *The Countess Cathleen* could (or should) be criticized on the basis of its representation of Irish history: 'It claims to represent neither historical personages nor particular periods, and cannot, therefore, be criticized as an outrage on either' (*United Irishman*, 29 April 1899: 1). Yet for others the fact remained that while Yeats's play was offensive in print (as the Royal University students encouraged their readers to see for themselves by consulting the 1895 edition at the Kildare Street (National) library) its offence was even greater when it was performed on stage. Here the fundamental condition of performance – the presence of spectators obeying the conventions of respectable audience behaviour – implies a level of cultural endorsement. Hence O'Donnell's insistence that his objection to *The Countess Cathleen* is not concerned with Yeats's literary reputation, but with 'the sort of ratification or consecration' that a performance of the play is bound to effect. Even the 'bare toleration of Irish audiences' implies an endorsement of the kind of anti-national and anti-Catholic discourses that the play articulates (O'Donnell 1899: 10). According to this logic the idea of silent disagreement in the theatre is simply a contradiction in terms: if protests were to be made, they had to be strident and vociferous. For some Irish Catholic intellectuals in 1899, therefore, the Irish Literary Theatre provoked strikingly ambivalent responses. As evidence of an Irish public sphere, a national literary theatre was a venture to be supported, but the appearance of *The Countess Cathleen* as that theatre's inaugural play seemed like a *coup de main* just as gratingly intolerable as the December 1901 unionist proposition that the Protestant Trinity College might function as Ireland's new national university (Morrisey 1983: 188).

Finally, in linking *The Countess Cathleen* to Yeats's earlier repudiation of Thomas Davis's didactic nationalist writings, O'Donnell's complaint implies that a cultural movement relevant to Ireland's struggle for nationhood is one that will run athwart a purely literary aesthetics. For the Royal University students as well, with their shouts of 'Thomas Davis' during the first performance of *The Countess Cathleen* (Hogan and O'Neill 1967: 6), this sense of an alternative, and explicitly pro-separatist nationalist literary tradition is also evoked. What begins to be articulated in the opposition to the play, then, is a gradual awareness that what may be more appropriate to an anti-imperial nationalism in Ireland is *not* the development of a public sphere (in Habermas's definition, that arena of public opinion free of political and economic interests to which the state claims to be accountable), but rather the development of what might be termed a *counter* public sphere in which articles of faith such as the autonomy and modernizing drive of the theatre are seen as unsuited to a country that does not yet possess political independence.

Part of the attractiveness of the Irish Literary Theatre as a 'national' theatre, therefore, was the widely held impression that serious theatre was that which was respectable and literary. But in Ireland, the project of a literary and cultural education was deeply problematic. Although its goal was the cultivation of individuality, individuality itself was the contested term. Tension arose not so much *between* the ideology of individualism and the presence or absence of representative state institutions, but *within* the notion of individualism. At once crucial to this phase of Ireland's modernization and yet marked by bitter sectarian dispute, individuality was seen as a quality that Protestants were thought to embody *par excellence*, but that Roman Catholics were thought to be fundamentally without. As many of the participants in the cultural revival at the turn of the century were themselves aware, the project of transforming the recalcitrant or pre-modern elements in Irish political culture was closely similar to Plunkett's programme for Ireland's economic modernization: his diagnosis of Ireland's problem as its 'tribal instincts' and absence of individual self-reliance and his promotion of the idea of 'association' as its possible remedy (Plunkett 1905: 167). Indeed, Plunkett himself regarded the literary and co-operative movements as mutually reinforcing, and records in his diary his desire to promote 'co-operation between the practical men and the dreamers of Ireland' (Plunkett Foundation: Diaries, 22 February 1899).

The protests directed against the first performance of *The Countess Cathleen* may be seen not as a product of an innate nationalist and/or Catholic myopia, but as a form of ideological critique. Put another way, the anti-Catholicism of the play's thematics threatens to expose the Irish Literary Theatre's dehistoricizing of Irish culture – precisely the function that was deemed to be so vital to its role in contributing to and rehearsing an Irish public sphere. In this respect, Yeats's setting of his play in Ireland at a time of famine was not only to evoke a painful national memory (Frazier 1990: 18–19), but was yet another reminder of divisive contemporary political issues. Maud Gonne and James Connolly had described in pamphlets and newspaper articles the mass starvation following an extensive failure of the potato crop on the Erris peninsula in 1897 as a famine. Indeed, it was on the basis of such descriptions that the anti-Parnellite MP,

John Dillon, petitioned Arthur Balfour for an emergency sitting of parliament to debate the issue. Balfour publicly rejected the petition, and Plunkett's and Gregory's diaries express their extreme private irritation at Dillon's move (Plunkett Foundation: Plunkett Diary, 2 October 1897). For Gregory, Plunkett and Balfour, therefore, 'famine' was an emotive and historically loaded term that marked a fracture line that they were unwilling to acknowledge: between the alliance of constructive unionism and constitutional nationalism and a more militant combination of agrarian socialism and anti-imperialist nationalism. That the setting and thematics of Yeats's play should evoke so notorious an instance of Protestant anti-Catholicism as famine 'souperism' meant that the Irish Literary Theatre's claim to exist 'outside all the political questions that divide us' (Yeats 1997: 124) was placed under immense strain.

The difficulty for nationalists as far as the Irish Literary Theatre is concerned arises less because of some of the theatre's flagrant contradictions as a representative national institution, but because *The Countess Cathleen* reveals the conscience of the protagonist as inscribed with an innate Protestant superiority (Frazier 1990: 10–12). Individual conscience was a primary term in this phase of Ireland's nationalist modernization, and is regularly presented in nationalist plays as homologous to the nation. The unusual feature of Yeats's play is that this is given a distinctive anti-Catholic gloss. To this extent, the breaking of the statue of the Virgin Mary in *The Countess Cathleen* was by no means gratuitous. On the contrary, this action – amended in the 1901 printed version of the play to Shemus Rua crushing the icon with his foot (Yeats 1997: 380) – merely foregrounds a point that Yeats and Gregory considered the Irish theatre to be about: the education of a predominantly Catholic audience away from its superstitious clinging to traditional structures of political and religious authority and towards a recognition of certain universal, literary values independent of the many vagaries and crises of Irish history. The problem was that with its inaugural 1899 performance of *The Countess Cathleen*, Ireland's national literary theatre appeared, albeit briefly, not as a site of consensus and as an instrument of modernization, but as an institution promoting the sectional interests of Ireland's minority, predominantly Protestant élite. Many of the other, later plays in the Irish Literary Theatre repertoire also reflect Irish Ascendancy and unionist preoccupations, but without *The Countess Cathleen*'s disquieting denominational perspective.

After the damage inflicted on the Irish Literary Theatre's

nationalist credentials by *The Countess Cathleen* controversy, Yeats planned (according to Gregory) to do something to 'violently annoy the upper classes to redeem his character' (Gregory 1974: 358). Two months later, in April 1900, Yeats condemned Queen Victoria's impending visit to Ireland as an anti-Boer recruiting drive: 'whoever stands by the roadway cheering for Queen Victoria cheers for that Empire, dishonours Ireland, and condones a crime' (Yeats 1997: 509). If Yeats's letter was designed to ruffle unionist feathers, it was an instant success. Within days, Lecky, the Irish Literary Theatre's most prominent unionist guarantor, publicly withdrew his support (Frazier 1990: 29–30). Even Gregory, who was irritated by Yeats's letter and to whom Lecky was a close friend (Saddlemyer 1982: 103; Gregory 1974: 352), accepted that the MP's withdrawal might do the theatre some good (Gregory 1974: 368); she commented, resignedly, that the Irish Literary Theatre needed 'all the aids to popularity we can get' (quoted in Yeats 1994: 74). The following year, in May 1901, Yeats met with George Moore, Frank Fay and others to discuss the possibility of forming a 'Gaelic dramatic touring company' (Yeats 1994: 72). Yeats's subsequent correspondence with Fay sounds all the right nationalist notes. He concedes the necessity of Irish-language drama as the basis for a national theatre, mentions that he hopes to collaborate with Hyde on a play written in Irish, and speaks with reassuring disparagement of his unionist relatives in Sligo: 'They look on us all in much the same way – "Literary Theatre" "Gaelic League" are all one to them' (Yeats 1994: 98).

If Yeats's nationalist pronouncements were wisely opportunistic (Frazier 1990: 30), they were so because the cultural parameters of any nationalist theatre project were now unequivocally representational. Indeed for Frank Fay (Fay 1970: 53–5), D. P. Moran[14] and George Moore (see Frazier 2000: 302–3), there existed a checklist of prerequisites: plays performed for a national theatre should be written in Irish, should engage positively with Irish nationalist politics and should be performed by Irish actors. To this end, Fay went so far as to distinguish between the Irish Literary Theatre as the place of Anglo-Irish dramatists, and an Irish national theatre that would be concerned exclusively with plays written in the Irish language (Fay 1970: 56–7). In addition, Martyn and (for a time) Moore insisted that a truly Irish national theatre should be subject to the involvement and supervision of the Catholic church (see Frazier 2000: 305–6; Hogan and Kilroy 1975: 119–25). Remarkably, Yeats's disapproving response to this suggestion is so muted as to be hardly noticeable:

> If Mr Moore should establish a national theatre with an
> ecclesiastic for a censor, and ask me to join the management
> I shall refuse, but I shall watch the adventure with the most
> friendly eyes. I have no doubt that a wise ecclesiastic, if his
> courage equalled his wisdom, would be a better censor than
> the mob, but I think it better to fight the mob alone than to
> seek for a support one could only get by what would seem to
> me a compromise of principle.
>
> (Yeats 1994: 119)

Even the *United Irishman* was taken aback by this extraordinary
circumspection, and proceeded to criticize Yeats for not taking the
'highest ground' in denouncing such obvious and blatant attempts at
clerical interference (*United Irishman*, 23 November 1901: 3).

Yeats in private maintained exactly the opposite point of view.
In his letters to Gregory in the same period he expresses strong
reservations about a politically nationalist theatre – 'I have always felt
that my mission in Ireland is to serve taste rather than any definite
propaganda' (Yeats 1994: 74) – and about audiences that prefer 'the
Freeman's Journal to [?]Ruskin, a mob that knows neither literature
nor art' (Yeats 1994: 118). Yeats's puzzling moderation towards
precisely the kind of national theatre that in all other contexts he
regards as anathema (a Catholic church-influenced theatre of
nationalist political propaganda) points both to Yeats's skills as a
consummate tactician and to the extensive politicization of national
culture that was then taking place.

By October 1901 Yeats attempts to reconcile these conflicting
private and public views. Arguing that the time is ripe for a more
organized national theatre movement, Yeats claims that one option
is to have a small Dublin-based company of Irish actors presided
over by an English professional in charge of literary excellence.
Another option is to have a more amateur, nationalist organization
along the lines of the propagandistic model advocated by Frank Fay
in the pages of the *United Irishman*. Less dependent on financial
backing, this latter option would 'build up an Irish national theatre
from the ground, escaping to some extent the conventions of the
ordinary theatre' (Yeats 1901: 5). Only in Yeats's insistence that those
who write for the stage must study the 'dramatic masterpieces of
the world' (Yeats 1901: 6) and in his negative criticism of two plays
written in Irish (by Fr. Dineen and Alice Milligan) does Yeats hint
at a preference for the former (see Yeats 1994: 714). Despite the
conciliatory efforts of Yeats and Gregory, anxieties in relation to the

future direction of the national theatre movement were exacerbated rather than allayed by the Irish Literary Theatre's final two productions in October 1901. While Douglas Hyde's *Casadh an tSúgáin* was performed in Irish by Gaelic League amateurs, directed by W. G. Fay, and was greeted with general enthusiasm, the London-based Benson company's bland mispronunciations of Irish words in Yeats's and Hyde's English-language *Diarmuid and Grania* underlined the inappropriateness of having an English theatre company, however skilful, perform an Irish play.

Strongly dissenting opinion from this judgement was the playwright J. M. Synge. In a French language review for *L'Européen* on 31 May 1902, Synge implies that in *Casadh an tSúgáin* the theatre was being used for completely different cultural and ideological ends from those articulated in the Irish Literary Theatre's 1897 manifesto. He claims that the popularity of Hyde's play is attributable solely to the audience's homogeneous nationalist orthodoxy, and that the play itself is no more than '*une petite pièce charmante*' (Synge 1982a: 381). Synge is especially scathing about the composition and behaviour of the audience, and refers acidly to the women of the Gaelic League 'chattering in bad Irish with youths quite pale with enthusiasm' (Synge 1982a: 381). The most significant aspect of Hyde's play, he argues, is not the play's narrative action, but rather the extent to which that action provided an occasion for the theatre's takeover by the *petit bourgeois* aspirants of the Gaelic League. Contrast this, Synge observes in the next sentence, with the inadvertent and far more revealing cultural expression evident in the songs sung spontaneously by the audience during the interval of *Diarmuid and Grania* (Synge 1982a: 381–2). Synge's description compares the audience's recourse to lyrical atavism as prompted by Hyde's and Yeats's English language plays to the brash vulgarity of Gaelic League enthusiasm as prompted by the play in Irish by Hyde.[15] For Synge, both plays are memorable principally because of the performative response that each generates in the audience. As with the shouts of 'Thomas Davis' during the protests against Yeats's *The Countess Cathleen*, what Synge seems to have found so disconcerting about the first performance of *Casadh an tSúgáin* was the play's reconfiguration of theatre as a vehicle for the politics of the Gaelic League. By contrast, what Synge found so inspiring about the performance of *Diarmuid and Grania* was its stimulation of what he saw as an essentially timeless and apolitical national identity.

Synge's scathing review of *Casadh an tSúgáin* suggests a rapidly emerging tension between a dominant theatre aesthetic and an alternative or counter-aesthetic. The tension between these two conflicting ideas of theatre is especially evident in the early years of the century, and is illustrated further by the first performance of Yeats's and Gregory's play *Cathleen ni Houlihan*. Performed on 6 April 1902 by members of the nationalist women's group, Inghinidhe na hÉireann (the daughters of Ireland), in co-operation with Frank Fay's theatre group, the National Dramatic Society, the immense popularity of this production helped to propel Fay's group into the more formally constituted Irish National Theatre Society. It also did much to restore Yeats's nationalist credentials. Indeed, the nationalist militancy of this 1902 production is uncontested. Key figures in the 1916 rebellion like Constance Markiewicz and Padraic Pearse recall Maud Gonne's portrayal of the title figure in the first April 1902 production as memorably inspirational (Markiewicz 1934: 241; Dudley Edwards 1990: 101).[16] Others who attended or were involved in that production describe Gonne's performance as breaking the bounds of ordinary theatre: more like 'acting' in a transitive sense, than the 'acting' that is usually associated with a theatre. 'In her', wrote Máire Nic Shiubhlaigh, 'the youth of the country saw all that was magnificent in Ireland. She was the very personification of the figure she portrayed on stage . . . the inspiration of the whole revolutionary movement' (Nic Shiubhlaigh 1955: 19).

Written in the aftermath of the 1898 Local Government Act and in the period immediately preceding George Wyndham's 1903 Land Act (both events that witnessed a dramatic and visible decline in the political power of the Irish Ascendancy and an equally conspicuous rise in peasant proprietorship) the narrative of *Cathleen ni Houlihan* depicts a propertied peasant family on the eve of new prosperity. Crucial to their social advancement is the impending marriage of the play's Michael Gillane and Delia Cahill. It is this projected alliance that motivates Michael's father to plan the purchase of a further ten acres for stock, and that inspires Michael's mother to consider educating their younger son, Patrick, as a priest. Peasant *arrivistes* in the thrall of Roman Catholicism and plotting social Ascendancy was Irish unionism's appalling vista. But what forestalls this traumatic prospect is the play's nationalist call to arms: the eponymous Cathleen ni Houlihan transforming herself into a young girl functions, that is, both as a nationalist trope and as the play's unionist *deus ex machina*. Demanding total and submissive obedience ('If anyone would give me help he must give me himself, he must give me all' (Yeats 1953: 84)), the cause of Cathleen or Ireland cancels the marriage to Delia, paralyses the Gillane's social ambitions, and, most crucially, forestalls the worrying prospect of Catholic peasant ascendancy. It is as if nationalism, experienced exclusively in terms of transcendence and political sublimation, is here presented as a force capable of pre-empting the far more forbidding prospect of nationalism as a programme for radical social change.

The play's portrayal of gender roles operates a similar ambivalence. In terms of the national struggle, women are presented either as sources of support and inspiration, or as potential obstacles. In neither case, however, do they possess individual volition. That the Poor Old Woman seeks help and cannot act on her own behalf is a point that is repeatedly emphasized. Remarkably consistent with stories of male imperial adventure at the turn of the century (see Showalter 1990), the threat of Michael's looming domestic claustrophobia is miraculously dispelled when Michael leaves the confines of the cottage and answers the call to military action. Once escaped from the real Delia, Michael is rewarded with the perpetually youthful Cathleen: 'a young girl . . . [with] the walk of a queen' (Yeats 1953: 88). The same process is at work in the play's dramaturgy. Considerations relating to the local context and setting of the play (the County Mayo town of Killala in 1798) are subsumed by the apparent universality of its conclusion (Michael surrendering himself to the nation). To this extent, the charismatic presence of Cathleen has much the same effect on the spectator as it does on Michael. In both cases, the desire for individual and national freedom is transmuted into a matter of specular projection, thereby dissolving the local context into insignificance. From this point of view, *Cathleen ni Houlihan* was nationalist certainly, but nationalist in a way that is broadly compatible with the political interests of constructive unionism.

And yet, notwithstanding this aspect of the play and the conventional roles allocated to women in the text of *Cathleen ni Houlihan,* the fact of the play's 1902 production indicates an alternative set of competing meanings. That this performance took place under the banner of Inghinidhe na hÉireann (a golden sunburst on a blue ground) and that the political activist Maud Gonne took the title role further underscored a role for women in Irish nationalism that was far from passive or traditional. The actress Máire Nic Shuibhlaigh remarks how Gonne's flouting of theatrical conventions by walking in costume from the street through the auditorium and onto the stage a few minutes before the play began, irritated Frank Fay, but added greatly to the political frisson of the occasion (Nic Shuibhlaigh

1955: 17). For the spectator it was as impossible to separate the action of the play from the propaganda work of Inghinidhe na hÉireann as it was to separate the role of the Poor Old Woman from the political activism of Maud Gonne. Gonne's unconventional entrance may have appeared to Fay as an unprofessional stunt, but it also served as a memorable image of a nationalist and gender defiance that was central to the group's political agitation. The 1902 performance concluded with the audience singing the popular nationalist song 'A Nation Once Again' (O'Sullivan 1988: 12). In short, the text and performance of the 1902 production of *Cathleen ni Houlihan* exhibit a tension between nationalism as a *modus vivendi* of constructive unionism, and nationalism as a popular and potentially revolutionary movement.

The result, Gonne perceived, was a dynamic opportunity for political subversion: 'impromptu in the sense that the players were not working from a script, yet it had been well prepared and rehearsed, and was more daringly rebel than would have been safe on a political platform' (quoted in NLI, Czira Papers: 6). As Arthur Griffith was to put it in the *United Irishman, Cathleen ni Houlihan* proved the existence of 'our Irish theatre' and thus served as a public declaration of a national cultural independence (*United Irishman,* 8 November 1902: 1). All that it is now required, he added a month later (and also with some slight apprehension) is 'the support of the people to make it permanent and paramount' (*United Irishman,* 6 December 1902: 1).

2

J. M. SYNGE AND THE COLLAPSE OF CONSTRUCTIVE UNIONISM, 1902–9

In the Theatre there lies the spiritual seed and kernel of all national and poetic and national moral culture. No other branch of Art can ever truly flourish or ever aid in cultivating the people until the Theatre's all-powerful assistance has been completely recognized and guaranteed.

(Wagner, as cited by W. B. Yeats in *The Arrow*, June 1907)

Seven months after the nationalist euphoria of *Cathleen ni Houlihan*, Yeats was at pains to reject the idea that an Irish national theatre should be a political one. His November 1902 essay 'The Freedom of the Theatre' argues that a national theatre cannot exist as a vehicle for the expression of majority national views, but must function instead as the means for their critique. Like shoving a stick into a beehive, writing plays in a spirit of sincerity entails upsetting the views of the majority (Yeats 1902: 5). The problem with Ireland at the moment, Yeats's essay insists, is that the norms of 'recognized criticism' are unobserved. Instead, a lamentable situation arises in which audiences feel free to judge according to their own lights; the result is that 'every newspaper man, every crossing-sweeper, thinks himself a moralist' (Yeats 1902: 5). Evoking *The Countess Cathleen* controversy as an example of the way in which good drama is frequently unpopular and, necessarily, a disturber of orthodoxies, Yeats also hints that an Irish national literary theatre will be an institution that is, of necessity, at odds with Roman Catholicism. But in resurrecting the 1899 controversy and by portraying the protestors against *The Countess Cathleen* as unimaginative and dogmatic, Yeats's essay intervenes directly in a hotly contested contemporary debate concerning religion and culture in Ireland. Theatrical art, it is strongly suggested, is fundamentally incompatible with the myopic tendentiousness of Roman Catholic religious belief. To this extent, however, Yeats pitches his argument in 'The Freedom of the Theatre' in a manner that suggests – albeit inadvertently – that aesthetic norms are themselves historically determined, and that they can and do vary from one political constituency to another.

This is also how it appeared to the journalist and Irish Parliamentary Party member, Tom Kettle. In 'Mr Yeats and the Freedom of the Theatre', Kettle responds to Yeats's article in the *United Irishman* by accusing Yeats of misrepresenting the Royal University protestors against *The Countess Cathleen* and of ignoring Irish history. Irish Catholicism, Kettle insists, is not a collection of abstractions and theological dogma, but an experience of 'determinate historical value' – an experience, that is, still burdened by the memory and continuing legacy of political discrimination (Kettle 1902: 3). The objectors to *The Countess Cathleen* were motivated not by 'bat-eyed literalism,' as Yeats claims, but rather by a keen sense of injustice. To suggest anything otherwise is to ignore the extent that criticizing national orthodoxies means one thing for a nation that has political autonomy, but something else entirely for a nation that does not. For Kettle, such an activity is not the exercise in cultural refinement that Yeats's essay so clearly implies, but is an act of almost facetious irrelevance and an anti-democratic upholding of the status quo. 'Only when we have reached our full growth as a nation', Kettle concludes, can '[t]his melancholy analysis of the prescriptive, the traditional . . . be harmlessly indulged' (Kettle 1902: 3). Kettle's point, however, is not to assert that an Irish national drama should be deferential to the views of the majority, but rather to insist on theatre as an activity that intervenes in a given historical and political situation. There is no such thing, therefore, as a timeless aesthetic and 'no play that is an impartial transcript' (Kettle 1902: 3). Although unmentioned in any subsequent account of the theatre or cultural history of the period, Kettle's essay is an important indication of the extent to which some intellectuals and political activists of the time were prepared to challenge the idea of a literary aesthetic as the necessary and only basis of Ireland's national theatre.

They did so because an Irish national theatre was viewed proleptically in terms of competing definitions of political independence. With an increasing impression of the inevitability of some form of self-government, the idea of a national theatre was contested by a constructive unionist view of home rule as a limited form of administrative devolution within a British context (and one that would retain and reinvigorate Ireland's traditional ruling élite) and the more constitutional and separatist definition of home rule, as posited by the Irish Parliamentary Party and, from 1905, by Sinn Féin. The aesthetic ideology of a national theatre, therefore, was a matter of acute political importance. If it could be accepted that the primary function of a national theatre was to criticize the views of the majority, then this was a consolation to the unionist and nationalist social élites that sponsored the literary theatre movement in the first place. But if Ireland's national theatre developed into a forum for nationalist political propaganda, then this augured a more radical form of democratic majoritarianism. In both cases, Ireland's national theatre institution was seen as rehearsing, and, to some extent anticipating, the future political organization of Irish society.

Kettle's essay did not stimulate further debate. Yeats simply ignored it and continued on the offensive. In numerous public state-ments during the 1902–3 theatre season, Yeats reiterates the view that a national literary theatre exists not for bolstering nationalist self-confidence, but for the purpose of national self-interrogation. It was to this end that, in February 1903, Yeats supported W. G. Fay's call for an alteration to the ending of Padraic Colum's anti-recruiting play *The Saxon Shillin'* (Hogan and Kilroy 1976: 50–1). Colum's play attempts a similar emotional effect to that of Yeats's and Gregory's *Cathleen ni Houlihan*. Set in the peasant interior of a house on the estate of Lord Clonwilliam in the west of Ireland, two frightened, white-faced young women are discovered on stage awaiting eviction. They are the victims of Clonwilliam's extortionate demands that his tenants pay their rent plus his legal costs accrued in a court action against them. With their father arrested for Fenian activities and their brother Hugh having taken the 'saxon shillin' by joining the British Army, the young women are helpless and bereft. But the bulk of the play concerns Hugh's unexpected return and the arrival of the landlord's representative with a final ultimatum. Faced with the impending eviction of his defenceless sisters, Hugh experiences a Pauline political conversion. From one who described himself as 'not a Nationalist', Hugh moves to a position of armed anti-landlord resistance: 'I'll defend the place till the last. For land an' home, Irishmen join me' (Colum 1902: 3). Hugh then stands in the doorway with a gun, but is shot dead by British soldiers before he can muster any further support. The final tableau is of Hugh's body slumped across the threshold and 'the two girls cling[ing] to each other in the centre' (Colum 1902: 3). It was this melodramatic tableau that was the problem. Fay complained to Yeats that the ending was dramaturgically weak, but did not elaborate; he then added (possibly to please his correspondent) that 'Political life in Ireland doesn't call for Heroism of any sort. If anyone wants to see trouble here, let them tackle Mother Church . . .' (Hogan and Kilroy 1976: 50).

But there may have been another reason for Fay's discomfort. Colum's narrative of evicted tenants in the west of Ireland bears close resemblance to a long-running dispute involving Ireland's chief agrarian agitation group, the United Irish League, and the County Roscommon landlord, Lord French De Freyne. This dispute had intensified in the previous winter of 1901–2 with De Freyne insisting on summonses being issued against some of his tenants for unlawful assembly and intimidation and for refusing to pay their rents (O' Brien 1976: 132–3). Within this recent context, and on the heels of *Cathleen ni Houlihan*, a performance of *The Saxon Shillin'* by the Irish National Theatre Society (INTS) might well have suggested that the theatre had a militantly nationalist orientation. But whatever the political reason for Fay's objection, Yeats upheld the decision not to perform Colum's play and, predictably enough, nationalists were incensed. Colum's play had won a Cumann na nGaedhael contest for anti-British propaganda (Saddlemyer 1982: 38), and for Griffith and Maud Gonne it appeared quite outrageous that a national theatre organization would not perform it (Synge, 1983: 70; MacBride 1992: 162). Griffith responded by resigning from the INTS altogether and by offering the acid suggestion the Society's audience might now consist of the Senate of Trinity College Dublin (*United Irishman*, 14 February 1903: 1). Most importantly, this bitter disagreement over *The Saxon Shillin'* led to a severing of the link between the INTS and the nationalist umbrella group, Cumann na nGaedheal (Saddlemyer 1982: 313).

The struggle to determine the primary ideological function of Ireland's national theatre became increasingly acrimonious. Not least of the factors involved was the financial sponsorship of the INTS from 1904 by an English philanthropist, Annie Horniman, who was also passionately opposed to all shades of Irish nationalism (see Frazier 1990). The convolutions and extraordinary effects of Horniman's subsidy are documented in detail by Adrian Frazier who argues convincingly that the literary aesthetic of the Abbey Theatre was viewed, from the beginning, as an anti-nationalist cultural endeavour (Frazier 1990: 75–9; 149–55). Another factor that contributed to the development of an exclusively literary ideology of the INTS was its change in September 1905 to a limited company. Initiated by Yeats, this was not simply a matter of nomenclature:

limited company status made it clear that the ownership of the society now rested exclusively with those who had contributed the most to it financially (see NLI: MS 10952(1) I). And with this important alteration, the term 'home rule', at least in Annie Horniman's parlance, became a byword for enforcing a more hierarchical and autocratic form of management. Horniman wrote to Yeats in the summer of 1906 that 'there is now complete Home Rule and a subsidy from London for the Abbey Theatre' (NLI: MS 10,952(1) ii). But Horniman's use of the term 'home rule' denotes not independence or democratic autonomy, but the reverse: a guarantee that she and the INTS directors would have sole control over all the national theatre's business and artistic affairs (Frazier 1990: 132–3). For Yeats and Gregory, however, the most important contribution towards establishing Ireland's national theatre as an exclusively literary institution is the playwright J. M. Synge and, in particular, the controversies arising from Synge's *In the Shadow of the Glen* (1903) and *The Playboy of the Western World* (1907). In Gregory's *Our Irish Theatre* and in Yeats's essay 'Synge and the Ireland of his Time' (1911), the figure of Synge is rendered inseparable from the idea of the Abbey as an artistic and literary institution set apart from the vociferous expediencies of Roman Catholic nationalist Ireland.

The first performance of *In the Shadow of the Glen* on 8 October 1903 did indeed mark a decisive step away from political nationalism (Frazier 1990: 79; Grene 1999: 72). Maud Gonne complained that *In the Shadow of the Glen* had 'been forced on the Company by a trick' and wrote to Yeats asking if she could 'gently withdraw' from her position as the INTS's Vice-President (MacBride 1992: 174). Her objection was that Synge's play had been accepted for production without being approved by the INTS's Reading Committee and that this unorthodox method of selection was yet another example of the Society's newfound hostility to nationalist cultural groups such as Inghinidhe na hÉireann and Cumann na nGaedheal. Gonne argued that Willie Fay was now increasingly concerned with placating Yeats's friends, 'many of whom are unionists' (MacBride 1992: 176), and that the INTS's new dispensation seemed to have forgotten that the original inspiration for the Society lay in nationalist cultural agitation: 'Members of Cumann na nGaedheal personally gave money & collected money for the Company & all this because we wanted a NATIONAL Theatre Co to help us combat the influence of the low English theatres & music halls' (MacBride 1992: 176). A suspicion that Synge's play signalled a decisive reorientation of the national theatre movement towards a more unionist political position may have also been aroused by the prominent opening night attendance of the Irish Chief Secretary, George Wyndham; Frazier points out, for example, that that night's seating arrangements had Wyndham ensconced in a throne-like red armchair (Frazier 1990: 72–3). But had Yeats and Gregory decided to accept Wyndham's subsequent request for the INTS to deliver a command performance for the King's visit to Dublin in April 1904 then such a reorientation would have been even more intolerably conspicuous (Yeats 1994: 519). Flattered nonetheless by Dublin Castle's overture – 'it means . . . that we are going up in the world' – Gregory and Yeats decided, very wisely, to refuse (Yeats 1994: 519).

Gonne's objection was that Synge's play represented the beginning of a new unionist agenda at the INTS. Her concern was shared by two members of the acting company, Dudley Digges and Maire Quinn, who both refused to perform in *In the Shadow of the Glen* and walked out in protest during its opening night (Fay 1958: 60). They also resigned their positions with the INTS, and together with Gonne and Griffith, established the short-lived Cumann na nGaedheal Theatre Company (Yeats 1994: 717; see Welch 1999: 24–5). Despite (and also because of) the increasingly rancorous relationship between the two companies, Yeats was delighted. 'I think that a political theatre will help us greatly in the end by making it easier for us to keep a pure artistic ideal', he wrote to Frank Fay. 'It will satisfy the propagandist feeling and at the same time make plain the great effectiveness of our work' (Yeats 1994: 425).

What nationalists found galling about *In the Shadow of the Glen* in performance was the play's modernist exposure of the problems of Irish society. In its depiction of Nora Burke as a young woman imprisoned in a loveless alliance with an elderly husband, Synge's play suggests that Irish peasant society is, quite literally, incapable of reproducing itself. The play's action exposes the way in which the aged Dan Burke acrimoniously suspects that Nora has a friendship with a neighbouring and more youthful sheep farmer, Michael Dara. Hoping to prove and punish Nora's infidelity the old man enlists the help of a tramp so as to feign his own death and so discover the affair. Nora returns with Michael and, as she speaks bitterly of Dan's coldness to her, Michael speculates on the joys of expanding his landholding by linking it, through marriage, with hers. Synge's surprising twist to what was otherwise a familiar enough narrative of peasant folklore (Greene and Stephens 1961: 158) is that when the Nora/Michael Dara alliance is revealed, Michael abandons Nora and instead pledges his friendship to the old man. Spurned by her former lover, Nora allies herself with the Tramp with whom she leaves the house for an uncertain future. The play's final image, however, is of Dan Burke and Michael Dara drinking whiskey together beside the hearth. Such a tableau implies that as far as propertied small-farmer Ireland is concerned, the homosocial bond is likely to be more tenacious than the bond that is heterosexual. This was a scathing indictment of Irish peasant purity, and of the nationalist view that peasant oppression in Ireland was a result of British imperialism. If, as Margaret O'Callaghan puts it, agrarian political resistance in Ireland depended on a 'rural agrarian language of excoriation' (O'Callaghan 1994: 5), Synge's play turns this language on its head. The social problem evident in *In the Shadow of the Glen* is not land-lords, gombeen men and grabbers, but an indigenous land-obsession.

With marital infidelity and rural dysfunctionalism as its choice of theme, Synge's *In the Shadow of the Glen* offers a very different kind of theatre to that evident in Colum's *The Saxon Shillin'* or in the first performances of Hyde's *Casadh an tSúgáin* or Yeats and Gregory's *Cathleen ni Houlihan*. Instead of an ideological project designed to show the customs and practices of a localized peasant culture as homologous to an envisaged Irish nation state, Synge's play suggests exactly the opposite. It shows a local and indigenous way of life as internally skewed and underlines an urgent need for that culture's sceptical reappraisal. Social introspection of this sort is a thematic preoccupation more akin to the avant-garde theatre of Ibsen's *The Doll's House* or Pinero's *The Second Mrs Tanqueray*, than to the historical pageants and peasant plays favoured by the Gaelic League. And whereas the volition of the female characters in *Cathleen ni Houlihan, Casadh an tSúgáin*, and *The Saxon Shillin'* is conspicuously passive, Synge's Nora is quite different. She, it is heavily hinted, is sexually active to the point that she considers adultery first with Michael Dara and then (and most outrageously for a nationalist bourgeois audience) with an unpropertied vagrant, the Tramp (Grene 1999: 75). Like a riposte to Kettle's essay of eleven months earlier, it is as if Synge's play assumes that Irish political autonomy has already been achieved, and that the time has now arrived for a bracing programme of national self-examination. The setting up of the INTS in August 1902 may well have been a result of what Padraic Colum later described as an 'imponderable nationalist enthusiasm' (Colum 1926: 275), but its immediate subsequent development owes much more to a growing critique of that enthusiasm.

Arthur Griffith's *United Irishman* castigated *In the Shadow of the Glen* as anti-national on the grounds that it was a slander on Irish womanhood and a reworking of a narrative derived from non-Irish sources (Hogan and Kilroy 1976: 78–9). Under the *nom de plume* 'Conn', Griffith published a short playlet, *In a Real Wicklow Glen*, as a theatrical reply. Griffith's play consists of a short scene set outside a small thatched cottage in County Wicklow and features a 'town-bred' young woman 'dressed for climbing' who encounters an elderly peasant (Mrs O'Shaughnessy) whom she asks for a drink of water. The old woman insists that the young lady must have a cup of fresh milk, and sends her neighbour, Norah, on an errand to fetch one. While they are waiting, Mrs O'Shaughnessy reveals that Norah was the eldest of six girls whose father was unable to care for them, with the result that Norah had to choose between service in Dublin ('and that is a bad place') and marrying an elderly husband when she was nineteen. She married the old man and he treats her dreadfully ('he was a hard man and wanted nothing but a slave' (Griffith 1903: 3)). Nevertheless, Norah is now happy ('when she was sick he showed more nature') even though her former lover, John Kavanagh, still lives in the vicinity. This is the cue for the wooden entrance of John Kavanagh, much the worse for wear because of despair-induced alcoholism. Norah pleads with him to give up the drink and Kavanagh replies that he will ... perhaps ... if only she will give him a kiss. Norah rejects him at once. Mrs O'Shaughnessy then comforts Kavanagh by revealing that she once married an old man, endured years of unhappiness, but then, after his death was proposed to again by the lover of her youth. On the basis of this story, Mrs O'Shaughnessy urges Kavanagh to be a man, and he declares that now he will indeed forswear alcohol.

Griffith's short play is everything that Synge's is not. It shows up the importance of the peasant for an urban middle-class audience and insists on the importance of female morality as the repository of national pride. Its specific lesson is one of deferred fulfilment. The father of Griffith's Norah is destitute and so Norah has had to defer her own wishes and marry the old man; besides, the corollary of this action is that the probity of her subsequent behaviour offers the only chance to ameliorate her lover's drink problem. Some rural social problems do exist, Griffith's playlet seems to acknowledge, but they can be ameliorated – if not alleviated altogether – by female sexual rectitude. But the action of Griffith's play is without excitement or humour, the characters are vapid mouthpieces, and its dramaturgy does little to disturb or challenge the audience's expectations. That *In a Real Wicklow Glen* was written in the first place is a measure of the nationalist offence caused by Synge's play, but its maudlin narrative also makes it easier for the cultural significance of this offence to be forgotten. As with Griffith's protest at the inclusion in *Samhain* of quotations by English critics and his complaint that Synge's play was based on non-Irish sources, the impression thus conveyed is of a nationalism that is prudish and myopic. Gregory's *Our Irish Theatre* (1993a) strongly reinforces this impression. The validity of Griffith's objections is undermined on two counts: by arguing for the authenticity of Synge's narrative – Gregory reports how the elderly maidservant of a Yale professor swears to the story's veracity (Gregory 1913a: 110–11) – and by evoking such objections as an illustration of a more general restrictiveness from which Irish nationalism must be educated.

But Griffith's objection to *In the Shadow of the Glen* was by no means the only one. For other objectors, such as James Connolly and Maud Gonne, the basis of disapproval was quite different. For the latter, it is less a case that the *source* of Synge's play is non-national than that the play fails to engage with the majority indigenous culture; not so much that evoking English critics for approval is reprehensible because these critics happen to be English, but that the standards of literary criticism are inappropriate to the writings of an independence movement. Nationalists do not require dogmatic conformity to a formula of 'green coats and tin pikes', Connolly insists in 'National Drama', nor is it required that Irish dramatists surrender their autonomy. Instead, a national dramatist should be one whose own culture differs from that of the people in degree rather than in kind (Connolly 1903: 2). Like Kettle's 1902 article, Connolly dismisses the idea of intrinsic literary merit, and argues instead that in a national theatre it must be the audience and not the theatre directors who decide whether or not a play deserves to be called national. Gonne's 'A National Theatre' outlines a similar position. She rejects Yeats's view that literature must be personal by arguing that such a view is singularly inappropriate for a country like Ireland where the struggle for independence is collective and one in which the 'majority of the people . . . are personally and passionately engaged' (MacBride 1903: 3). Within the circumstances of political struggle an Irish national theatre will be one that will, of necessity, run athwart the principles of English literature. In this respect modern Irish writers must 'forget so much they have learned' (MacBride 1903: 3). Although neither Gonne nor Connolly develop the point, both essays imply that an Irish national theatre involves the formulation of an aesthetic practice that may well run counter to the standards and norms of English literary criticism.

This was absolutely not the way it appeared to Yeats. Distributed to each member of the audience at Synge's play was a copy of the September edition of *Samhain* containing two articles (Yeats's usual miscellaneous theatre notes as well as his March 1903 lecture, 'The Reform of the Theatre') that underline the theatre's aesthetic autonomy in the face of nationalist reductionism. 'Beauty and truth are always justified in themselves', writes Yeats, 'and their creation is of greater service to one's country than writing that compromises either in the seeming service to a cause' (Yeats 1903: 9). Disclaiming the majority of Gaelic League plays as 'mere propaganda', Yeats returns again to his idea that an Irish national theatre should function as a forum in which a minority ('the half dozen minds, who are likely to be the dramatic imagination of Ireland for this generation' (Yeats 1903: 7)) may set out to critique the views of the majority. And, in a move that further emphasizes the contrast between the new INTS and Cumann na nGaedheal, Yeats's 'The Reform of the Theatre' argues that English theatre is demoralizing not because it is English, or because it is controlled by capitalist syndicates based in England, but because English drama is sometimes badly written (Yeats 1903: 11). Deftly avoiding Kettle's 1902 argument, Yeats contends that nothing is intrinsically wrong with the English theatre's thematic preoccupation with 'the husband, the wife and the lover' (Yeats 1903: 11), and there is no reason whatsoever, except a borrowed English puritanism, why it should be opposed by Catholic Ireland. Indeed, if literature is the 'conscience of mankind' (Yeats 1903: 11), then its opposition to institutions that organize opinion, such as the church and political parties, is axiomatic. Conspicuously not mentioned by Yeats on this occasion are Irish unionism and the role of the British state. For Yeats, the 'voices of the mob' are, exclusively, the product of nationalist politicians and newspapers aided and abetted by 'the rough and ready conscience of the pulpit' (Yeats 1903: 11). Written for a lecture delivered six months *before* the protests against *In the Shadow of the Glen*, Yeats's remarks reiterate an analogy that is centrally important to the national literary theatre movement in this period: that of an art beset by philistines and the plight of Ireland's Protestant and non-nationalist minority.

That analogy is also underlined by Yeats in a series of three articles published in the weeks following the first performance of *In the Shadow of the Glen*. In a manner that suggests that the controversy concerning Synge's play was fostered as a *cause célèbre* even as it was then taking place, Yeats argues that political nationalism cannot be used as a criterion for the selection of plays since its preference for 'salutary rhetoric' subordinates literary merit. He appeals to the educated reader: just as a comparison of the popular Irish ballad collection *The Spirit of 'The Nation'* with John Keats's 'Ode to a Grecian Urn' is an obvious solecism, so drama with a patriotic intention is, by the same token, 'mere journalism . . . in dramatic form' (Yeats 1962: 116). As for his own notoriously patriotic play *Cathleen ni Houlihan,* Yeats declares that this was written not to assuage any external necessity, but because it arose from a dream. Any putative political effect is simply adventitious (Yeats 1962: 116). Again evoking the protests that greeted the 1899 production of *The Countess Cathleen,* Yeats condemns the literary ignorance that he sees as endemic to a Catholic and politically nationalist mentality: 'the very girls in the shops complained to us that to describe an Irish-woman as selling her soul to the Devil was to slander the country' (Yeats 1962: 121). Against the Catholic priest for whom 'literature is nothing' Yeats thus sets the man of letters as a heroic idol-breaker.

> The man of letters looks at those kneeling worshippers who have given up life for a posture, whose nerves have dried up in the contemplation of lifeless wood. He swings his silver hammer and the keepers of the temple cry out, prophesying evil, but he must not mind their cries and their prophecies, but break the wooden necks in two and throw down the wooden bodies.
>
> (Yeats 1962: 120)

Yeats's arresting image of the artist as a Protestant messiah figure decapitating the graven images of Catholic idolatry illustrates his point concerning the cultural function of a national theatre. Because a theatre's most important role is to cultivate individuality, idol breaking and icon smashing *must* be its vital characteristics. If this is offensive, the offence itself is a measure of the extent to which a national theatre is needed. Individuality needs to be encouraged because the 'noble nationalism' of the past has been replaced by an anti-intellectualism emanating from three overlapping systems of ignorance: that of the Gaelic propagandist, the Roman Catholic priest, and the nationalist politician. In contrast to Synge's uncom-promising verisimilitude and perspicacity ('Everyone knows who knows the country-places intimately, that Irish countrywoman [sic] do sometimes grow weary of their husbands and take a lover' (Yeats 1975: 307)) a nationalist aesthetic is one that portrays Irish rural life as artificially as 'a young lady's water-colour' (Yeats 1975: 308). Synge's *In the Shadow of the Glen*, it is implied, possesses exactly the opposite qualities to those supposed to emanate from Yeats's female water-colourist.

In the same vein, John Butler Yeats – the poet's father and a man whom Synge later identified as the best person to write an introduction to his play (Synge 1984: 47) – argues that *In the Shadow of the Glen* is to be welcomed as a respite from the inexorable monotony of nationalist consensus. Ireland, the elder Yeats claims, is now 'out of the dock', 'sufficient to itself', no longer in a state of oppression. In the wake of recent land and local government reforms, the country would do well to cease clamouring about its past sufferings and concentrate instead on the many problems of its own making: 'rent contracts', he adds caustically, 'are not the only ones in need of revision' (*United Irishman*, 10 October 1903: 2). From John Butler Yeats's perspective, therefore, Synge's play offers a salutary and long overdue investigation of the problems of Irish society and of a characteristically Irish institution: 'the loveless marriage'. Its only weakness is that it does not go far enough: 'he [Synge] did not make it quite clear that the wife will not return to the house into which she should never have entered, a view of the play I would earnestly commend to Mrs MacBride' (*United Irishman*, 10 October 1903: 2). This gossipy reference to Maud Gonne's recent (and apparently disastrous) marriage to the Boer war veteran and popular Irish nationalist, John MacBride, was also a sideswipe at the apparent collusive inseparability of political nationalism and the Catholic Church. John Butler Yeats's assessment of *In the Shadow of the Glen* as a mordant diagnosis of the contemporary state of Ireland was exactly to the point. What was so offensive for nationalists was not just its unflattering depiction of Irish peasant society; it was that with this production, the INTS appeared to accept that Ireland was indeed 'sufficient to itself', and thereby contributed to a contemporary discrediting of nationalist political demands.

There is an additional point. John Butler Yeats's defence of *In the Shadow of the Glen* may have appeared to align Synge's play to a growing Irish unionist critique not just of the Irish Parliamentary Party, but of the conciliatory efforts of Wyndham's Irish policy. For unionists in 1903, there was good reason to feel disenchanted. Instead of killing home rule by kindness, the Tory government's policy of reform and conciliation seemed to have achieved the opposite; accelerating the advance of the Catholic middle classes and reinvigorating home rule (Buckland 1973: 159). Like his predecessor, Gerald Balfour, Wyndham embraced the philosophy of constructive unionism: that is, Wyndham viewed the creation of a peasant proprietary and the fostering of indigenous institutions as a crucial means of strengthening the workings of the British state in Ireland, of pacifying rural discontent and of developing badly needed support for the Irish Unionist party. Wyndham's major legislative achievement, the Land Act of 1903, was directed towards this end. It provided for a massive use of state credit in order to make up the difference between a purchase price that tenants could afford and the price at which landlords might find it profitable to sell. But despite its reforming impetus this legislation generated considerable political opposition. The Irish Parliamentary Party, urged on by the United Irish League, argued that Wyndham's provision of a twelve per cent bonus for landlords indicated that the Land Act's true purpose was that of rehabilitating Ireland's traditional ruling class.

Unionists also viewed Wyndham's reforms as a source of dissatisfaction. Instead of conciliation leading to an improvement in the political situation, many Irish landlords and unionists noted with dismay the dramatic rise in rural intimidation organized by William O'Brien and the United Irish League. The unrest at Lord De Freyne's estate at Frenchpark in County Roscommon was an especially bleak reminder of the adversarial years of the Land War (see Bew 1987: 89; Gailey 1987: 182); moreover, as early as September 1902, forty nationalists were imprisoned and over half the country, including the cities of Dublin, Cork, and Waterford, had been proclaimed under the Crimes Act (Gailey 1987: 180). Pro-unionist newspapers, such as the *Irish Times* and *Daily Express*, reacted by calling on the government to respond decisively to the degenerating law and order problem. British government policy towards Ireland may not have altered radically in the early years of the century, therefore, but what had changed, and changed decisively for the worse, was the political space available for the conciliatory policies of constructive unionism (Gailey 1987: 180). This was to become an important context for the reception of Synge's plays at the INTS.

Another factor that contributed to the animated controversy generated by Synge's *In the Shadow of the Glen* was the on-going campaign for a Catholic university. This remained a deeply contested political issue (see Paseta 1999: 5–27). Some prominent unionists such as Sir John Ross, believed that the provision of a Catholic-controlled education system was crucial to putting a brake on the revolutionary potential of the United Irish League (Gailey 1987: 211–12). But the university question was even more important for Ireland's expanding middle-class population for whom the negative effects of not having a separate university appeared to be borne out by the census figures for 1901. (Within the medical and legal professions alone there remained a huge disproportion in favour of Irish Protestants (O'Brien 1982: 40, 282–3).) But while the issue was an obvious choice for inclusion in Wyndham's programme of reform and was perceived as critically important by Wyndham himself (Wyndham 1915: 29, 48, 52), it was also politically explosive. Many in the British cabinet were vehemently opposed on the grounds that it would strengthen the hold of the hierarchy and undermine the workings of the state. There was opposition also from Trinity College in Dublin, Queen's College in Belfast, from most unionist politicians in the north-east of the country, and from a substantial share of the British electorate. In February 1903, seven months prior to the performance of *In the Shadow of the Glen*, the Royal Commission appointed to look into the matter concluded that establishing a Catholic university would be inadvisable (Morrisey 1983: 194). For nationalists, it appeared that once again the just claims of Catholics had been sacrificed to anti-Catholic intolerance and the Ascendancy bigotry of Trinity College (Gailey 1987: 194, 202): stark evidence, in fact, that the university question could only be resolved within the context of an indigenous parliament with a Catholic majority (Gailey 1987: 202). Kettle, who may by no means be described as a strident nationalist or Catholic triumphalist, pointed to the British Prime Minister's denial of a University Bill as an 'insolent' abrogation of a fundamental principle of democratic politics: that the will of the majority should overrule that of the minority (Kettle 1937: 3).

As far as the conciliatory efforts of constructive unionism were concerned, then, the non-resolution of the university issue was a disaster. Not only did it increase the linkage between the Irish Parliamentary Party and the Catholic hierarchy, and foster a new spirit of religious intolerance (Gailey 1987: 306–7), but this, in turn, added to unionist fears that Irish constitutional nationalism was 'Rome rule' in disguise. Indeed, from a broadly unionist perspective, Wyndham's Land Act and the campaign for a Catholic university appeared, almost wilfully, to be missing the point. Seeking to provide a separate university was retrogressive to Ireland's modernization since it was bound to consolidate the already alarming control of education by the Catholic hierarchy. John Redmond and the nationalist members of parliament were 'practically under the heel of the hierarchy', complained one unionist pamphleteer four years later, and so what was needed in Ireland was not reform and constitutional change, but self-examination (see Miller 1909: 10). For this writer, as also for John Butler Yeats in his defence of *In the Shadow of the Glen*, Roman Catholicism remained Ireland's overwhelming 'medieval' barrier to progress.

Unionist criticism of Wyndham's policies and of the nationalist political campaign is popularized in M. J. F. McCarthy's vituperative social histories, the popular economics and journalistic accounts of P. D. 'Pat' Kenny, and the political commentaries of Canon J. O. Hannay (the novelist George Birmingham) and Sir Horace Plunkett. All held one view in common: constitutional changes to Ireland's political status should follow a radical change in Irish character and not – as Wyndham's reforms seemed to imply – the other way around. Thus 'Pat' argues that the first priority of the Irish is to confront their internal tyranny ('the hidden forces that make justice as well as democracy impracticable among them' (Kenny 1907: 24)) and argues that it is only when a robust self-criticism is practised and tolerated in Ireland that home rule should be contemplated (Kenny 1907: 53). Irish character must be released from the 'twin tyrannies' oppressing it, writes Hannay, 'the tyranny of the priest [sic] & the tyranny of the political boss' (Buckland 1973: 161) while McCarthy describes the power of the priest as 'the one unspeakable, unmention-able thing' (McCarthy 1902: xii). The popular (1905) edition of Plunkett's *Ireland in the New Century* is just as trenchant: only by opposing Catholicism's 'moral servitude' will Ireland achieve the necessary maturity for constitutional change (Plunkett 1905: 296, 300, 312–13). What is so much needed in Ireland, Plunkett grumbles, is not political home rule but 'just a little home rule in the region of thought' (Plunkett 1905: 299). As with John Butler Yeats's defence of *In the Shadow of the Glen*, what is here suggested is that the real source of Irish backwardness lies not so much in English misrule, as in indigenous social problems such as insanity, rural alcoholism, postponed marriages and priestly domination. Against Wyndham's misguided quixoticism, and the mounting demands of nationalist politicians for a Catholic university, the views of Plunkett, McCarthy, 'Pat' and Hannay present themselves as clear-sighted, analytical and faithfully empirical. 'If Ireland is to be saved', remarks 'Pat' with a quasi-missionary zeal, 'it is by the truth' (Kenny 1907: 25).

These views did not go unchallenged. Revd Dr M. O'Riordan strongly criticized Plunkett's *Ireland in the New Century* by arguing that its recourse to empiricism was not at all non-partisan, but rather a disguise for its support for the political status quo (O'Riordan 1906: 2) and by pointing out that attacking Catholicism 'in the shadow of an epidemic of slander against Irish Catholicism' was itself a political act (O'Riordan 1906: 14–15). As the Plunkett–O'Riordan debate suggests, anti-Catholicism was the hidden fulcrum around which a range of socio-economic issues were discussed. This is not to say that the criticism of clericalism in Ireland was unwarranted or that it was exclusively the preserve of unionists. Nationalist writers like John Eglinton, Francis Sheehy-Skeffington and Fred Ryan, and publications such as the *National Democrat*, the *Peasant*, and *Dana* were all vigorously opposed to the influence of the Catholic church on Irish political and civic life. Even separatist nationalists, like D. P. Moran and Arthur Griffith, were well known for their opposition to clericalism. But the basis for the nationalist objection tended to be that clericalism interfered with political organization, that it impeded independent thought and that it stood in the way of democracy. For the majority of unionist critics, the point was somewhat different: it was not just clericalism but Catholicism *per se* that impeded individuality and retarded Ireland's development (Plunkett 1905: 301).

The campaign to establish the INTS as an exclusively literary institution cannot be separated from this broader contemporary context. Just as a fundamental point for some Irish intellectuals was that individuality was not fully developed in Ireland because of the sclerotic influence of the Roman Catholic church, so for Synge the scandal of Irish life lay in the 'squeamishness' of its refusal to confront nationalist pretensions and Catholic hypocrisy (Synge 1983: 74). Like Eglinton, Sheehy-Skeffington and Ryan, Synge also believed that the country should face up to its many contemporary failings – the 'percentage of lunatics in Ireland and causes thereof' (Synge 1983: 74) – and that Ireland was in a state of 'a dismal morbid hypocrisy' (Synge 1983: 76). But what allies Synge more to unionist writers such as McCarthy, Kenny and Plunkett is the strong impression that this is part of an overall anti-nationalist objection. Indeed, even in a play like *Riders to the Sea*, which is regarded as sympathetic to an indigenous Irish culture and which audiences considered unobjectionable, it is possible to detect Synge's anti-nationalist edge.

Written in the immediate aftermath of the first performance of

Cathleen ni Houlihan (Synge 1982b: xv), *Riders to the Sea* is like the earlier play's antithesis. Instead of Yeats's and Gregory's narrative of a community regenerated by nationalist sacrifice, Synge's play shows a peasant community caught up in an atavistic cycle of despair and resignation. And whereas *Cathleen ni Houlihan* turns on an old woman transformed into youth, *Riders to the Sea* charts the relentless undermining of an old woman's hope that somehow her community will be regenerated. When, in March 1904, Frank Fay requested that Synge write a 1798 play 'as much alive as *In the Shadow of the Glen* and *Riders to the Sea*' but similar to *Cathleen ni Houlihan* showing 'what the peasantry had to endure' (Synge 1968: 215), Synge responded by reminding Fay that the primary objective of the INTS was literary: 'The whole interest of our movement is that our little plays try to be literature first – i.e. to be personal, sincere, and beautiful – and drama afterwards' (Synge 1984: 81). And when his friend Stephen McKenna advanced the Tom Kettle-like argument that 'literary nationhood' should precede 'frieze-clad Ibsens' (Synge 1983: 75), Synge defends the need for a theatre of Ibsenite social analysis and rejects outright a theatre of nationalist utopian projection:

> I do not believe in the possibility of 'a purely fantastic, unmodern, ideal, spring-dayish, Cuchulainoid National Theatre', because no drama – that is to hold its public – can grow out of anything but the fundamental realities of life which are neither modern or unmodern, and, as I can see them, are rarely fantastic or spring-dayish.
>
> (Synge 1983: 74)

The literary aesthetic of the INTS therefore had a distinct ideological significance. It bespoke cultural autonomy in the face of majority demands and it insisted on the representative authority of an educated minority. Indeed, the truth-value and empirical basis of Synge's writings were points that the dramatist reiterated on each occasion that his plays were performed or criticized. This was not simply a question of Synge's often-painstaking concern with the details of theatrical authenticity. When in July 1904 the actress Mary Garvey objected to a line in *The Well of the Saints* that referred to a priest pretending not to notice a drunken man and a girl in a ditch, Synge responded with pedantic emphasis that the simile was based on his actual experience (Synge 1983: 90–1). Catholic priests regularly beat their parishioners, Synge maintains, but they just as easily ignore the misdemeanours of those categories of people who would be likely either to fight back (as in the case of tinkers, strangers, sailors or cattle drovers) or who might be liable to press charges (as in the case of an Irish Protestant). He himself had witnessed two priests pretending not to notice the indecent approaches of a young man to a girl in Galway, and the incident struck him as typical of the 'many attitudes of the Irish church party' (Synge 1983: 91). Whether or not this was intended as a criticism of the Roman Catholic church in Ireland or of the Irish Parliamentary Party (the ambiguity is itself revealing), Synge's remark points to an almost institutionalized Irish hypocrisy: a Catholic nationalist obsession with home rule government without any consideration whatsoever of the many faults and problems of Irish society. Synge considered Catholic myopia to be a pervasive feature of Irish life, including the INTS. In a letter to Gregory on 11 September 1904, for example, Synge refers to Frank Fay's nationalist opposition to *The Well of the Saints* as evidence of 'a Neo-patriotic-Catholic clique' (Synge 1983: 94) and makes the unsubstantiated argument that the INTS actress, Helen Laird, was the subject of anti-Protestant discrimination.[1]

Later on that year, Synge was commissioned by the *Manchester Guardian* to write a series of articles on rural impoverishment in the west of Ireland. Accompanied by Jack B. Yeats (the poet's brother) as illustrator, Synge travelled in Mayo and Galway where he recorded his particular object of dislike, the rising Catholic middle class: 'the groggy-patriot-publican-general-shop-man who is married to the priest's half-sister and is second cousin once-removed to the dispensary doctor . . . the type that is running the present United Irish League anti-grazier campaign' (Synge 1982a: 283). In roughly the same period (December 1904/January 1905) Synge wrote two unperformed and unpublished scenarios that contain further scathing satirical attacks. Synge's scenario for 'Deaf Mutes for Ireland' conveys this well:

> [SCENARIO]
> The Gaels have conquered. A Pan Celtic congress is being held in Dublin. A large prize is offered for any Irishman who can be proved to know no English. A committee is sitting to try them. They bring in each man in turn, throw a light on him and say 'God save Ireland' and 'To Hell with the Pope'. Men are detected again and again. One is found at last who baffles all tests. In delight the congress is called in glorious

robes; the victor is put up to make a speech in Irish, he begins talking on his fingers – he is deaf mute and advocates a deaf mute society as only safeguard against encroaching Anglo-Saxon vulgarity!

(Synge 1968: 218)

Another scenario from the same period – 'National Drama—A Farce' – includes a raid on a group of Trinity College professors by 'a gang of cattle maimers from Athenry' (Synge 1968: 219). Such dystopian imaginings (reminiscent of Lady Gregory's anxiety-ridden 1893 pamphlet, 'A Phantom's Pilgrimage, or Home Ruin') convey a strong impression of Synge's unenthusiastic and, at times, embittered relationship with middle-class Catholic Ireland. In the case of both authors, there is a nightmarish fear of being overrun by a heartless (and philistine) majority.

For Yeats, Gregory and Synge, then, developing individuality was the primary goal of the literary theatre movement and was an issue with an ever-present denominational aspect. To 'get the right for every man to see the world in his own way admitted' (Yeats 1954: 447) was, first and foremost, a broadly Protestant endeavour: an objection to the 'medieval' and 'superstitious' faith of Irish Roman Catholicism. The production of Synge's plays functioned as the spearhead for this cultural mission (Yeats 1954: 447–8).

In February 1905, a few weeks after Kettle's attack on Arthur Balfour's anti-democratic denial of a Catholic University Bill, Synge's next play, *The Well of the Saints*, was first performed at the Abbey Theatre. Set in 'some lonely mountainous district on the east of Ireland, one or more centuries ago' (Synge 1968: 69), the play focuses on two married beggars, Martin and Mary Doul who, blind and on the margins of society, live their lives in a world that is materially impoverished but also enriched by their imaginative narrative skills. Most importantly, Martin and Mary are convinced of each other's extraordinary physical beauty. This blissful state ends abruptly when a visiting Saint cures them of their blindness by sprinkling them with holy water. As a direct consequence of this miracle, they discover each other as ugly and old, and the community in which they live as tawdry, acquisitive and mean-spirited. Eventually, however, their blindness starts to return and with it the consolation of their fictionalizing abilities. When, at the behest of the community, the Saint returns with his can of holy water determined to cure Martin and Mary with finality, Martin Doul *'with a sudden movement strikes the can from Saint's hand and sends it rocketing across the stage'*

(Synge 1968: 147). Horrified at this blasphemous action, the community rejects Martin and Mary. Although Mary is despondent, Martin leaves defiantly and the play ends with the community dutifully following the Saint, in procession, back to the church (Synge 1968: 151).

Rocketing a can of holy water across the stage of Ireland's national theatre was iconoclasm of a most direct and literal kind. For Arthur Griffith *The Well of the Saints* was 'a decadent wail with a Calvinist groan' (*United Irishman*, 11 February 1905: 1), and even Yeats expressed some concern that the profusion of 'Almighty Gods' in the play might 'weary and irritate the ear' (Yeats 1994: 636). More predictably, Edward Martyn, who was a devout Catholic, found 'all this sneering at Catholic practices . . . utterly distasteful' (quoted in Foster 1997: 334). But cavilling at Synge's tactlessness is missing the point. Not only is anti-Catholicism a fundamental aspect of the ideological impetus underlying Synge's plays and the INTS in this period, but it is an expression of the fraught, and increasingly sectarian, nature of the contemporary political scene in the wake of the devolution crisis of winter 1904. This crisis arose, in September 1904, when the Irish Reform Association proposed a scheme for devolution (Gailey 1987: 221). The scheme had been drawn up by Lord Dunraven assisted by the Under Secretary, Sir Anthony MacDonnell; what was so controversial was that their report reversed traditional unionist thinking. They argued that constitutional reform had to *precede* Ireland's political education and, to that end, a limited form of devolution was an absolute necessity. The outcry that followed the detailed publication of the report in the *Irish Times* was calamitous to the immediate future of constructive unionism in Ireland (Gailey 1987: 253). Dunraven's proposal for a twin (financial and legislative) council in which government nominated (mainly unionist) members would outbalance elected (mainly nationalist) members was denounced by nationalists as unacceptably partisan in favour of unionism (Lyons 1948: 6; Gailey 1987: 223). For the unionist establishment, however, the devolution proposal was an outrageous example of MacDonnell (and Wyndham) pursuing, without mandate, an unacceptably pro-nationalist Catholic position (Gailey 1987: 217). By early 1905, MacDonnell, himself a Roman Catholic, had become a unionist hate figure (Lyons 1948: 9; Gailey 1987: 229–31) even to the extent that a British cabinet minister described MacDonnell, albeit in his diaries, as a 'disloyal papist' (Arnold-Foster quoted in Gailey 1987: 263). By March Wyndham's own position had become so untenable that he submitted his resignation (Lyons 1948: 20). Within this acrimonious political and sectarian context, the ending of Synge's play with his imaginative blind beggars walking away from a society dominated by religious superstition and material acquisitiveness had a strong contemporary element.

The fall of Wyndham and the subsequent Liberal victory in the British General Election of December 1905 was a mixed blessing for Irish politicians. The extent of the Liberal majority (between 80 and 100 votes more than all of the other parties combined) meant that the Irish Parliamentary Party no longer enjoyed its former political leverage (Bew 1987: 124–5); for Irish unionists, however, there was the worry of the Liberal Party's long-standing support for home rule. In February 1906, the *Church of Ireland Gazette* condemned the Liberal policy on Ireland as 'disquieting and mischievous' (23 February 1906: 153) while other organs of Irish Protestant and unionist opinion, such as the Dublin *Daily Express* and the *Irish Times* urged the government not to reform the Royal Irish Constabulary, and petitioned instead for stronger security measures against politically fomented agrarian unrest. As Irish unionists insisted on protection from the intimidatory tactics of the United Irish League and the belligerence of Sinn Féin, Yeats and Gregory underlined the vital importance of artistic autonomy and the freedom of the theatre. But in articulating as their primary concern the tension between independent thought and organized opinion, they were also expressing an anxiety concerning the role and outcome of a minority within the context of majority self-government. More than any other cultural event in this period, the first production of Synge's *The Playboy of the Western World* crystallized these wider political concerns.

The narrative of *The Playboy of the Western World* begins with Pegeen, the daughter of a rural publican, preparing for her wedding to a local man, Shawn Keogh. Keogh's priest-fearing ineptitude makes him terrified of any action that might be construed as improper. It soon becomes clear that Pegeen is impatient with Keogh's frequent invocations of Fr. Reilly, and that she regrets the extent to which the virility and glamour of the past has now disappeared. Early on in Act I, the action is interrupted by the arrival of a young man, Christy Mahon. Impressing the locals with his fantastic story of having killed his father with the blow of a spade, and without any corroborating evidence to support him, Christy quickly achieves the status of a folk hero. So in awe is the local publican that he insists that Christy should spend the night as a protector for Pegeen. His daughter now properly protected by a man who has just killed his father, the publican removes himself to the all-night debauchery of a local wake. The only protest against this precipitous and unorthodox chaperon arrangement comes from Pegeen's fiancé and is based exclusively on his fear of Fr. Reilly. This is dismissed curtly by Pegeen and with each retelling of the parricide, Christy's self-esteem and rhetorical abilities increase proportionately. The arrival of Old Mahon, Christy's very undead father, is the play's comic denouement and is positioned in the midst of Christy's successful courtship of Pegeen (Synge 1982b: 157). Confronted with indubitable evidence that the parricide is a fabrication, Christy offers to kill his father 'again' (Synge 1982b: 165). But now the response of the local community, including Pegeen, is unanimous: they reject outright the person they had previously considered as a hero. And, in an action that echoes the concluding scene of a play that Synge loathed, Hyde's *Casadh an tSúgáin*, the locals attempt to tie Christy with a rope and drag him from the house. With this abrupt change in the play's dramaturgy, Pegeen (who had engaged earlier in lyrical exchanges with Christy) now attacks him by burning his leg with a sod of turf (Synge 1982b: 171). What produces this adverse change in the community's attitude to Christy is not so much the people's realization that Christy's story is a fabrication, but that it has been exposed as a fabrication. The local people do not object to violence as long as it is part of a narrative, but they recoil altogether when it is committed directly in front of them.

Pegeen's lament, 'there's a great gap between a gallous story and a dirty deed' (Synge 1982b: 169) encapsulates the point. This rural County Mayo community regenerates itself through narratives of violence that, absurdly, glamorize brutal local crimes within a larger narrative of 'holy Ireland'. But the actuality of violence with which the community is then threatened when Christy offers to kill his father 'again' belongs to a wholly different category of experience. For Christy, as for the audience, the local community is exposed as ugly, mean-spirited and cowardly. Synge's final *aperçu* is that the strength and maturity of the individual is directly proportionate to the individual's resistance to the will of the peasant community. Christy comes to maturity not only by asserting authority over his father, but by condemning the locality as mentally impoverished. At the same moment that local Connacht society is revealed as craven, priest-fearing and hypocritical, Christy is revealed as a fully integrated individual.

The shebeen setting of Synge's Act I – a commercial premises licensed to sell beer, wine and spirits – offers a tawdry commercialized version of the pastoral cottage kitchen settings of earlier peasant dramas like *Cathleen ni Houlihan, Casadh an tSúgáin,* and Synge's own *Riders to the Sea* (McCormack 2000: 312, 320). Despite its chronological vagueness the setting of *The Playboy of the Western World* – 'a village, on a wild coast in Mayo' (Synge 1982b: 55) – advertises a potentially contentious subject matter. Mayo was one of the western counties most associated with the agrarian warfare of the Land War and with a network of clandestine political organizations. It had the greatest concentration of congested districts, and was the principal area for the activities of the United Irish League. Moreover, for the Abbey Theatre's bourgeois and metropolitan audience, Mayo suggested both a place of unsullied national integrity and the location of sporadic and apparently inexplicable acts of violence. Incidents such as the Maamtrasna murders in 1882 (in which the killing of an entire family in a remote cottage was linked to a local secret society (see Waldron 1992)), or the notorious 1894 case of James Lynchehaun from Achill (who viciously attacked his English landlord employer by biting off her nose (see Carney 1986)) were well known throughout Ireland. The Lynchehaun case, by which Synge claimed that *The Playboy of the Western World* was partly inspired (Synge 1983: 333), dominated newspaper headlines well into the new century (Carney 1986: 158–87). The story achieved further prominence in 1902 when, on 7 September, Lynchehaun made a daring escape from Maryborough (now Portlaoise) prison and then smuggled himself to the United States. He was arrested a year later in Indianapolis. There followed a much-publicized court case which culminated in the decision by the United States Supreme Court on 2 May 1904 to refuse the British government's application for Lynchehaun's extradition on the grounds that the Achill assault was politically motivated (Carney 1987: 200–3). The Irish emigrant group, Clann na Gael, was jubilant, heralding Lynchehaun as a political exile (Carney 1987: 205). For unionist commentators, however, the Lynchehaun episode was a disgraceful sign of the times: a brutal criminal attack glamorized as nationalist insurgency.

There is a connection between this outraged response and Pegeen's speech in the first scene in which she laments the passing of the heroic virility of former days: 'Where now will you meet the like of Daneen Sullivan knocked the eye from a peeler, or Marcus Quinn, God rest him, got six months for maiming ewes, and he a great warrant to tell stories of holy Ireland till he'd have the old women shedding down tears about their feet' (Synge 1982b: 59). As Nicholas Grene's reading of the play points out, the violence that Pegeen here celebrates is a mixture of the gratuitously barbaric and the political (Grene 1999: 86–96). Assaulting policemen and wounding animals were regular occurrences during the Land War and both forms of violence were remembered, widely feared and still sometimes practised in the context of the contemporary anti-grazier activities of the United Irish League.

Synge's earliest version of *The Playboy of the Western World* is a manuscript draft, 'The Murderer: A Farce'. It is thought to have been written in Autumn 1904 (Synge 1982b: 295), that is, a few months after the extensive publicity concerning the Lynchehaun extradition case and at the beginning of the devolution crisis. This draft version of the play contains a few sketched paragraphs in which 'Christy O'Flaherty' appears to kill his father, boasts about the killing to such an extent that the police are afraid to prosecute him, and then is elected as a local county councillor. As he is about to make his first pre-election speech, his father appears and exposes Christy as a liar. The scenario ends with Christy being led off in handcuffs by the police (Synge 1982b: 295). This brief outline suggests a combination of political anxieties concerning the increasing nationalist militancy of Ireland's newly established county councils, and a particular worry that any form of national independence or self-government might entail an extension and broadening of the powers and responsibilities of county councillors as well as licence a continuation of the intimidatory tactics of the United Irish League. In the wake of the devolution controversy and the victory of the Liberal Party in January 1906, worries such as these were widely shared. Just a week before *The Playboy of the Western World* was performed in January 1907, Plunkett's *The Irish Homestead* complained angrily about 'Wexford's "glib councillors".' Plunkett denounces their suggestion that they, as elected representatives, would be better able to run the Irish Agricultural Organization Society, rather than people of proven leadership abilities like George Russell and himself (Plunkett 1907: 45–6). With a combination of chagrin and Ascendancy hauteur, Plunkett refers to 'this fellowship of butchers, traders, and livery stable men' and concludes by warning that the democratic principle in Ireland should be restricted only to local organizations. National institutions, by contrast, must be established according to a meritocracy: 'Local bodies are to look after local affairs, the mending of roads, the raising of rates, etc., but they are not to take up a great national problem' (Plunkett 1907: 45–6).

The controversy concerning *The Playboy of the Western World* was closely related to this raising of unionist anxiety in relation to home rule. Repeatedly in Irish Protestant and unionist organs of opinion, like the *Irish Times*, the *Church of Ireland Gazette*, the Dublin *Daily Express*, or in Lindsey Talbot-Crosbie's *After the Battle or Imperial Home Rule* (1906) or Lord Ashtown's *The Unknown Power Behind the Irish Nationalist Party* (1907), home rule is defined not as the political freedom and independence that follows from democratic majority rule, but as the enslavement of the individual and the destruction of independent opinion.[2] Such fears arose partly because of the now blatant links between the Catholic hierarchy and the leadership of the Irish Parliamentary Party, and partly because of the aggressively separatist positions of the United Irish League and Sinn Féin. For a *Church of Ireland Gazette* editorial in January 1906 John Redmond was the puppet of the Roman Catholic hierarchy (12 January 1906: 32–3) because Redmond had refused to challenge his rival candidate T. M. Healy on account of Healy's support from Cardinal Logue and Archbishop Walsh.[3] Synge's *The Playboy of the Western World* does not address these concerns explicitly, but it is motivated by the view that an impoverished peasant community – one regarded by nationalists as paradigmatic of Ireland's political oppression – regenerates itself through tales of violence, but collapses altogether when confronted by the prospect of its physical expression. In this respect *The Playboy of the Western World* allays a contemporary unionist anxiety concerning the relationship between the agrarian outrages of the United Irish League and the nationalist rhetoric of the Irish Parliamentary Party. Most importantly, in suggesting that the rhetoric of violence so beloved of Irish peasant society collapses when confronted by its brute reality, Synge's play crystallizes a contemporary 'law and order' view that agrarian insurgency might also collapse when and if it too were stoutly confronted by the violence of the state (Bew 1987: 144). *The Playboy of the Western World* controversy was a chance for unionists to take a stand against the majority, and to insist further on the protection of the police and of the courts in defence of the playwright's individual right of expression. But for nationalists, the main issue of objection in relation to *The Playboy of the Western World* was that Synge's play was a disgraceful slur on Irish womanhood and a betrayal of the Abbey Theatre's status as a national institution. To nationalist newspapers such as the *Freeman's Journal* and *The Leader* the spectacle of an Irish national theatre guarded, and its audiences invigilated, by the pro-unionist Dublin Metropolitan Police was a scandal. It revealed in particular the extent to which the newly renamed National Theatre Society (NTS) appeared to have been perverted by its English owner and by its Protestant and Ascendancy directors. (That the word 'Irish' had just been dropped from the national theatre's title at Horniman's insistence (Frazier 1990: 187) may also have contributed to the offence). In any case, the protests that followed the first performance of *The Playboy of the Western World* were an opportunity for nationalists to insist that a national institution like the NTS should be sensitive, if not wholly responsive, to majority opinion. For Yeats and the defenders of the theatre, however, it was a matter of principle not only that the police be invited to the theatre and asked to make arrests, but that those arrested should be prosecuted in the courts (Frazier 1990: 215–17).

Yeats, the *Irish Times* and the prominent Catholic unionist and judge, Sir John Ross, all regarded Synge's play as taking a stand for the freedom of the individual and intellectual independence. As against the intimidatory and para-legal methods of nationalist political groupings was set the Abbey Theatre whose operation was independent and transparent. For Yeats as reported in the *Freeman's Journal*, the problem is that there are no longer great leaders to be obeyed, but rather the dictatorship of the 'mob'. What was happening in the theatre, therefore, was symptomatic of what was happening to society as a whole, and those who caused the disturbance 'merely carried out a method which is becoming general in our national affairs' (quoted in Kilroy 1971: 33). For the *Irish Times* as well, the Abbey was to be commended for taking a stand against 'the clap-trap patriots' (quoted in Kilroy 1971: 37): 'bodies which seek to introduce into the world of the mind the methods which the Western branches of the United Irish League have introduced into politics' (quoted in Kilroy 1971: 37). To this broadly unionist and non-nationalist community, Synge's play was perceived as taking a stand against the threatening tactics of the United Irish League and of the newly established political party, Sinn Féin. As Judge Ross was reported to have said to Lady Gregory, 'You have earned the gratitude of the whole community – you are the only people with the pluck to stand up against this organized intimidation in Dublin' (NYPL: Berg; Robert Gregory to Lord Gough, 3 February 1907).

P. D. Kenny (or 'Pat') argued that *The Playboy of the Western World* was an outstandingly accurate analysis of Ireland's contemporary malaise and praised the 'merciless accuracy' (quoted in Kilroy 1971: 37) with which Synge illuminated that which nationalist Ireland insists on covering up: a priest-ridden country from which all of those with initiative have emigrated.

> He has led our vision through the Abbey street stage into the heart of Connaught, and revealed to us there truly terrible truths, of our own making, which we dare not face for the present. The merciless accuracy of his revelation is more than we can bear. Our eyes tremble at it. The words chosen are, like the things they express, direct and dreadful, by themselves intolerable to conventional taste, yet full of vital beauty in their truth to the conditions of life, to the character they depict, and to the sympathies they suggest. It is as if we looked in a mirror for the first time, and found ourselves hideous. We fear to face the thing. We shrink at the word for it. We scream.
>
> (quoted in Kilroy 1971: 37–8)

Kenny's assessment of the play was not the only one to take this attitude. John Quinn, a wealthy New York patron of Synge and Yeats, regarded the play in a similar light. Writing to Synge, Quinn argued that what was wrong with the protestors was that they 'can't stand the truth' (TCD: MS 4425/364, John Quinn to J. M. Synge, 23 August 1907: 3).[4] In these circumstances it was hardly surprising that Synge's play should occupy such a central role in the social and political life of the day. The thematic core of *The Playboy of the Western World* – the freedom of the individual as the basis of the rule of law, and the tyranny of majority rule – was also the main issue of the play's controversy.

But not all non-nationalists were as delighted. Canon Hannay described Synge's scathing indictment of the west of Ireland in *The Playboy of the Western World* as 'a Comedy of Hell' (TCD: Hannay Mss 3454/397), and Plunkett considered the play as 'clever, but foolish' (Plunkett Foundation: Diary, 14 June 1907). John Quinn may have hoped that the NTS would develop as a forum for satirizing the separatist pretensions of Sinn Féin, but there is little evidence that this was a view shared by Yeats or Lady Gregory. Nor was their concern with the Abbey Theatre's nationalist identity simply a matter of box-office expediency (Foster 1997: 368) or of political opportunism. For Yeats and Gregory, the ideological importance of the NTS lay in its ability as a national institution to lay claim to the cultural and symbolic apparatus of an envisaged Irish state. Certainly, Yeats's lecture to the British Association in

September 1908 referred to the NTS's production of *The Playboy of the Western World* as 'our Belfast address' (Yeats 1975: 369) and thus invited analogy with Lord Randolph Churchill's dictum, 'Ulster will fight, and Ulster will be right'. But this does not mean that Yeats regarded the first performance of *The Playboy of the Western World* as a declaration of opposition to home rule, or that he viewed this as the Abbey Theatre's cultural objective. On the contrary: the controversy concerning the 1907 production of *The Playboy of the Western World* and its later representation by Yeats and Gregory served as vitally important mechanisms for declaring an interest in any new nationalist dispensation. Churchill's maxim functioned well as a rallying call for Ulster unionism, but it served no similar purpose for those southern Irish unionist politicians such as Plunkett or Dunraven for whom some form of Irish independence, however limited, was a matter of inevitability and for whom, therefore, negotiation and accommodation were fundamental realities. To this extent, the Abbey Theatre's more eirenic engagement with nationalism in the period 1907–9, as evident in its performance of *The Rising of the Moon, Cathleen ni Houlihan* and Thomas McDonagh's *When the Dawn is Come* (1908) and its co-operation (for a time) with the Theatre of Ireland (Foster 1997: 399), was perfectly consistent with the NTS's production of *The Playboy of the Western World*.

This helps to explain the undisguised relish with which Yeats and Gregory defied Dublin Castle by insisting on a performance of G. B. Shaw's *The Shewing Up of Blanco Posnet* during the week of the Royal Dublin Horse Show in August 1909. The English censor, the Lord Chamberlain, had banned Shaw's play, but the ban did not apply to Ireland. The NTS decided to perform it in Dublin, and Lady Gregory's refusal to back down on the issue shocked the representatives of the Chief Secretary's office who felt that this would make a mockery of English law. Gregory's stubborn insistence that the play's performance should go ahead may well have been an embarrassing and inexplicable affront to the authority of the Lord-Lieutenant (Lord Aberdeen) and his Under Secretary (Sir James Dougherty), but it made perfect sense to Yeats and Gregory. In defying Dublin Castle by putting on a performance that was attended on its opening night not only by prominent unionists such as Lord Iveagh, but also by the wife of the Commander-in-Chief of the British Forces in Ireland, Lady Lyttelton (McDiarmid 1994: 27), Gregory and Yeats were making the point that Ireland operated, or at least ought to operate, according to a different political régime to that imagined by London.

Most importantly, performing *The Shewing Up of Blanco Posnet* against the wishes of a stuffy British administration demonstrated that Gregory and Yeats were an integral part of such a régime in waiting. Performing Shaw's play against the wishes of Dublin Castle was no radical act of anti-establishment defiance (McDiarmid 1994: 33), but it was a coup nonetheless.

3

NTS, LTD AND THE
RISE OF SINN FÉIN,
1910–22

Our dramatists, like our lyric poets, seem to be obsessed
with a passion for facts. They will not look at life through
rose-coloured glasses. Their tragedies are tragedies of naked
realism. Their comedies – and they produce comedies with
sparkle – are relentless exposures of our pettiness, our
meanness, and our narrow outlook upon life. No literature
known to me is less touched with sentimentalism than our
Irish drama. . . . The drama is the Irish art of the twentieth
century, and our dramatists are so determined to rub salt
into our wounds that they scarcely give us credit for having
any whole part in us.

(Birmingham 1912: 63–4)

In May 1910, the first phase of Ireland's national theatre movement
at the Abbey Theatre concludes, somewhat oddly, with the demise
of the reigning British monarch, King Edward VII. This situation
arose because Annie Horniman, the NTS's wealthy English patron
since 1904, decided to cease subsidization upon discovery that the
theatre had not cancelled its performances as a token of monarchal
respect. What incensed Horniman in particular was that the NTS
directorate (W. B. Yeats, Lady Gregory and Lennox Robinson) had
compounded their error by not publishing an apology in the daily
newspapers (Frazier 1990: 232–40). And, yet two days after the
King's death, on 13 May 1910, the following notice appeared in the
Irish Times:

The directors and manager regret that owing to an accident
the theatre remained open on Saturday last. Lady Gregory,
who was in the country, had wired immediately on receipt
of the news of the King's death, and of a telegram asking
for instructions, desiring it to be closed; but this was late in

the day; the matinée had already been put on, and it was
considered too late to stop the evening performance.

(*Irish Times*, 13 May 1910: 7)

Horniman deemed this notice to be inadequate as an apology,
demanded the dismissal of Robinson as manager and, when this
also was refused, responded by cancelling payment of the June
instalment of the subsidy. The Abbey Theatre was plunged into
crisis.

What is so remarkable about this affair, however, is not its
precipitousness. For Yeats and Gregory, Horniman's volatility, her
long-standing animus against all shades of Irish nationalism, and
her desire from 1909 to withdraw from the NTS itself were all
tediously well known (see Frazier 1990; Welch 1999: 50, 53). What
is surprising about the Horniman withdrawal, rather, is the extent
and fulsomeness of the explanations offered by the Abbey authorities.
Despite accusations of sycophancy from Arthur Griffith ('The
Englishwoman who subsidizes the Abbey Theatre has flogged
the directors of that institution in public and they have taken the
flogging with a smile', *Sinn Féin*, 21 May 1910: 1), Gregory and
Yeats conceded that keeping the theatre open on the day after the
king's death had been unintentional – even a mistake – and that they
were prepared to state publicly their regret. Moreover (as Gregory
was careful to emphasize in a subsequent legal attempt to have the
subsidy restored) this explanation had already been accepted by
'leading unionists,' and thus, she argued, there was no reason why the
non-closure of the Abbey should be seen as 'political' (NYPL, Berg
Collection: Draft of letter by Augusta Gregory for Whitney and
Moore). For Francis Sheehy-Skeffington, a well-known socialist,
pacifist, and campaigner for women's rights, Gregory's attitude
represented 'the dry rot of flunkeyism' eroding the status of the
Abbey Theatre as a national institution (*Irish Nation*, 21 May 1910:
3). In apologizing for the theatre's non-closure (albeit in a phraseology
not quite obsequious enough to satisfy Horniman), and in the
subsequent legal attempt to regain the subsidy, Yeats, Gregory and
Robinson show little concern that the Abbey Theatre might now be
perceived as a unionist and pro-British cultural institution.

There is a similar insouciance in Yeats and Gregory's establishment
of the Abbey Theatre Endowment Fund. Quickly set up in reaction
to Horniman's cancellation of the subsidy, this was a funding system
designed to ensure that future donations would take the form of
unencumbered gifts rather than subsidies or subscriptions. The

Abbey Theatre Endowment Fund was advertised extensively in England and, at its inauguration in Dublin, was supported by the Lord-Lieutenant, Lord Aberdeen, the Chief Secretary, Augustine Birrell, and by a leading unionist and prominent member of the Irish judiciary, Sir John Ross (see *Irish Times*, 28 October 1910: 7–8). Yeats and Gregory then registered the NTS in November 1910 as a limited liability company, 'National Theatre Society, Limited', and thereby became the theatre's sole directors and owners (*Irish Times*, 28 November 1910: 5). This removed the last vestiges of the NTS's once uncommercial and co-operative origins (Foster 1997: 423): Ireland's national theatre was now strictly private property (Malone 1929: 108), a limited liability company with unionist political support. For Sir John Ross, the Abbey Theatre was 'a centre of light all over Ireland' because of its steadfast resistance to nationalist political protest (*Irish Times*, 28 October 1910: 8). Yet, neither the privatization of the Abbey Theatre nor its support by key members of the British establishment in Ireland aroused controversy in the main nationalist newspapers. Why, one might well ask, should papers like the *Freeman's Journal* and the *Daily Independent* show such a marked lack of concern?

The answer lies not so much in any newfound nationalist credibility for the Abbey Theatre in this period, but in Ireland's changed political circumstances. The January and December 1910 general elections diminished the Liberal Party's parliamentary majority and consequently raised the fortunes of the Irish Parliamentary Party (IPP). Under the leadership of John Redmond, the IPP now occupied a pivotal position within the Westminster parliamentary arithmetic and so the success of the long-awaited third Home Rule Bill seemed a virtual certainty. In this context – that of the IPP's co-operation with the Liberals at Westminster and its preparation at home for some measure of national autonomy – the idea that an endowment fund for Ireland's national theatre should be launched by the British Chief Secretary and supported by unionists did not seem the scandalous or controversial affair that it might once have appeared. Nor was there any worrying contradiction between Gregory and Yeats establishing themselves as the sole owners of Ireland's national theatre and a new Catholic élite preparing itself for power. Both groupings realized that naturalizing the prestigious status of Ireland's dwindling Ascendancy also functioned as a way of naturalizing the idea of an élite as such. And while a list of those attending Lady Gregory's 'at home' at the Abbey on 22 November 1910 reads like an extract from Debrett's *Peerage*, the notable guests also included John Redmond's daughter, Johanna, and the wife of the nationalist MP, T. M. Healy (*Irish Times*, 22 November 1910: 8). That the Redmondite weekly, the *Freeman's Journal*, reported this event not only without criticism, but with a certain unctuous deference to Gregory ('her ladyship') indicates the extent to which Irish social and political life had changed (*Freeman's Journal*, 22 November 1910: 10). As the third Home Rule Bill progressed its way to the statute book, conciliation was, once again, the order of the day (McDowell 1997: 51).

It may have been for this reason that the Abbey playwright, William Boyle, characterized Yeats's and Gregory's decision to stage Johanna Redmond's play *Falsely True* in March 1911 as straight-forward political opportunism (NLI: ms 22,404 [ii]).[1] But support for the Abbey Theatre was a reciprocal process. That Yeats and Gregory were as interested in cultivating an alliance with the élite of constitutional nationalism as the élite of constitutional nationalism was interested in cultivating an alliance with them, is also suggested by the Abbey Theatre's ambivalent treatment of Synge. Since his death in 1909, Synge had become a byword for the NTS's literary achievement. More particularly, Synge was associated with a defence of artistic value against (as Yeats continually insisted) the reductive philistinism of the mob. Yeats's *Synge and the Ireland of his Time* (1911) and Gregory's 'Synge' (1913b) present this writer as the NTS's master dramatist. But for almost a decade to follow, the Abbey directors avoided performing Synge's more disputed plays in Ireland. Apart from occasional short performances of *The Playboy of the Western World* in 1911, 1914 and 1916, Irish productions of this play and of *The Tinker's Wedding* were avoided. What did take place, and took place regularly and defiantly in this period, were numerous productions of Synge's more controversial work in England, Canada and the United States. For Yeats, performing these plays amongst Irish emigrant communities abroad was evidence of 'a new patriotic, educated Ireland . . . insisting on its standards being recognised'; opposition and protest (something which Yeats claimed disingenuously no longer took place in Ireland) instance a bigoted nationalism, twenty years out of date (*Irish Times*, 20 January 1912: 8).[2] Apart from Sinn Féin, which in the period 1910–14 was no more than a small nationalist faction (Lee 1989: 8) and D. P. Moran's inimitably cantankerous references in *The Leader* to 'the Shabby Theatre,' Irish nationalists in Ireland had no special difficulty with this line of argument. Home rule was now a unifying slogan with a wide variety of political meanings (Fitzpatrick 1977: 93). What was important to the Abbey's nationalist supporters like John Redmond, John Dillon and T. M. Healy, *and* to some Protestant Ascendancy figures such as Sir Horace Plunkett and Canon Hannay, was its role as an instrument of modernization. An underlying agreement about this cultural function allowed Gregory to write confidently of the Abbey Theatre as 'our' Irish theatre while at the same time hinting at an analogy between her role in instigating the Irish Literary Theatre and the imperialist philanthropy of her distinguished friend, Lady Enid Layard (Gregory 1913a: 8). Just as Redmond thought of Ireland under home rule as 'an autonomous nation within the Empire' and thus as beneficial to the empire (quoted in Bew 1994: 128), Gregory considered a national literary theatre as a consolidation rather than a weakening of the union between Ireland and Britain. The only issue that threatened this consensus was the adverse publicity of Abbey Theatre tours in the United States (see *Freeman's Journal*, 21 November 1911: 8). From the arrival of the Abbey players in the United States in September 1911 to their departure from Philadelphia in March 1912, certain performances (especially those of T. C. Murray's *Birthright* and Synge's *The Playboy of the Western World*) were the subject of repeated protest that culminated, in January 1912, with the arrest of the Abbey players who were charged with immorality (Everson 1966: 84).

This is also the period of Gregory's seminal work of Irish theatre history, *Our Irish Theatre* (1913a). Hurried into publication so as to coincide with the second Abbey Theatre tour of the United States in 1912–13,[3] Gregory's story of the national theatre movement is an almost unbroken narrative of conciliation and agreement. Opening chapters are at pains to emphasize the extent to which support for the 1899 Irish Literary Theatre came from a wide variety of political backgrounds – from the former Fenian, John O'Leary, to unionist luminaries such as W. E. H. Lecky and Sir Frederick Burton – while the book's later chapters maintain this impression of consensus by balancing nationalist displeasure at Synge's *The Playboy of the Western World* in 1907 with the displeasure of Dublin Castle at the Abbey première of G. B. Shaw's controversial *The Shewing Up of Blanco Posnet* in 1909. At the same time, however, Gregory follows Yeats's lead in describing the various protests against the Abbey as 'riots' and in explaining their motivation in terms of an endemic, Irish cultural myopia. Defined as a kind of pre-modern, literal-mindedness that is unable to comprehend the nature of symbolic representation, and from which audiences, and Irish Catholic audiences in particular, must be educated, it was precisely against this myopia that the Irish theatre movement was established. Hence, for Gregory, the steadily diminishing rate of theatre protests in contemporary Ireland is a salutary indication that the conflict between artistic freedom and Ireland's cocktail of recalcitrant nationalism and unbending (Roman Catholic) religiosity is slowly being dissolved. Commenting, for example, on the way in which her own play, *Spreading the News*, was objected to when it was first performed in December 1904, Gregory notes that Abbey Theatre audiences have been sufficiently 'educated' so that they 'know now that a play is a selection not a photograph and that the much misquoted "mirror to nature" was not used by its author or any good play-writer at all' (Gregory 1913a: 91). As for the protests directed against the Abbey Theatre on tour in the United States, these are portrayed in similar terms: a conflict between recently arrived immigrants and rabble rousers,[4] and a more established, more socially integrated, and better educated United States population – such as the professors and students of wealthy eastern universities, politicians like the Republican Party leader, Theodore Roosevelt, and influential public figures like the New York lawyer, John Quinn. (This was, of course, precisely the readership for whom *Our Irish Theatre* was intended). What prevents the stark facts of recurring popular opposition to Ireland's national theatre from appearing to contradict the idea of the Irish theatre as an expression of consensus, then, is the overriding importance of a literary education. Unlike the often sectarian and apocalyptic warnings of Edward Carson or M. J. F. McCarthy,[5] or the cataclysmic forecasts of the Irish Unionist Alliance (McDowell 1997: 46), Gregory's tone in *Our Irish Theatre* is one of sang-froid.

But what helps Gregory allay the widely held unionist anxiety that home rule is Rome rule is not just constructive unionist moderation. It is her assumption that in so far as the Irish theatre is literary it enshrines the notion that patriotism is neither agreement with 'the people', nor an expression of their current orthodoxies, but rather quite the reverse: a forum for the critique of majority views (Gregory 1913a: 66–7). Other southern Irish Protestant intellectuals held similar opinions. In an address to the Royal Dublin Society in February 1912, for example, the novelist, Canon J. O. Hannay (George Birmingham) remarked that art was now one of the few areas of Irish life in which the majority was not necessarily always right and that artistic autonomy should, therefore, be carefully cultivated and protected (*Irish Times*, 8 February 1912: 7). And in his 1911 lectures in the United States, Yeats emphasized the importance of Synge for an 'independent Irish culture' (Foster 1997: 445) and related the performance of Synge's *The Playboy of the Western World* to 'an educated patriotic Ireland . . . insisting on its standards being recognised' (Foster 1997: 454). Gregory places such a degree of emphasis on this point that by the time of the conclusion of *Our Irish Theatre*, the pronoun of the book's title signifies not so much the collective nationality for whom the Irish theatre is intended, but the extent to which the NTS remains indebted to the leadership and initiative of that largely Protestant Ascendancy of which Gregory, by virtue of her birth, religion and husband's baronetcy was a titled and prominent representative. As a *literary* institution, then, Ireland's national theatre adumbrates within the public sphere the special place and potential vetoing power of Ireland's traditional leadership class. In this important respect, Gregory's conception of the Abbey as the national theatre looks forward to the initial role of the Senate in the Irish Free State:[6] that of expressing the still relatively privileged position of Ireland's ex-unionist minority.

Gregory's *Our Irish Theatre* was not, therefore, concerned exclusively with theatre history. As with the two Abbey Theatre tours of the United States in this period, the book also served to petition support for a version of home rule that regarded national independence less as political autonomy and more as imperial integration. It carried the implicit argument that any system of Irish self-government should not be reduced to the common denominator of the democratic franchise and was directed primarily towards a North American audience. As the most important arena outside of Ireland for competing versions of Irish independence in the first two decades of this century, the United States comprised an important location for defining what home rule might reasonably entail. Here, the anti-imperialistic version of home rule promoted by the Irish immigrant group Clann na Gael existed in constant battle and the pro-imperialistic version of national independence supported by the British authorities and by President Roosevelt (see Ward 1969: 61; Foster 1997: 445). Less than nine months prior to the first Abbey tour of the United States in 1911, T. P. Gill, former editor of the *Daily Express* (1898–1900) and from 1900 a senior civil servant at the Department of Agriculture and Technical Instruction in Dublin, sought and received reassurance from Roosevelt that the former American president's position on Irish home rule had not changed (see Morison *et al.* 1954: 209–10). Roosevelt himself was a keen supporter of the Abbey Theatre players. At a performance of *The Playboy of the Western World* in New York in November 1911, the

President visited the theatre to demonstrate his support for the Abbey in the face of Clann na Gael opposition and then went on to praise the Abbey players for their work on behalf of 'the dignity of Ireland'. These were important public gestures. Most importantly, Roosevelt's presence at the play bolstered the idea of the Abbey Theatre as a national institution that was defiantly *outside* the dictates of popular or majority objection.[7] Yeats was all too well aware of this, remarking to Gregory that Roosevelt's gesture had done much to stave off 'the danger of a regular open clerical campaign against us' (quoted in Gregory 1974: 461). Unquestionably, therefore, the 1913 publication of Gregory's *Our Irish Theatre*, and the Abbey Theatre's battles with Clann na Gael while on tour in the United States, were all about helping to establish the national pre-eminence of the NTS. But this was also related (albeit more subtly) to maintaining and protecting a special position for Ireland's southern unionist minority.

Back in Dublin, the plays that now predominate in the Abbey Theatre repertoire are those dealing with themes of rural backwardness and national introspection. Lennox Robinson's *Harvest* (1910) and *Patriots* (1911), Padraic Colum's *Thomas Muskerry* (1910), T. C. Murray's *Birthright* (1911) and *Thomas Harte* (1912) all work to expose Ireland's new rural proprietorial class as acquisitive, imaginatively impoverished, and as beset by contradictions of its own making. Robinson's *Harvest*, for example, features a cottage setting that is described by one of the play's characters as looking 'just like a scene in the Abbey Theatre' (Robinson 1911: 2), but the play's action reveals a peasant family crippled by debts acquired through their over-ambitious programme of self-education and social advancement. As first generation *petit bourgeois* of peasant stock, the younger Hurley family from West Cork is unhappy and in crisis. Jack Hurley is a chemist's assistant in Dublin but is married to the daughter of a Protestant Ascendancy British Army colonel; perpetually short of money, Jack finds it impossible to relate successfully either to his rural past or to the more comfortable upper middle-class background of his wife. The only daughter of the family, Mary, lives in London where her family believes her to be working as a lady's maid. Another brother has been educated as a priest, another is a solicitor, and a fourth works in England as the personal assistant to an Earl. When Jack arrives home hoping to effect a loan from his farmer brother Maurice, he finds that the family farm has been bankrupted because of the expenses incurred in educating his brothers, sister and himself and that, for various reasons, none of his siblings is able, or prepared, to assist in repaying the debt (Robinson 1911: 14–15). Blame for this entire catalogue of disaster rests with the well meaning but naïve local schoolteacher, William Lordan, who has dedicated his life to educating a former peasant class into an emergent, and primarily urban, bourgeoisie. A final, devastating disillusionment comes when it is revealed that Mary (described by Lordan as 'the best scholar I ever had' (Robinson 1911: 31)) – has spent the last few years working not as a lady's maid, but as a society prostitute. Ironically, it is her gift of £50 that allows Maurice to retain the farm, and that allows Lordan's cycle of education, unhappiness and emigration to continue: to the end, Lordan remains unaware that his educational 'harvest' is, in fact, a catastrophe (Robinson 1911: 57–61). Very bluntly, Robinson's play suggests that Roman Catholic, Irish peasant society would be much happier without the traumatic upheaval of its current social and educational advancement. Robinson's project is an ironic under-mining of what the dramatist perceives is an established glamorization of Irish rural life. But, in fact, sentimentalizing the Irish peasant was a phenomenon strikingly *absent* from previous Abbey Theatre productions (Hogan *et al.* 1979: 17). Moreover, while the acerbity of Robinson's analysis of Irish rural life 'out Synges Synge' (Hogan *et al.* 1979: 33), the play's overall effect is one of regret for the passing of an impoverished, but stable, peasant society. In the play's final scene, for example, when Mary prepares to return to London where she intends to resume her clandestine occupation as a prostitute, the spectator is left in no doubt that the Hurley family from West Cork would be much happier if their ambitions to overreach themselves socially had somehow been curtailed. Even moderate nationalists found the revisionist lessons of *Harvest* hard to accept: Robinson should have his neck wrung, advised the *Evening Telegraph* (O'Neill 1964: 58).

Rural demystification was a preoccupation that continued apace at the NTS although not always with Robinson's polemical fervour. T. C. Murray's *Birthright* (1910), for example, concentrates on the rivalry between the younger and elder Morrisey sons for the inheritance of the farm belonging to their parents, Bart and Maura, and is a scathing indictment of the idea of Irish peasant life as imaginative, noble or autochthonous. Bart Morrisey is so embittered by his work that he fails to appreciate the sporting and cultural achievements of his elder son, Hugh, and encourages his younger son, Shane, to think of the family farm as belonging more rightfully to him. The play's climax is a fight between the two brothers in which Shane unintentionally kills Hugh with a hurley stick (Murray 1998:

57). In all of this, Murray's focus is on Ireland's primogenital system of rural inheritance within which, the play's narrative suggests, there is no possibility that the idealism of national regeneration and the practicalities of agricultural labour will ever be reconciled. What the play does not address are the reasons for primogeniture in thirty years of tardy land reform, nor its history since the mid-nineteenth century, nor the political arguments put forward by the anti-grazier movement for changing it. Instead, *Birthright* concentrates on the fatal inevitability of primogeniture within the Irish social system and on its tragically divisive consequences.

This is a general trend in the plays of Colum, Murray, Robinson and a handful of lesser known dramatists like R. J. Ray or John Guinan. The social problems of Irish rural life are portrayed as internecine: a consequence of inherited social systems that can only be removed by means of an accelerated process of cultural modernization. As Yeats stated in an interview with the *Pall Mall Gazette* in June 1911, the 'Cork Realists' (Murray, Ray and Robinson)[8] were 'men . . . studying the conditions and problems of our national life' (quoted in Hogan *et al.* 1979: 126). But in their suggestion that rural dysfunctionalism is not a political, but an ontological problem, these plays tend to reflect the contemporary interests of constitutional nationalism. Indeed, the strength of the Irish Parliamentary Party in this period was proportional to the extent to which it subsumed, or attempted to subsume, a network of traditional and often localized political allegiances such as those of the United Irish League and anti-grazier movements while at the same time underlining the need for an exclusively parliamentary politics (see Foster 1997: 461). The IPP's restraining force on land agitation and rural activism was not always successful, and sometimes led to considerable tension between local activists and their more conservative parliamentary representatives (see Varley 1994: 195–8).

It is not at all surprising, therefore, that plays performed at the NTS show political militancy as dangerous and irrelevant. Ingeniously, Robinson's *Patriots* castigates the acquisitive materialism of contemporary Ireland and the militant nationalism that it has displaced by suggesting that it was the extremism of this militancy that made such materialism inevitable in the first place. Nationalist militancy is not just anachronistic, Robinson's play suggests, but it is the source of contemporary acquisitiveness. Set in a provincial town, *Patriots* deals with the Rip Van Winkle effect of a former Irish Fenian, James Nugent, after he is released from prison. During his incarceration, Ireland has become a nation of shopkeepers and thus

Nugent's repeated question, 'How are we off for arms?' (Robinson 1982: 43), is met by his colleagues with disbelief and embarrassment. 'I drilled secretly twenty years ago for Ireland,' one League member admits, 'now I make bread for Ireland – that's progress' (Robinson 1982: 56). Finally, Nugent realizes that the entire tradition of republican militant opposition to British rule has been a terrible mistake and, in the context of Ireland's contemporary acquisitiveness, is also an anachronism (Robinson 1982: 62). At a time when the majority of those engaged in Irish agriculture were, in fact, struggling at subsistence level – in 1910, for example, 50 per cent of Irish farm holdings were under 15 acres, and 72.4 per cent were under 30 acres (Crotty 1966: 251) – the preoccupation of Abbey Theatre plays is a lament for the materialist and social ambitions of rural modernization, but also an acceptance of the inevitability of the modernization process itself.

It is not so much that themes of anti-imperialism are entirely absent from the NTS repertoire in this period, but that popular motifs associated with anti-imperialism tend to be portrayed within an exclusively internecine social context. In Murray's *Birthright*, for example, the word 'grabber' (Murray 1998: 57) is used to denote not someone who advances him- or herself by colluding with a *system* of exploitation, but rather an individual who acts exclusively in his or her own interests. Yet it is the extent to which the former, more political meaning cannot fully be expunged, that triggers the play's tragic ending: Shane's fatal attack on his older brother (Murray 1998: 57). Similarly, Redmond's *Falsely True* deals directly with the stigma that attaches itself to the role of informer, and suggests that this stigma is misplaced. Through the case of the play's main character (Shaun) who reneges on his comrades to save the life of his brother, Redmond's play suggests that informing can be altruistic in some situations. But although Shaun's devoted and patriotic parents accept this point of view, it is also clear that it will take much longer before the local community forgives him. Another illustration of this trend of historical reappraisal is the workhouse setting of Colum's *Thomas Muskerry*. As Ireland's principal institutional reminder of famine and rural impoverishment, the workhouse is reinterpreted in Colum's play not as a monument to British misrule, but as a contemporary icon of bourgeois acquisitiveness. The play's grim, melodramatic ending – Thomas Muskerry, the former workhouse master, now relegated to a pauper's bed – occurs not because of an iniquitous political or economic system, but because of the unstoppable greed of Muskerry's own blood relatives. And in St John Ervine's *Mixed*

Marriage (1911), one of the most popular plays in the NTS repertoire in this period, the politically sensitive topic of anti-Catholic pogroms in Belfast (and their relation to the anti-Catholic rhetoric of unionist leaders such as Sir Edward Carson) is avoided by Ervine's exclusive concentration on the domestic. Sectarian prejudice is seen as a problem that arises from individual personalities, rather than as related to the structural or political features of Irish society.

In general, then, the thematic emphasis of plays performed at the Abbey Theatre in the period 1911 to 1915 reflect the political interests of the IPP, and its informal alliance with the constructive elements of the southern Irish social élite. That the narrative of Robinson's *Harvest* suggests the impossibility of any such alliance taking place at the level of personal relationships (Mildred, the daughter of an Irish unionist, and Jack the son of a peasant realize that their marriage will not survive unless they emigrate) disguises the fact that such associations were already well under way within the spheres of business and local politics.[9] George Birmingham's 1912 remark that contemporary Irish drama was gratuitously rubbing salt into old wounds (Birmingham 1912: 63) or George Russell's (AE) comment that 'All this is helping is our natural pessimism and self-mistrust' (quoted in O'Neill 1964: 61) missed the point. Celebrating modernization and interrogating a predominantly rural way of life was now closely related to the NTS's cultivation of Ireland's new political élite. Yeats and Gregory's view of the actors as social inferiors, and their idea of the Abbey acting troupe as 'temperamentally unfitted to undertake roles representing men and women of the upper classes' (quoted in Hogan *et al.* 1979: 139), certainly contribute to the dominance of the Irish peasant play in this period. But the Abbey Theatre's conception of itself as an instrument of national modernization is also a vitally important factor. Under the imprimatur of Synge, and within the optimistic political context of impending home rule, a crucial index of literary achievement at the NTS is the sharpness of a play's critique of Irish rural life. As this was a point of broad agreement between nationalists and constructive unionists, it was no wonder that Gregory could describe the NTS as 'our Irish theatre'.

But this political consensus did not last for long. Although the third Home Rule Bill was placed on the Westminster Statute Book in September 1914, it was accompanied by two debilitating qualifications: first, an insistence that the Act could not come into operation until after the war and, second, an undertaking that the issue of the government of the six north-eastern counties of Ulster still remained to be considered. Redmond did his best. By urging his followers to support England's war effort, join the British Army, uphold the empire at its hour of need, Redmond tried to maintain the alliance between the Irish Parliamentary Party, the British Liberal Party and the progressive or 'constructive' minority of southern Irish unionism. Redmond's endorsement of British Army recruiting was itself supported by a panoply of influential Irish bodies and institutions including the Roman Catholic hierarchy, Dublin Corporation, Dublin Chamber of Commerce, University College, Dublin and the two principal nationalist newspapers, the *Irish Independent*, and the *Freeman's Journal* (O'Brien 1982: 254–5). But although for southern unionists this was positive proof of the conciliatory and pro-imperial face of constitutional nationalism, their optimism diminished sharply with the progress of the war. Rumours of impending conscription (O'Brien 1982: 256; Townshend 1983: 280–1; Bew 1994: 122) and a strengthening of the impression that home rule had now been postponed indefinitely (Lee 1989: 23) eroded the basis of political consensus. An accumulation of grievances, such as those that stemmed from the British Treasury's severe curtailment of the land distribution scheme of the Congested Districts Board (Varley 1994: 201–2) or from the British Army's blunt refusal to countenance Redmond's petitions for Irish military divisions, strengthened Sinn Féin's argument that Redmond and the IPP had been out-manoeuvred and that home rule was now even further off than it had been before. For Sinn Féin's growing separatist constituency, the British Army's recruitment campaign did not illustrate a unifying political alliance that spelled hope for the future, but was a clear demonstration of the deleterious effects of 'coalitionism' (*The Spark* 1.25 [25 July 1915] 1) and of British government high-handedness.

For unionists also there was disillusionment: an awareness that patriotism in the context of the European war meant one thing for them, but quite another for Irish nationalists (McDowell 1997: 54). But, for nationalists, defending the 'rights of small nations' and 'protecting Catholic Belgium' merely begged the question: what about Catholic Ireland and its right to self-government? (Townshend 1983: 280). Instead of imperialist consensus, in other words, the political gulf in Ireland had widened. From mid-1915, southern unionist opinion castigated the lukewarm response to recruitment in the south and was especially critical of the IPP for not assisting with its considerable political machine. What was revealed by the IPP's ineptitude, argued the *Irish Times* in January and February

1916, was the fundamental 'triviality' of Irish public life (see McDowell 1997: 55).

Within this context, the Abbey Theatre adopted a confidently pro-British position. There were benefit concerts for the troops (O'Brien 1982: 255), the October 1915 appointment of St John Ervine (an outspoken northern unionist) as General Manager,[10] and in November 1915, a brief, unpublicized controversy concerning Shaw's anti-war play, *O'Flaherty, V.C.* The British military authorities warned Ervine that Shaw's play was unhelpful to army recruitment and should therefore be withdrawn. Although Shaw himself urged the NTS to oppose the Dublin Castle directive (as had been done so forcefully in the 1909 case of *The Shewing up of Blanco Posnet*) and claimed that Dublin Castle's view was based on a serious misreading of his play, the unanimous opinion of Yeats, Gregory and Ervine was that *O'Flaherty, V.C.* should not be performed. For Ervine in particular, the slightest prospect that a Sinn Féin element in the audience might misinterpret certain passages of the play in an anti-British light was reason enough for cancellation. Should Sinn Féin accuse the NTS of pro-British censorship, Ervine's answer was simple: the Abbey Theatre must stand firm (Hogan *et al.* 1979: 384–9). Risking Sinn Féin opprobrium was far less important than the risk, however slight or ill-founded, of undermining Britain's hard-pressed recruiting campaign.

But the most striking evidence of a change in the cultural politics of the NTS in this period was Ervine's speech to the Dublin Literary Society in February 1916. Commenting initially and with approval on the Abbey Theatre's improved finances and expanded middle-class audience ('He was pleased to say that the theatre was now very well and Rathmines seemed to have discovered it at last'), Ervine turned to a more controversial topic: the NTS's reputation as a 'disreputable institution organized by people who hated Ireland and were forever maligning the Irish people'. The problem, Ervine argued, lay not so much with the dramatists, but with the present condition of Ireland.

> When a nation was healthy and vigorous, that nation could stand strong plays. But when a nation was weak and decadent, that nation could not stand strong plays; it could not stand anything; and that was the state Ireland was in now. The Irish people had completely lost their sense of reality.
>
> (*Irish Times*, 12 February 1916: 4)

Echoing and adding to Yeats, Ervine concluded that Irish maturity would be gauged in terms of the country's readiness to accept 'strong drama' without protest or objection (quoted in Hogan and Burnham 1984: 12). But Ervine's insensitivity to Irish nationalist sentiment is not simply maverick northern tactlessness ('the Ulsterman was a stronger man, a better man, though, perhaps, not so charming'). His comments about weak Irish plays as a symptom of an innate national weakness also articulate Yeats's and Gregory's own views that the NTS was concerned, above all, with criticizing majority orthodoxies from a broadly unionist political position.

As far as generating social and cultural consensus was concerned, Ervine's remarks were a disaster. Ervine's own stirring up of political controversy was again evident just one month after the 1916 Easter Rising. Four weeks after insurgents affiliated to the Irish Volunteers and to James Connolly's Irish Citizen Army took control of a number of strategic buildings in Dublin and proclaimed the existence of an Irish republic from the steps of the General Post Office, and only two weeks after the imposition of martial law and the phased execution of fourteen of the rebellion's leaders, Ervine insisted on an unscheduled performance of Synge's *The Playboy of the Western World*. Here was a play, still well known in Ireland for its perceived anti-Catholicism and anti-nationalism (and for this reason 'shirked . . . for years by the Abbey management' (Gregory 1974: 546)), which Ervine now demanded should be performed on the first month's anniversary of the rebellion. (That the first month anniversary of bereavement has a special significance for Irish Catholics ('the month's mind') may well have added to the offence.) Thus, when Ervine insisted that the actors should attend additional rehearsals so as to prepare Synge's play for performance, the Abbey Theatre players simply refused to attend. Instead, on Monday, 29 May 1916, they issued their own 'proclamation' protesting against Ervine's dictatorial policy (Hogan and Burnham 1984: 22–3). In an interview with the *Freeman's Journal*, a representative of the players (Arthur Sinclair) stated that one of the primary causes of their friction with Ervine was his 'dabbling in politics' and their 'disapproval' of his speech to the National Literary Society (*Freeman's Journal*, 30 May 1916: 4).

Ervine responded to the players in kind – that is, with his own version of martial law – and dismissed the entire company forthwith (Hogan and Burnham 1984: 22–5). Yeats and Gregory did not contradict these orders of dismissal although, six weeks later, Yeats suggested that it would be better if Ervine did not renew his position as manager. Yeats's letter cites the 'commotion' at the Abbey and Ervine's 'impatient temperament' as the reason (quoted in Hogan and Burnham 1984: 33). Privately, Gregory was especially dismayed: attempting to perform *The Playboy of the Western World* in 1916, she wrote in her journals, was 'snatching a mean triumph . . . just as those who have attacked it are in prison' (Gregory 1974: 546).

The Easter Rising was therefore an unpromising context for the Abbey Theatre to function as a national cultural institution. As Yeats remarked in its immediate aftermath, the 1916 insurrection dealt a fatal blow to the unifying and conciliatory project of the Irish literary movement. 'All the work of years has been overturned, all the bringing together of classes, all the freeing of Irish literature and criticism from politics,' he wrote to Gregory, 'I had no idea that any public event could so deeply move me – and I am very despondent about the future' (Yeats 1954: 613). But Yeats was overly pessimistic, and there is no evidence of any corresponding trauma in the NTS. Aside from Ervine's dismissal, and Gregory's occasional worries about plays that might be 'too political' for Sinn Féin audiences (Hogan and Burnham 1984: 93, 101), there is no sudden change of tack in the plays performed at the Abbey in this period, or in the way in which the NTS presents itself as an Irish institution. And while the extraordinary rise in political support for Sinn Féin in this period might lead one to surmise that the Abbey Theatre would avoid the peasant plays that Sinn Féin has previously considered anathema, this was not in fact the case. By December 1916, the NTS had staged revivals of Synge's *The Playboy of the Western World* and *The Shadow of the Glen*, as well as a first performance of Robinson's *The Whiteheaded Boy*.

Described by Robinson as 'political from beginning to end' (quoted in Robinson 1982: 14), *The Whiteheaded Boy* is like a comic version of *Harvest*. Like the earlier Robinson play, the narrative of *The Whiteheaded Boy* works to expose the folly of the social ambitions of Ireland's rapidly expanding, middle-class, Catholic bourgeoisie. Denis Geoghagan is the 'whiteheaded boy' of the play's title – his mother's cherished or favourite son – whose bohemian life as a feckless Trinity College medical student has been supported by his hardworking, shopkeeper brother. The play's narrative begins with the family's discovery that Denis has, once again, failed his exams and their determination to support him no longer. But what the subsequent action reveals is that it is not so much Denis who is to blame for his life of dissipation, but rather Mrs Geoghagan's absurdly ambitious notions of social improvement. Denis himself did not wish to be so favoured: he has been forced into this role by his family's expectations. It is precisely this issue – the grandiose social ambitions of the Irish *nouveau riche* – which is the core feature of the play's comedy. The play's satire extends from the knowing vernacular of Robinson's stage directions ('Here she comes. Isn't she a great lump of a girl? She's thirty if she's a day, but she doesn't look it – 'tis the way she dresses, I suppose' (Robinson 1982: 69)) to Aunt Ellen's pretentious desire to establish a co-operative shop, and Mrs Geoghagan's solecistic grasp of the peerage (Robinson 1982: 76).

There is no evidence, then, of any rowing back in the NTS's propensity for rural satire. Prominent productions in the period 1917–20 include revivals of Murray's controversial *Birthright* (October 1920) and *Maurice Harte* (13 November 1917) as well as a performance in January 1918 of Murray's one-act play *Spring*. The latter deals with a peasant family anxious to improve itself, but debilitated by poverty to such an extent that the woman of the house, Jude, insists that her father-in-law, Andreesh, must be ejected from the family home and sent to the workhouse. Set in rural Ireland in 1908, the play makes it clear that Jude's cruelty is a result of her poverty ('Twenty years o' struggling an' rearing children on a starved bit of a mountainy farm, as she says herself, would make any creature bitter in the end' (Murray 1956: 9)) and that it is this that has led to her violation of the country tradition of hospitality. What is significant about *Spring* (at least in relation to nationalist plays like *Cathleen Ni Houlihan*) is that it portrays rural impoverishment as a basic and permanent condition of Irish peasant existence not linked to any external or political cause. Such an impoverishment leads directly to the erosion of precisely those traditional qualities of hospitality and solidarity that the peasant was most associated with in traditional nationalist discourse. Within this internecine and destructive cycle the only solution is the *deus ex machina* of the British Liberal government's granting of an old age pension (Murray 1956: 24). Andreesh dies from shock, but the play ends with Jude agreeing, despite the expense, to a traditional Irish wake. Ironically, it is an action of the British government that revives Irish traditions.

In this period, the Abbey Theatre appears, if anything, to be more self-confident about its public role in national affairs. With the NTS's announcement of a series of Monday night lectures on issues of Irish cultural life, the theatre was widely supported as a forum for national education, and cultural improvement. In 1918, for example, a series of lectures on 'The Catholic Theory of the State' and

'National Taste' were enthusiastically championed by the new Sinn Féin weekly, *New Ireland*. Its editor, P. J. Little, remarked that the Abbey played a central role in thinking out 'the problems of social order and cultural ideals for Ireland in the future. No platform could afford a better market-place [sic] of ideas than the Abbey Theatre. No atmosphere could be freer and more favourable for the energetic discussion of the real necessities of Irish life in the future' (*New Ireland*, 13 April 1918: 364–5; *New Ireland*, 25 May 1918: 37). By September 1918, *New Ireland* described the Abbey as 'a centre of cultural activity' (*New Ireland*, 21 September 1918: 317). This is a far cry from the 'dry rot of flunkeyism' of eight years earlier.

This growing importance of literary culture and the Abbey Theatre for Sinn Féin is also linked to the party's 1918 electoral strategy: abstention from the Westminster parliament, the establishment of a national council or assembly, and an attempt to secure recognition for Irish independence at the post-war Versailles Peace Treaty (Mitchell 1995: 5). All three objectives depended on Sinn Féin's reliance on 'national solidarity, on . . . growing cohesion and determination' (*New Ireland*, 27 July 1918: 181). Yeats's dire prediction that the 1916 rebellion would overturn the ideological work of the Irish literary revival thus ignored the considerable ideological importance of the NTS for those within Sinn Féin – people like P. J. Little and Desmond FitzGerald – who stressed the party's conformist agenda. The contrast between the attitude of Sinn Féin to the Abbey in the period 1910–14 with the attitude of *New Ireland* in the period 1916–18 is remarkable. Whereas in the case of the former, the Abbey Theatre was simply to be condemned, for the latter it was recognized as having an important ideological role in preparing Ireland for statehood.

Again, what had changed was not so much the modernizing project of the NTS, but the political and cultural policies of Sinn Féin. The Abbey Theatre's viability as a national institution, which Yeats had considered as under threat, was revived by Sinn Féin's retreat in 1917–18 from many of the radical commitments of the 1916 Easter proclamation (Lee 1989: 38). As with the IPP in 1911–14, there was a particular tension in this period between the Sinn Féin leadership (mainly drawn from the professional middle classes) and local rural-based militants responsible for actions such as cattle driving, tree felling and forced ploughing (Townshend 1983: 317–18; Kostick 1996: 30–1). Contentious issues, such as the promise of 'equality of social and economic opportunity' were shelved, postponed or ambiguously rephrased. Moreover, as Sinn

Féin established links with the leadership of the Irish Trade Union Council (Kostick 1996: 35–7), helped to organize a general strike for 23 April 1918, and began to take over the local organization of the IPP (Townshend 1983: 315), the party placed an increasing emphasis on presenting itself as a socially inclusive national organization. This was the political context for the noticeable change in the attitude of Sinn Féin to the Abbey Theatre and to literary culture in general. Certainly, critics such as David Munster and John McDonough continue to attack the NTS for its over-reliance on plays that indict rural life and its avoidance of other non-peasant aspects of Irish social life. But other writers, such as Ernest Boyd and P. J. Little in *New Ireland*, also argue that Sinn Féin must revise its traditional opposition to the Abbey Theatre in the light of the party's newfound conformity to the norms of European national statehood. Thus, for Little, the Abbey Theatre's role in 'refining' Irish culture was far more important than its past controversies and, in particular, the disputes that arose concerning the first performances of Synge's *The Playboy of the Western World* or Yeats's *The Countess Cathleen*:

> People in the past have quarrelled with our poets and 'dreamers'. They have been condemned, but the tragic farce of our quarrels is that real evils have remained neglected. Whilst we were denouncing the views, possibly even the mistaken views, of men whose whole energies were directed towards refining culture, the filth of commercialised vulgarity and obscenity paraded, and still parade, our streets, our theatres, our newspapers. . . . in the future Ireland must have the will to build her own culture for herself.
>
> (*New Ireland*, 13 January 1917: 157).

Similar, in this respect, to the work of the National Vigilance Association, the NTS is here conceived of as a way of counteracting the vulgarities of mass culture and as the basis for building a new national culture. And, like the campaign to have Sir Hugh Lane's art collection returned to Ireland[11] – a project which at a meeting at the Mansion House in Dublin in January 1918 had the support of unionists *and* Sinn Féin – the Abbey Theatre as a national institution is seen to demonstrate the existence of a socially and politically united Ireland. Ireland's national literature, argued A. S. Green in the course of his Abbey lecture on national taste, proved the existence of a unified consciousness 'one and indivisible' (*New Ireland*, 22 June 1918: 102–3). Yeats's 1916 pronouncement had indeed been unduly pessimistic. The unifying, ideological role of literary culture was just as important to Sinn Féin in 1917–18 as it had earlier been for the IPP, and thus the NTS remained central to the vitality of Ireland's national life.

Yeats himself recognized this. His autumn 1919 essay, 'A People's Theatre: An Open Letter to Lady Gregory' (Yeats 1962: 244–59) argues that the modernizing function of the NTS is now unstoppable. Despite Yeats's disparagement of the Abbey as a 'people's theatre' dominated by realism, and his advocacy of an alternative theatre that would be élite and esoteric, Yeats points to the vitally important effect of realistic plays. Written for the most part by 'National School' educated dramatists and performed by similarly lower middle-class actors (Yeats 1962: 248), such performances bestow on their audiences a temporary 'objectivity' thereby allowing them to see themselves in relation to the state as a whole: 'For certain hours of an evening they [Dublin playgoers] have objective modern eyes' (Yeats 1962: 253). This was 'cultivating the people' with a vengeance. As Yeats put it in his public lecture of 5 May 1921: 'The object of the realistic drama was to show man as he appeared in the eyes of a just man, and in his own eyes' (quoted in Hogan and Burnham 1992: 26). Yeats's support for the Abbey's 'dogged realism' at the same time as his advocacy of an alternative and élite poetic theatre is less of an irony than a consistent ideological position: a recognition that the realism of the Abbey Theatre was vital to an agenda of modernization and state preparation. Hence Yeats's belief that while a modernist and international drama was indeed desirable in Ireland, it was also crucial that this be established within an institution *separate* from the Abbey, 'the centre of Irish truth'. '[Irish] dramatists must get their inspiration and form from this country – from Murray or Synge rather than Ibsen', Yeats argued, 'the international drama was not wanted on *that* [Abbey] stage as the normal or natural thing' (my emphasis, quoted in Hogan and Burnham 1984: 195). Strongly supporting the formation of the Dublin Drama League, which promoted a repertoire of international and modern drama in Ireland (see Clark and Ferrar 1979), Yeats also insists that the Abbey Theatre should remain exactly as it is. And, in the same year as he promotes an esoteric dramaturgy based on Japanese Noh plays, Yeats remarks that Murray's *Maurice Harte* is 'a masterpiece' which 'all young dramatists should study' (Hogan and Burnham 1984: 196).

During the war of independence (January 1919 to 11 July 1921) and most notably throughout the subsequent truce and Anglo–Irish peace negotiations (July–December 1921), the NTS maintained a

scrupulous balance between the broadly progressive unionist affiliations of its directors and some of its principal supporters, and the
political and publicity needs of Sinn Féin. The theatre's ability to
operate from June 1921 was due exclusively to a £500 donation from
a prominent Dublin unionist, Lady Ardilaun (Gregory 1978: 270),
but Lady Gregory was vigilant in ensuring that the NTS should
act in a manner that was publicly sympathetic to the first Dáil. In
September 1920, for example, after Terence MacSwiney, the Sinn
Féin Dáil member and Lord Mayor of Cork, went on hunger strike
to protest at his arrest and detention, Gregory issued instructions that
the Abbey Theatre must close in the event of the hunger strike
ending in death (Gregory 1978: 187). On 24 February 1921 (some
four months after his eventual death), the Abbey mounted an
elaborate production of MacSwiney's play *The Revolutionist*.
Although Yeats felt that it 'was not a good play', he also definitely
wanted the Abbey to perform it, and regarded the play as important
for the Abbey Theatre's profile.[12] Addressing MacSwiney's widow
Muriel, Gregory described *The Revolutionist* as 'a national play of fine
quality' and compared its Abbey performance to 'laying a wreath
upon . . . [his] grave' (quoted in Hogan and Burnham 1992: 35).
When Robinson suggested two days after the truce that the Abbey
might also produce *The Playboy of the Western World*, Gregory was
flabbergasted at Robinson's insensitivity: 'I wouldn't have any
contentious play at this moment of goodwill' (Gregory 1978: 277).
And while Gregory did postpone a second production of *The
Revolutionist* for the same reason, not only was MacSwiney's play
soon performed (whereas *The Playboy of the Western World* was not)
but the takings from the production were given to the (republican)
Prisoners' Dependants' Fund (Mitchell 1995: 301).

This was not the torturous balancing act that it may seem. Not
only did the period of the Truce and the establishment of the second
Dáil (in August 1921) entail a considerable reining in of the radical,
left-wing elements of the counter-state (Mitchell 1995: 322), but it
also involved the appointment of a Minister for Fine Arts (Mitchell
1995: 302; Kennedy n.d.: 5) designed precisely to improve the
image of Sinn Féin and to emphasize the party's appeal to a broad
social constituency. In de Valera's words, 'it was very important . . .
that the constructive work of the Government in literature and the
arts should get attention. It gave the appearance of stability and
progressiveness to their affairs if they set up a Ministry of Fine Arts'
(quoted in Mitchell 1995: 304). In this context, maintaining
equilibrium between the broadly progressive unionist affiliations of

the Abbey Theatre and the republican credentials of Sinn Féin was not an especially difficult or disingenuous process. Indeed this was precisely the objective that both political constituencies wished to achieve. It is entirely unsurprising therefore that when General Michael Collins visited the theatre for a performance of MacSwiney's *The Revolutionist* in October 1921, Gregory declared herself to be delighted. Finally (and yet once again) the Abbey was 'a real national theatre' (Gregory 1978: 298).

4

CUMANN na nGAEDHEAL AND THE ABBEY THEATRE, 1922–32

We have slain Frankenstein, and buried him. We have shed all our illusions about 'the Ireland of Saints' and 'Rich and rare were the gems she wore'. We know now that we are just like other people, that the beast in us is restrained only by the same sanctions and conventions which restrain men elsewhere. We have for the first time responsibility and the reality of government.

(O'Hegarty 1998: 125)

For many in the early years of the 1920s, it was Ireland's regular recourse to a kind of theatricality, as evident in the legacies and continuing existence of republican and labour militancy, that remained the country's most acute cultural and political problem. Cardinal Logue lamented that 'the people of Ireland were running wild after visions, dreams and chimeras and turning the country upside down in the process' (quoted in O'Callaghan 1984: 227). The unionist-oriented *Irish Times* described the operation of the first Dáil Éireann as 'a stage play at the Mansion House' (quoted in Kostick 1996: 49) and even the guerrilla leader and nationalist politician Michael Collins remarked that Padraic Pearse's 1916 proclamation of an Irish republic had had an inappropriate 'air of a Greek tragedy' about it (Foster 1989: 482–3). Such comparisons were commonplace. Maintaining the counter-state of the first Dáil Éireann while fighting a guerrilla war of independence in the years 1919–21 may well have necessitated a form of politics that was rhizomic, clandestine and decentralized, but the reforming agenda of the new post-Treaty Irish Free State (or Saorstát Éireann) demanded a wholly opposing set of priorities. The challenge facing the nation builders of the new state was that of engendering a form of Irish identity that would be transparent, centralized and constitutional. This challenge was especially urgent given the limitations to the Irish Free State's political autonomy: a partitioned, self-governing dominion within the British Commonwealth (Cronin and Regan 2000: 1–2). Moreover, for Cumann na nGaedheal, the main government party and the renamed pro-Treaty wing of Sinn Féin, this was a period of reining in revolutionary expectations and reconciling the population to constitutional government.

For Horace Plunkett's resuscitated *Irish Statesman* the cultural reformation of the Irish Free State is a recurring theme. Edited by AE and incorporating the Irish co-operative movement's periodical *The Irish Homestead*, the *Irish Statesman* repeatedly emphasizes the need to abandon militancy and adopt what is presented as a more reasonable (i.e. constitutional) approach to political action. Plunkett's weekly was openly supportive of the Anglo-Irish Treaty[1] and opposed to republican and trade union militancy; its overall project entailed outlining a possible leadership role for what remained of southern unionism within the newly independent Irish Free State (see Brown 1985: 120–9). As Yeats remarked in 1925, Ireland's modernity now rested, once again, on the intellectual fortitude of its minority élite: 'the centre of intellect and the pivot of its unity' (Yeats 1975: 452). In a conscious resurrection of the constructive unionist philosophy of almost two decades earlier (and in a frankly sentimental desire to return to the more harmonious politics of pre-1914) the *Irish Statesman* argued that boycotts, strikes or political violence would never achieve Irish unity and that what was most needed instead was a programme of education towards a 'social order in which there will be a real sense of identity of interest among our citizens' (*Irish Statesman* 1.1 [15 Sept. 1923]: 4). Ireland's fundamental handicap, argues AE in a subsequent article, lies in its lack of a 'national culture'. This lack is lamented not only because of the socially homogenizing power of a national culture (*Irish Statesman* 1.8 [3 November 1923] 229–30), but because 'national culture' offers an antidote to Ireland's unfortunate tendency to take action as if for its own sake, and without any proper consideration of consequences. 'We are continually taking to action without prior thinking', wrote AE, 'rushing to action without the slightest conception of what was to follow action, and trusting to luck to find some way out of our next troubles' (*Irish Statesman* 1.8 [3 November 1923] 229). National culture, in this definition, is a means of maintaining the vitally important distinction between play-acting and real life, between theatrical and non-theatrical action. Yeats's insistence that what Ireland needed most in the post-independence period was 'education in the most common and necessary subjects' (Yeats 1975: 455–6) took this, the distinction between symbolic and real action, as its core principle. The role of the Abbey Theatre as an Irish national institution in the early 1920s was viewed increasingly as enforcing and maintaining that important distinction.

The educational role of the National Theatre Society, Limited in the life of the Irish Free State was also a point that Yeats and Gregory repeatedly emphasized in their campaign to achieve an annual subsidy from the post-Treaty Cumann na nGaedheal government (Hogan and Burnham 1992: 97). Gregory considered the issue of the subsidy as a matter of urgency and regularly lobbied politicians on the theatre's behalf while Yeats, who had been appointed a senator in November 1922, promised to make the theatre a major issue during his political tenure (Yeats 1954: 678; Fitzpatrick 1975: 161). As early as 10 January 1922, Gregory records a discussion with Desmond FitzGerald, Minister for External Affairs, concerning the possibility of handing over the theatre to the new state and records her relief when FitzGerald reassured her that the government already viewed the Abbey as 'the National Theatre of Ireland' (Gregory 1978: 319). Nevertheless, and despite considerable sympathy for the Abbey Theatre from important political figures like Eoin MacNeill (Minister for Education), Ernest Blythe (Minister for Finance) and Tom Johnson (leader of the Labour Party), the government's initial response to the campaign was unfavourable. On 27 January 1923 MacNeill reported to the Executive Council that the Abbey had applied for a subsidy as well as 'for official recognition as a national theatre' (NA: CAB. C. 1/36). On 13 July 1923, however, Lennox Robinson reported back to Gregory that although the Department of Education was enthusiastic about funding the NTS, the President of the Executive (William Cosgrave) had advised against it (Hogan and Burnham 1992: 158). All that MacNeill and his chief executive officer could offer by way of consolation was to advise the Abbey directorate to apply the same pressure on Cosgrave as had been applied by those campaigning for a government grant for Trinity College (Hogan and Burnham 1992: 158). Even 'the Republicans would have supported a theatre', Gregory complained despondently in her journals, but then added as an afterthought: 'they might probably have wrecked the theatre by putting their own people in' (Gregory 1978: 469).

But Yeats, Gregory and Robinson were well aware that state control of the theatre would also mean considerable adjustments to the theatre's repertory and aesthetic autonomy. Notwithstanding Robinson's 1924 claim that the Abbey Theatre had never modified its programme to suit any Irish government for the past decade (*Observer*, 3 February 1924: 11), Robinson advised Yeats on 24 April 1922 that petitioning the government for financial support was contingent both on the theatre offering to help establish an Irish language theatre and on it being prepared to give performances on special occasions as well as 'accept suggestions from them as to the plays given on such occasions' (quoted in Hogan and Burnham 1992: 94).[2] Yeats and Gregory endorsed the broad outline of Robinson's advice, and Robinson's draft memorandum to the government included a clause indicating that the Abbey directors 'would give special performances on such occasions as the Government would require' (Hogan and Burnham 1992: 98). Moreover, by 1924, and for the first time, the Abbey Theatre facilitated the regular production of plays in Irish (Ó Siadhail 1993: 63; Welch 1999: 85–6; 91). These performances by the Dublin-based Irish language theatre group, An Comhar Drámuíochta, were a permanent feature of the Abbey repertoire in the 1920s.

It was not until August 1925 that the Abbey Theatre was granted a modest annual subsidy of £850. Yeats responded immediately, by delivering a speech (previously agreed with Blythe (NLI: 20,704 acc 3164)) in praise of the government for 'this new manifestation of their courage and intelligence' (*Irish Times*, 10 August 1925: 5). In December, the *Irish Times* underlined the educational benefits of the Abbey Theatre in purging the 'superstitions and prejudices which are relics of a barbarous age' and also in helping to improve Anglo–Irish relations (quoted in NLI: ACC nfc 98 vol (4) 1924–32). But what is so surprising about the government's accession to Yeats's and Gregory's request for state support is not the length of time that it took to achieve, but the fact that the subsidy was granted at all. Dogged by economic difficulties and already famous for its policies of fiscal rectitude (Brown 1985: 14–15), the Cumann na nGaedheal administration in the 1920s was not known for initiatives of this kind. As recently as September 1924, Blythe had taken the extremely unpopular measure of reducing the old-age pension by one shilling simply in order to balance the budget (Foster 1988: 519; Regan 1999: 209–11). And similar projects to the funding of the Abbey Theatre, such as Horace Plunkett's campaign to re-establish a Department of Fine Arts, had been blocked repeatedly by the Department of Finance in the 1920s (see Kennedy n.d.: 9–11). It is true that An Comhar Drámuíochta had been awarded a state subsidy of £600 at the end of 1924 (Ó Siadhail 1993: 63), but this was consistent with the government's official policy of cultural de-Anglicization (Kennedy 1992: 16–17; O'Callaghan 1984: 229–30); the NTS at the Abbey Theatre, with its three Protestant directors, its regular performance of plays by Shaw and Gregory and its history of defiant anti-populism, was a very different form of cultural endeavour.

It is likely that a major factor in the cabinet's approval of a subsidy to the Abbey Theatre was its recognition of the theatre's important ideological role in relation to the new state. At a time when the legitimacy of the Cumann na nGaedheal government lay under constant threat from anti-Treaty republicans, the NTS was an important institutional supporter. While during the war of independence the theatre had done its best to maintain a scrupulous, but nationalist-oriented impartiality (Gregory 1978: 136), this altered radically after the signing of the Anglo–Irish Treaty in December 1921. From here on, and with the establishment of the Provisional government in January 1922 and the November appointment of Yeats to the Senate, the Abbey offered unambiguous support to the new Irish state. Alone among Dublin theatres it closed for the state funeral of Arthur Griffith in August 1922 (Hogan and Burnham 1992: 65) and in March 1923 it was the only Dublin theatre to stay open in defiance of a republican ban (Hogan and Burnham 1992: 134). In addition to such overt declarations of political fidelity to the new state, the Abbey Theatre included in its immediate post-independence repertoire plays that were directly concerned with satirizing republican anti-Treaty militancy. There was a revival of Lennox Robinson's tendentious *Patriots*, for example, as well as first productions of George Shiels's *First Aid* (December), Sean O'Casey's *The Shadow of a Gunman* (April) and O'Casey's *Cathleen Listens In* (October); all of these plays were openly critical of nationalist anti-Treaty ideology and rhetoric (Hogan and Burnham 1992: 150–3). No longer hampered by the need to appease both the progressive and reformist elements of Sinn Féin (see Hogan and Burnham 1992: 135, 137) or of avoiding Labour criticisms of the nationalist agenda (Gregory 1978: 651, 309), the Abbey Theatre appeared to be injected with a new sense of purpose.

This reinvigoration of the NTS repertoire in the early 1920s was assisted considerably by the three Dublin plays of Sean O'Casey: *The Shadow of a Gunman* (1923), *Juno and the Paycock* (1924) and *The Plough and the Stars* (1926). *The Shadow of a Gunman* was performed (under armed guard) in April 1923, just one month after the theatre critic for the *Sunday Independent* declared that the Abbey Theatre was dead (Hogan and Burnham 1992: 137). The play is set, not in the Abbey's all-too-familiar peasant kitchen, but in a rented room of a Dublin tenement house and its action takes place in the immediate context of Ireland's recent war of independence. As one of the first occasions in which a naturalistic dramaturgy was applied to a contemporary urban setting,[3] this play marked a new departure. The play addresses itself explicitly to the relationship between literary culture and political violence. Donal Davoren, the protagonist, is a likeable but inept Shelleyean poet whose futile endeavour is his attempt to achieve the seclusion that he believes is vital for literary composition. Instead, Davoren has to endure a series of comic interruptions not only from the room's principal occupant, the garrulous Seamus Shields, but from other tenants of the house, neighbours and finally from a British Army raiding party. In the politically and socially tumultuous world of recent Irish history, Davoren's romantic aesthetic is farcically outdated. Nevertheless, while Davoren resolutely eschews any engagement with contemporary nationalist or republican ideology – 'we've had enough of poems . . . about '98 and of Ireland, too' (O'Casey 1960: 90) – he succumbs almost immediately to playing the role of a republican gunman once he realizes that by so doing he will gain both glamour and charisma within his community. The problem with Ireland, O'Casey's play suggests, is that nationalist anti-Treaty militancy is inspired simply by self-aggrandisement: self-indulgent role playing with no attention to consequences. The sheer irresponsibility of such militancy is the point that Davoren and the audience learn at the end when Davoren's admirer, the guileless Minnie, is shot dead by the British military.

One of the play's most farcical scenes occurs when Davoren, believed now to be a republican gunman on the run, is compelled to officiate over a republican court. Such alternative arbitration courts had been one of the most successful instruments in establishing the legitimacy and authority of the counter-state in the period 1920–1 (Mitchell 1995: 141). Instigated as a result of popular agitation in the west and endorsed, *post facto*, by Dáil Éireann, republican courts comprised an extensive judicial network throughout Ireland (some with full civil and criminal authority) and were widely supported. Even Sinn Féin's unionist and British opponents regarded them as remarkably effective and even-handed (Mitchell 1995: 137–47). But with the outbreak of civil war in 1922 these Dáil courts were suppressed and were replaced by government-appointed District

Courts (Kotsonouris 1994: 14–15). O'Casey's play, in which the activities of the republican courts are reduced to the dimensions of farce, reflects this new pro-government initiative. In O'Casey's scene Mrs Henderson and Mr Gallogher submit a malaprop-laden request for armed action to be taken against a neighbour's noisy children.

> While leaving it entirely in the hands of the gentlemen of The Republican Army, the defendant, that is to say, James Gallogher of fifty-five St. Teresa Street, ventures to say that he thinks he has made out a Primmy Fashy Case against Mrs. Dwyer and all her heirs, male or female as aforesaid mentioned in the above written schedule. N.B. – If you send up any of your men, please tell them to bring their guns.
>
> (O'Casey 1960: 100)

O'Casey's treatment of a core feature of the Irish counter-state is farcical precisely because the play's characters are so strikingly unaware of consequences. And the scene in which Mrs Henderson and Mr Gallogher petition Davoren for IRA intervention suggests that Sinn Féin's radical pre-Treaty republicanism was also no more than a charade: a cultural phenomenon entirely lacking in serious political motivation, and an expression rather of egotism and pretentiousness. The hilarity of the scene, and the familiarity of its stage conventions, enjoins the spectator's ready agreement. In so far as the political motivation of anti-Treaty Irish republicanism is addressed at all by the play, it is evoked in Minnie's defiant resistance to the British soldiers in the final scene. Apart from Minnie, however, the play's one republican activist (Maguire) appears only very briefly while Davoren merely pretends to be an insurgent. For Minnie, the decision to hide Maguire's Mills bombs in her room during a British military search is an act of heroic self-sacrifice. But, as O'Casey emphasizes throughout, Minnie's political commitment, like that of Davoren, is exclusively superficial. Her true motive is the desire to impress Davoren. And while Davoren is fully aware that his act is a theatrical pretence, Minnie is equally aware that her actions are not. The motivation for Minnie's resistance to the British soldiers and her 'shouting bravely, but a little hysterically, "Up the Republic"' (O'Casey 1960: 126), is presented simply as a subterfuge for narcissistic sexual desire. For the spectator, guided by O'Casey's earlier stage directions ('Her well-shaped figure . . . charmingly dressed' (O'Casey 1960: 39)) such a conclusion is consistent with Minnie's overall portrayal.

For contemporary intellectuals like Daniel Corkery and P. S. O'Hegarty the first performance of O'Casey's *The Shadow of a Gunman* was a landmark event. Corkery, writing from an anti-Treaty position, argued that it meant that the NTS could no longer be regarded as a national theatre (Maume 1993: 99), and he went on to denounce the play's cynical anti-nationalism as a symptom of a new 'literature of collapse' (Corkery 1924). But for O'Hegarty, a staunch supporter of the government, *The Shadow of a Gunman* re-established the Abbey Theatre's *métier*, the creation of 'true historical perspective'. He claimed that O'Casey portrayed contemporary events with 'that air of detachment and disillusionment which the historian aims at' (quoted in Hogan and Burnham 1992: 146). In the midst of writing his own account of this period, *The Victory of Sinn Féin* (1924), O'Hegarty mused aloud as to whether now, in the wake of O'Casey, it was even worthwhile bothering to write history again in prose. But as both O'Hegarty's own impressionistic account of the period and his extravagant praise of *The Shadow of a Gunman* in the *Irish Statesman* makes clear, O'Casey's play was welcomed as much for its immediate political effect as for its objectivity or skilful and entertaining theatricality. From O'Hegarty's perspective as a senior civil servant in the Cumann na nGaedheal administration[4] and as someone for whom Dublin was now 'full of hysterical women' and sea-green republicans (O'Hegarty 1998: 39), O'Casey's apotheosis was a straightforward and logical response.

O'Casey's success in satirizing the unmandated actions of anti-Treaty republicans is elaborated and extended in his next play, *Juno and the Paycock*. Performed in March 1924 and at a time when the Cumann na nGaedheal administration was desperate for credibility (Regan 1999: 183), *Juno and the Paycock* similarly deals with Ireland's recent political history within the context of an urban working-class setting. Again, the play's dramaturgical method relies on the audience's familiarity with long-established dramatic conventions: as in melodrama, O'Casey stresses the primacy of the domestic unit and shows republican or socialist activism as innately antagonistic to this domesticity. Here, as in the earlier play, women are presented both as the main tokens of ethical value and as the sum total of their sexual attractiveness and reproductive potential. The issue of this play is how, within the context of militant anti-Treaty opposition, an urban Irish working-class community may hope to reproduce itself. This is addressed by means of the two Boyle children: Johnny, a republican insurgent who has recently betrayed a fellow soldier to the forces of the state, and Mary, an activist within the labour movement. As with *The Shadow of a Gunman*, O'Casey's treatment of political militancy teeters between the comic and an impression of republicanism as an almost demonic threat. For the play's *miles gloriosus*, 'Captain' Boyle, republicanism is simply drunken bravado, whereas for Johnny, the arrival of the shadowy republican mobilizer heralds his execution. What prevents this formula from collapsing into facetiousness (as it does sometimes in the earlier *The Shadow of a Gunman*) is the play's portrayal of republicanism as fundamentally antithetical to domestic value, and thus as ethically deleterious.[5] In the 'state o chassis' of Ireland during the civil war political 'hearts o stone' are set against domestic 'hearts o flesh' (O'Casey 1960: 72–3). Thus, Boyle's comic fantasy about having fought for Ireland in 1916 ('I done . . . me bit . . . in Easther week' (O'Casey 1960: 72)) would be amusing, and Johnny's guilty hallucinations concerning the murdered Robbie Tancred would be simply melodramatic, were it not for the play's insistence on the extent to which anti-Treaty republicanism intrudes and damages the domestic. A sentimentalized version of the patriarchal domestic unit, with women presented either as sexual commodities or as asexual mother figures, is proffered as the one and only benchmark of ethical value. In this respect, Mary's incipient syndicalism – her support for a victimized fellow worker (O'Casey 1960: 8) – is undercut from the beginning. Within the framework of O'Casey's stage directions, Mary is revealed by the action to be no more than she appears initially to the viewer: 'a well-made and good-looking girl of twenty two' (O'Casey 1960: 5). Her abiding self-absorption (the spectator's first impression of Mary is of her gazing with fascination in a mirror (O'Casey 1960: 5)) exposes Mary's trade union principles as no more than a trite slogan. Again, and with O'Casey's characteristic populism, the possibility of women's agency is undermined by a recourse to biology: it is Mary's pregnancy at the end of the play that offers the most compelling demonstration that her trade union principles are utterly irrelevant. In this respect, O'Casey's representation of female militancy coincides with the many pro-Treaty portrayals of women republicans as motivated by hysteria brought on by personal loss (see Ward 1989: 166; O'Hegarty 1998: 73–5).

As the mainstay of the Abbey Theatre repertoire in this period, the principle ideological achievement of O'Casey's *The Shadow of a Gunman* and *Juno and the Paycock* lay in their discrediting of political militancy by means of an appeal to social realism. 'Democracy', claimed the *Irish Statesman* in relation to *Juno and the Paycock*, has 'at last become articulate on both sides of the curtain. . . . The spectacle of the Abbey crammed to the doors on the first week in Lent is eloquent of the fascinations of his curiously composite dramaturgy' (*Irish Statesman*, 15 March 1924: 16). Moreover, not only did O'Casey traduce Sinn Féin republicanism – what O'Hegarty's book describes as Ireland's 'pseudo-republicans' (O'Hegarty 1998: 69–72) – but he did so by sentimentalizing Dublin working-class culture in a manner that was of considerable ideological benefit to the increasingly middle-class and business-oriented interests of the Cumann na nGaedheal party in the mid-1920s. As John Regan's recent study of élite formation in the 1920s points out, senior Cumann na nGaedheal figures including Blythe, Fitzgerald and Kevin O'Higgins (Minister for Justice and Vice-President of the Executive) also exhibited a strong reaction against republican and socialist politics by presenting 'themselves as constructive materialists fighting an ongoing war against destructive spiritualists' (Regan 1999: 181). Like O'Casey's down-to-earth female heroines, Cumann na nGaedheal in this period represented itself as closely in touch with fundamental social realities while, simultaneously, realigning itself with Dublin business and merchant interests (Regan 1999: 230). The destructive spiritualists were viewed as the anti-Treaty and nationalist aspirational politics of Sinn Féin.

What was so disconcerting about the cultural legacies of the Easter Rising, the clandestine institutions of the counter-state in the period 1919 to 1921, and the war of independence against the British was their continuing quasi-theatrical ability to inspire political opposition to the state. But the ideological benefit of O'Casey's *The Shadow of a Gunman* and *Juno and the Paycock* was that they reinterpreted such action in terms of a misunderstanding of the fundamental conventions of theatre. O'Hegarty's acerbic remark that 'they [the anti-Treaty faction of Sinn Féin] never meant to do anything but pose, or the majority of them have never done anything but pose' (O'Hegarty 1998: 70–1) is supported by the way in which Davoren, Minnie and 'Captain' Boyle are exposed as 'actors' who, absurdly, appear unaware of themselves as such.

With O'Casey's representation of political insurgency, in other words, the NTS proclaimed the aesthetic authority of the institutional theatre as the proper and only site of theatrical representation, and, simultaneously, underlined the importance of the state as the sole legitimate arena of political action. Within such a context, it is not difficult to understand how many within the Cumann na nGaedheal cabinet would have been sympathetic to the Abbey

Theatre's request for a subsidy. As the *Irish Times* put it in an editorial to mark the Abbey Theatre's twenty-first anniversary celebrations, it was this 'disillusioning art' and 'educational influence' that was the key to the theatre's modernizing success. The Abbey helped to purge the country of 'superstition and prejudices' and 'did more than any other agency to break up the mould of [Ireland's] mental dishonesty' (*Irish Times*, 24 December 1925: 4). Blythe put the matter more bluntly: the Abbey Theatre was 'an important national asset' (Hogan and Burnham 1992: 279) and it deserved to be rewarded for 'helping to rouse national feeling for the decisive stage in the struggle for independence' (UCD: Blythe papers, P24/289). This was also the point (although expressed from a strongly opposing perspective) of Corkery's unpublished essay 'The Literature of Collapse.' Corkery pointed out that, under the slogan '*Nil nisi verum*' (nothing but the truth), the new literature of Ireland nevertheless accorded remarkably with the approved sentiments of the Irish Free State (Corkery 1924: 3).

But aside from the ideological benefits of O'Casey's plays, there is another related and more complicated reason why the NTS may have found favour with the purseholders of a usually parsimonious Department of Finance. As a cultural institution, the Abbey Theatre possessed a reputation that was of particular symbolic importance to Ireland's ex-unionist and predominantly Protestant minority élite. On a par with other prestigious institutions such as the Royal Dublin Society and Trinity College, the Abbey Theatre represented one form of continuity between the positive nationalist contribution of the 'old Ireland' of Plunkett, Gregory, Balfour, Birrell and Redmond on the one hand, and, on the other, the new Irish Free State regime of ex-Sinn Féin revolutionaries like MacNeill, O'Higgins, FitzGerald and Blythe. Yeats himself drew attention to the analogy when he praised the constructive work of the Royal Dublin Society's series of concerts and of the Abbey Theatre in assisting what he regarded as Ireland's long-overdue process of modernization (Yeats 1975: 455–61). In this respect alone, government support for the Abbey Theatre was similar to Cumann na nGaedheal's offer of one-third of senate places to Ireland's unionist minority and former Ascendancy élite. And while the government's generous offer of senate places did not nearly meet the earlier demands of southern unionists as articulated in the Irish Convention of 1918–19 and the Anglo–Irish peace negotiations of 1921, the public stature of senators such as Sir John Keane, Sir Thomas Grattan Esmonde, Sir Andrew Jameson, the Countess of Desart and Sir Horace Plunkett did offer Ireland's ex-unionist population a considerable level of symbolic reassurance (see White 1975: 93; Fitzpatrick 1975: 160). Nor was the disproportionate political representation of Anglo-Irish gentry in the senate entirely symbolic since, to some extent, it matched their continuing relative economic advantage (and that of the Protestant population in general) within the state (White 1967: 20–1; Foster 1988: 534). Like the post-independence playing of 'God Save the King' at the Royal Dublin Horse Show and at Trinity College commencements or the appointment of former Indian civil servant James MacNeill as Governor-General in 1927 (McDowell 1997: 166–7; White 1967: 20), support for the Abbey Theatre with its three well-known Protestant directors – Yeats, Gregory and Robinson – was, at least partly, a valued recognition of a minority and élite tradition within Irish society.

Cumann na nGaedheal's benevolence towards the former southern unionist minority was not, of course, entirely altruistic. It served to underline the tolerance and inclusivity of the Irish Free State, and thus provided a reassurance to nervous English investors. It also naturalized the idea of post-revolutionary Ireland as a still class-based society. By the mid-1920s key figures in the Cumann na nGaedheal administration such as O'Higgins, Blythe and Fitzgerald worked hard to integrate into the government what remained of the former southern unionists as a way of opposing any potential backslide into nationalist revolutionary politics (Regan 1999: 246). For this influential cadre within Cumann na nGaedheal, the job of restoring normal society to Ireland in the 1920s was, crucially, about restoring the normality of a pre-revolutionary class hierarchy. By January 1926, as Regan points out, 'there were now more non-combative Clongownians (i.e. pupils of Ireland's famous Catholic upper middle-class private school) in the Cabinet than veterans of the 1916 rising' (Regan 1999: 252). To an extent, the granting of a subsidy to the NTS served as a formal acknowledgment of the overlap between the ideological requirements of this dominant element within the Cumann na nGaedheal party and the perceived social and cultural needs of Ireland's Anglo-Irish minority. That the latter were now grateful beneficiaries, and that the Cumann na nGaedheal ministers were the munificent benefactors, must have added considerably to the cultural frisson of the occasion.

But the granting of a subsidy in 1925 did not resolve the vexed issue of the Abbey Theatre's status as a representative Irish institution. On the contrary, the publicity surrounding its announcement helped to resurrect a public debate concerning how the Abbey Theatre related to Ireland's majority population. In February 1926, a former manager of the Abbey (G. N. Reddin) condemned the Abbey Theatre as 'Cromwellian' (a pejorative shorthand for Irish Protestant) and as unreflective of the entirety of Irish opinion.

> The Cromwellian tradition and the national tradition would never blend, and the continuance and consolidation in the direction of the destiny of the Abbey Theatre was, in his view, strangling its progress towards the achievement of its fuller and final ambition – namely, that of being the National Theatre of Ireland. (Cheers)
>
> (*Irish Times*, 24 February 1926: 7)

A truly national theatre, according to Reddin, would be one in which performances took place in the Irish language (what Ireland's 1922 constitution referred to as the 'national' language), and one that would abandon altogether performances involving the artificial Hiberno-English dialects of Synge and Gregory. Although the Abbey Theatre continued to host plays performed in the Irish language this did little to alter a general public perception (eagerly fomented by the bigoted denunciations of the *Catholic Bulletin*) that the NTS was an élite institution controlled by an unrepresentative and often hostile Protestant directorate.

But the government's subsidy to the NTS does not infer that the Abbey Theatre in the 1920s responded to the policies of the Cumann na nGaedheal government with Pavlovian agreement, or that its various productions met with blanket approval from the new, pro-Treaty Catholic élite. A national theatre may well have been regarded as an important way of illustrating the distinction between the legitimate actions of the state and the play-acting of anti-Treaty republicanism, but the libidinous physicality of the stage was also a source of official anxiety. Similar in some respects to the way in which the Roman Catholic hierarchy withdrew from the fraught issue of post-Treaty politics in the 1920s and concentrated instead on an obsessional campaign against dance halls, cinemas, 'company keeping' and motor cars (Regan 1999: 279–86), sexuality had become a key area for Irish intellectuals in articulating opposition to aspects of the Irish Free State's nationalist ideology. For writers such as Yeats, Robinson, O'Casey and Liam O'Flaherty or for the painter Jack B. Yeats (Brown 1985: 137), the mere proclamation of sexuality as a determinant of identity was a challenge to the Catholic-dominated ideology of the Irish state (see Howes 1996: 185). Similar to Yeats's fantasies of rape in 'Leda and the Swan', the stage directions in O'Casey's early plays lay emphasis on the physicality of the actresses' bodies as the basis of an anti-nationalist critique. But this is a critique that does not threaten the state's fundamental political or social structures (Howes 1996: 186). Indeed, this strongly patriarchal and misogynist version of sexuality caused offence to nationalist ideology to much the same extent that it expressed nostalgia for a world with a clearly demarcated gender hierarchy.

Within a few months of the formal announcement of the subsidy, it was clear (if it had not been before) that the Abbey Theatre would not function simply as a forum for cultural propaganda on behalf of the new state. Performed on 8 February 1926 – a few months before the tenth anniversary of the 1916 Easter Rising – O'Casey's *The Plough and the Stars* engaged directly and controversially with that insurrectionary event. Like O'Casey's two earlier plays, this later one presents a sentimentalized version of patriarchal sexuality as the ethical norm against which *all* forms of political militancy are found wanting. Jack and Nora Clitheroe are a recently married working-class couple who live in a Dublin tenement with Nora's neurotic uncle, Peter Good. Although Jack and Peter are labourers, they, like Nora, are impelled by notions of social advancement. For Nora, this is expressed in terms of her desire to improve her appearance and that of the apartment; for Jack and Peter the desire for social advancement is sublimated in terms of an obsession with military uniforms and rank. Peter struts around the room in the absurdly elaborate dress of the Irish Foresters – 'like somethin' you'd pick off a Christmas tree' (O'Casey 1960: 139) – and Jack takes an obsessive pride in his rank and uniform of the Irish Citizen's Army. The core dramatic tension of the play is established from the beginning: Nora, who is also pregnant, wants her husband to eschew political involvement and stay at home with her, whereas Jack, intoxicated by nationalist fervour, is determined to maintain his militancy. Apart from Fluther Good, a sanguine carpenter and entertaining opportunist, all the other male characters in the play are similarly affected. Even the Covey, who professes himself a Marxist and an anti-nationalist, is puffed up by the self-importance bestowed on him by extracts from 'Jenersky's *Thesis on the Origin, Development, an' Consolidation of the Evolutionary Idea of the Proletariat*' (O'Casey 1960: 165).

The destructive nature of male political commitment is elaborated on in the play's controversial Act II. In this scene, the banner of the

Irish Citizen's Army (the eponymous plough and the stars) and the tricolour of the Irish republic are brought into a public house by the ideologically intoxicated nationalist soldiers, Commandant Clitheroe and Captain Brennan of the Irish Citizen's Army and Lieutenant Langon of the Irish Volunteers. At the same time, a prostitute, Rosie Redmond, tries unsuccessfully to gain the attention of the politically committed. To the accompaniment of bloodthirsty extracts from speeches by the executed 1916 nationalist patriot, Padraic Pearse, Rosie's inability to make erotic progress in the context of political fervour is portrayed as the ultimate condemnation of all ideology (O'Casey 1960: 161–2, 178–9). As with the strange lack of interest in Rosie in Act II (her only client is the apolitical Fluther), women in *The Plough and the Stars* are portrayed as victims of this absurd male love of militarism and militancy. They are victims to the extent that their sexuality is ignored, and their domestic role as mothers (presented by O'Casey as the natural and only corollary of their sexuality) is wholly unprovided for. In Act III, Nora – 'Her eyes are dim and hollow, her face pale and strained looking' (O'Casey 1960: 183) – is distraught first at her husband's absence, and then at his rejection of her when she pleads with him to return home and when she accuses the republicans of cowardice (O'Casey 1960: 197). Abandoned, Nora suffers a miscarriage and is looked after by a neighbour, Bessie Burgess. Bessie's humanity and heroism is shown in her giving her life to protect Nora Clitheroe, her demented Roman Catholic neighbour; Protestant and loyalist, Bessie is the only character in the play who matches action and rhetoric (Kiberd 1995: 227). She is shot dead in the last scene, ironically by a soldier of the British Army that she so fervently supports. The play's concluding tableau underlines the irony: Dublin burns while the British Tommies drink tea and sing 'Keep the 'owme fires burning' (O'Casey 1960: 218).

The opening night of the production was 'thronged with distinguished people' including Kevin O'Higgins, Ernest Blythe and Lord Chief Justice Kennedy (Hogan and Burnham 1992: 287). But despite the play's attack on political militancy, there was a general impression that O'Casey's satire had gone too far (Hogan and Burnham 1992: 294). 'He makes the audience feel that it [the 1916 rebellion] was not worth it', commented the *Irish Times* not altogether disapprovingly (Hogan and Burnham 1992: 289), and even O'Hegarty remarked regretfully that *The Plough and the Stars* was 'an untrue picture' (quoted in Greaves 1979: 118). Republican protests against the play took place on the fourth night of the production. Yeats announced from the stage (and reading from a pre-prepared statement) the fame of O'Casey's 'genius'.

> 'Is this', he shouted, 'going to be a recurring celebration of Irish genius? Synge first, and then O'Casey! The news of the happenings of the last few minutes here will flash from country to country. Dublin has once more rocked the cradle of a reputation. From such a scene in this theatre went forth the fame of Synge. Equally the fame of O'Casey is born here to-night. This is his apotheosis.'
>
> (*Irish Times*, 12 February 1926: 7–8)

Despite Yeats's analogy, however, the protests against *The Plough and the Stars* were very different to the nationalist protests against *The Playboy of the Western World* almost twenty years earlier. They were organized by what the *Irish Times* referred to as 'a small minority' of republican women, some of whom were also feminists, and, with the assistance of uniformed Gardaí and the Special Branch (Ireland's newly established armed and plain clothed police), the protest was easily and quickly suppressed.

What the republican and feminist protesters against *The Plough and the Stars* objected to was the play's representation of the 1916 rebels as cowards principally motivated by vanity and self-love. But from the government's point of view as articulated by George O'Brien (the government's nominee on the Abbey board of directors), the most objectionable aspect of the play was its controversial presentation of prostitution (Hogan and Burnham 1992: 282–4).[6] On this point, however, the NTS directors would not relent. As O'Casey acknowledged on the opening night in his comments to the actress Ria Mooney, Rosie Redmond is crucial to the play's success (Hogan and Burnham 1992: 288). Indeed prostitution functions in the play as the index for assessing Irish nationalist, republican and socialist politics. In the pub scene of Act II, for example, it is Rosie *qua* prostitute who exposes both the inadequacy of Pearse's appeals for blood sacrifice, the Covey's recourse to Leninist theory and the Rosary-like incantations of Brennan, Langon and Clitheroe.

Yeats declared that the appearance of the prostitute in Act II was central to the play's technique and thus 'to eliminate any part of it on the grounds that have nothing to do with dramatic literature would be to deny all our traditions' (quoted in Hogan and Burnham 1992: 283). Yeats's comments on the dramatic importance of the prostitute to O'Casey's play, his reference to 'all our traditions' and the refusal of the NTS directors to excise or modify the role do not suggest any ready compliance to the political exigencies of Cumann na nGaedheal. Indeed, in the context of Yeats's robust opposition to the government's anti-divorce legislation of spring 1925, the importance of the prostitute in *The Plough and the Stars* is a revealing qualifier to the Abbey Theatre's support for the government. Some months earlier, Yeats's article, 'An Undelivered Speech' (published in the *Irish Statesman* in November 1925) argued that the President of the Executive, W. T. Cosgrave, had broken the 'religious truce in Ireland' by compelling a 'Catholic conscience [to] alone dominate the public life in Ireland' (Yeats 1975: 450–2). A key element in this article was Yeats's contention that the price of no divorce is a public opinion that tolerates prostitutes, but that in countries where divorce is made available, illegal relationships between the sexes are frowned upon (Yeats 1975: 450). What the government's anti-divorce campaign has revealed, Yeats concludes, is that Ireland's modernity depends 'upon a small minority which is content to remain a minority for a generation, to insist on these questions being discussed' (Yeats 1975: 452). What is established in *The Plough and the Stars* is something more than a feminized Protestant heroics that exposes Irish republicanism and socialism as a hollow sham. Through the play's blatant celebration of sexuality (albeit a sexuality that is sexist to the point of misogyny and that is resolutely defined by patriarchy) O'Casey's play constitutes a forceful attack on Cumann na nGaedheal's acquiescence to Roman Catholic social teaching.

To this extent, it is a daring ideological critique of nationalist orthodoxy, but it is also an exception to the majority of plays performed at the Abbey Theatre in the 1920s. Comedies of rural life, such as Brinsley MacNamara's *'Look at the Heffernans!'* (1926) or George Shiels's *The New Gossoon* (1930), psychological dramas like T. C. Murray's *Autumn Fire* (1924) or naturalistic 'issue' dramas, such as Lennox Robinson's *The Big House* (1926), Brinsley MacNamara's *The Master* (1928) or Denis Johnston's *The Moon in the Yellow River* (1931) do address issues of, for example, sexuality, rural property inheritance and gender relations, but in a manner that tends to dissociate such issues from a critique of the legitimacy of the state.

Murray's *Autumn Fire* is a case in point. Performed at the Abbey in 1924, the action of Murray's play takes place in the familiar setting of the standard Abbey Theatre farmhouse kitchen. The play deals with the collision between a traditionalist way of life represented in the stage setting, and an idea of individuality that is associated with

Ireland's modernization. The latter is represented in the character of Nance Desmond who has returned to the country with modern ideas. Nance presents a fundamental threat to the traditional, familial way of life that is represented by Ellen Keegan and the new Catholic/nationalist discourse of moral rectitude. Nance thus threatens precisely that which makes the 'beauty' and the 'homely simplicity' of the farmyard kitchen such an attractive icon of contemporary Ireland. The specific threat lies precisely in Nance's attractiveness as a stage character: her frank enjoyment of her physical appearance and of her attractiveness to men (Murray 1998: 123). Ellen is horrified, for example, when Nance expresses delight that her beads and glassy shoes may have distracted the men while at mass or when Nance says that she is looking forward to the threshing for the same reason ('I'll keep every nice boy from his work with my goings on' (Murray 1998: 124)). But for the spectator, watching silently from the darkened auditorium, Nance's attractiveness is also the basis of the play's theatrical pleasure. And while Ellen is associated with the new Catholicism of the 1920s and with the traditional social structures of rural Ireland (Murray 1998: 133), Murray's stage directions indicate the extent to which Ellen does not meet the spectator's approval.

In terms of the play's narrative, the conflict between traditionalism and individuality is soon put to the test when Owen Keegan (Ellen's father) falls in love with Nance and makes an arrangement to marry her. This causes consternation not only to Ellen, but also to Ellen's brother Michael who is himself infatuated with Nance. The marriage does take place, but Owen soon falls ill and Nance, now acting on the advice of a priest, persuades Michael that he must no longer entertain the idea of their having a relationship. But Owen discovers them just at the moment of their farewell embrace, and, reaching the conclusion that they are, in fact, having an affair, he retreats inconsolably into solipsism. Although the play shows that this unhappiness has arisen largely because of Ellen's Catholic moral rectitude, the ending of the play, with Owen Keegan completely isolated except for the consolation of his crucifix and rosary beards, suggests not so much the irrelevance of Roman Catholicism to Irish social life, but rather its absolute centrality. Similar to *The Plough and the Stars*, this is a denouement that suggests the need for desire to be regulated within traditional moral structures because the only alternative to this is presented as a state of moral and emotional destructiveness, but unlike O'Casey's play, Murray's gives this an unequivocally Catholic emphasis. In this respect *Autumn Fire* also works in support of the state, but in a manner that tends to endorse, much more than it challenges, the Catholic dominated nationalist ideology of moral purity and the sanctity of the family.

Brinsley MacNamara's popular comedy '*Look at the Heffernans!*' (1926) is similarly concerned with the relevance of traditional social structures to the exigencies of Irish modernization. At a time when Irish social and economic life was primarily rural (in 1926, 61 per cent of the population lived outside towns and villages while 53 per cent of all employed persons worked in agriculture (Woodman 1986: 30)), MacNamara's play considers directly the tradition of rural inheritance. Known as 'familism', this was a system of property inheritance in which farmers did not divide their land, but left all of the property to one son and dowered one daughter. As Arensberg and Kimball's famous 1940 study of familism in rural Ireland demonstrates, this pattern of land inheritance led directly to emigration, celibacy and late marriages. In MacNamara's play, the Heffernan family are prosperous farmers from County Meath whose economic prudence in not marrying (and so not dividing the family property) is so exemplary that the epithet 'Look at the Heffernans' has become a national aphorism. The play begins, however, with an announcement that such an attitude is no longer appropriate: instead of admiration, the community now views the Heffernans' celibacy as a cautionary warning. If everyone in the community acted like the Heffernans, explains the local tailor, not only would business begin to suffer but the community itself would start to expire. MacNamara's play thus taps into a growing anxiety in Ireland in the 1920s: that familism's insistence on maintaining the integrity of family property at all costs, and the consequent problems of emigration and celibacy, would lead to a form of 'race suicide' (see Howes 1996: 136). The play's comedy consists of a sequence of schemes and counter-schemes for marrying off the Heffernan family while allowing the family patriarch (James) to remain single. Ironically, the principle of familism is preserved while all the play's main characters are married off. '*Look at the Heffernans!*' played to capacity audiences despite Yeats's strong dislike of it: 'I have given orders that all the young women are to tousle their heads that we may not mistake them for whole women, but know them for cattle' (Yeats 1954: 713).

There is little indication that the Abbey Theatre in the mid- to late 1920s was eager to promote plays that would either confront or expose the Catholic-dominated nationalist ideology of the Irish Free State. To the contrary, the notorious rejection in 1928 of O'Casey's *The Silver Tassie* and of Denis Johnston's *The Old Lady Says 'No!'* may well have been motivated as much by the mordancy of these plays' satires of contemporary society, as it was because of Gregory's reputed dislike of their modernist and expressionistic dramaturgy. Indeed, Yeats's main objection to *The Silver Tassie* was in relation to the play's thematic emphasis: O'Casey had not experienced the First World War directly, Yeats claimed, and so he should not seek to represent it. 'You are not interested in the Great War', Yeats wrote to O'Casey, 'you never stood on its battlefields or walked its hospitals, and so write of your opinions. . . . The mere greatness of the world war has thwarted you' (O'Casey 1975: 268). Not least of the reasons why a Dublin performance of *The Silver Tassie* in 1928–9 might have been politically troublesome was that the First World War, and the manner of its commemoration, remained a matter of fierce political dispute. De Valera's newly formed party, Fianna Fáil, argued that while it respected the wish of ex-soldiers to honour their dead comrades, it did object very strongly to the exploitation of such commemorations for the purpose of celebrating imperialism (*The Nation*, 19 November 1927: 1). That some Dublin businesses persisted in flying Union Jacks on Poppy Day was a cause of particular dissension, as was the presence at a 1928 Dublin poppy day event of a contingent of uniformed British fascisti (*Irish Times*, 5 November 1928: 5). The commemoration of the First World War was an especially awkward political issue for the Cumann na nGaedheal government because this was also a period in which (in the wake of the disastrous 1927 General Election results) the party was forging a stronger link with ex-unionists. For the NTS to have sponsored a play that satirized the Roman Catholic liturgy *and* took a position on the First World War which resembled that of Sinn Féin would have been for it to adopt a singularly rebarbative position in relation to the state.

A similar argument can be put forward in relation to Denis Johnston's *The Old Lady Says 'No!'* which, although it attacks republican nationalism by portraying it as a form of play-acting, also offers an acerbic satire on the new Free State élite. Rejected for performance at the Abbey (ostensibly because of Gregory's view of it as confused and incomprehensible) Johnston's play was later performed on 3 July 1929 as the final production of the second season of Micheál MacLiammoir and Hilton Edwards's Gate Theatre. The force of Johnston's expressionistic satire is directed at the crass vulgarity of contemporary Ireland. In particular, the play attacks what it sees as Ireland's irredentist attraction to romantic nationalism with Irish political militancy portrayed pejoratively as a form of inappropriate or unacknowledged theatricality. At the opening of the play, for example, a collage of nineteenth-century nationalist ballads introduces what appears as a stereotypically melo-dramatic setting for the patriot Robert Emmet. Language, costumes, and stage setting all conform to the popular nationalist melodramas that were still regularly performed in Dublin in the 1920s at the Queen's Royal Theatre. But although this opening playlet suggests that the action that follows will conform to nationalist and melo-dramatic expectations, these expectations end abruptly when, within a few moments Emmet (the Speaker) is struck on the head by the villain, Major Sirr. As the play's succeeding action makes clear, the effect of this injury is to induce a peculiar state of concussion in which Emmet (who now believes completely in the role that he is playing) is forced to confront the prosaic realities of contemporary Dublin and of the Irish Free State.

Johnston's play implies that a sentimental attachment to Ireland's nationalist past prevents any proper or clear perception of the acquisitiveness of the contemporary situation. Thus, in Act I of *The Old Lady Says 'No!'* Cathleen ni Houlihan is presented as an old flower woman who is now more interested in her 'rights' (Johnston 1977: 43) and in selling off her 'four bewtyful gre-in fields' (Johnston 1977: 32), than in inspiring people to fight for the nation. Act II of the play satirizes the new Irish élite in its portrayal of a party hosted by the 'Minister for Arts and Crafts and his nice little wife' (Johnston 1977: 49), and its representation of the minister who 'bears a strange resemblance to the Stage Hand' (Johnston 1977: 50). Like Robinson's *The Big House*, what is portrayed as lost and neglected as a result of the banalities of a liberated Ireland is the Anglo-Irish and Irish Protestant tradition. This tradition is represented by the statue of Grattan played by the same actor who took the part of Major Sirr, villain of the nationalist melodrama of the opening playlet. The doubling of Sirr and Grattan (and the dramatic function of Grattan himself in the play as a whole) draws attention once again to the pernicious effect of Irish nationalism: 'Driven blindly on by the fury of our spurious moral courage! Is there to be no rest for Ireland from her soul?' (Johnston 1977: 34). Even if the inimitable O'Hegarty was delighted with *The Old Lady Says 'No!'* (Ferrar 1973: 21), it is likely that the broadening of Johnston's satire to include not just romantic nationalism, but the mannerisms and pretensions of Ireland's new political élite made this a difficult play for a national theatre to perform. Lady Gregory's dislike of Johnston's expression-istic dramaturgy was undoubtedly sincere, but as in the case of *The Silver Tassie*, *The Old Lady Says 'No!'* could also have occasioned an embarrassing disruption to the strengthening alliance in the 1920s of southern unionism and Cumann na nGaedheal.

Indeed, several of the most notable plays performed by the NTS in this period were attempts not at disrupting this connection, but at supporting and maintaining it. Plays such as Lennox Robinson's *The Big House* (1926), Brinsley MacNamara's *The Master* (1928) or Denis Johnston's *The Moon in the Yellow River* (1931), that is, work either to sentimentalize the relationship between Cumann na nGaedheal and southern unionism or to advocate support for the 'national' government of the Irish Free State as opposed to the recalcitrant and anti-modern forces of republican opposition. The most outstanding example of this kind of play is Robinson's *The Big House*. Less than three years after the burning of almost 200 Ascendancy houses in the period 1921–3, Robinson's play was one of the few occasions in twentieth-century drama in which a naturalistic dramaturgy was directed towards Ireland's former social élite. Performed by the Abbey on 6 September 1926, Walter Starkie described *The Big House* in the *Irish Statesman* as 'one of the most enthusiastic first performances that I can remember at the Abbey Theatre' (quoted in Brown 1985: 119). Like O'Casey's Dublin trilogy, *The Big House* deals with Ireland's recent political history. It is set in Ballydonal House and constitutes a historical survey of the recent history of an Anglo-Irish family (the Alcocks) from the end of the First World War in 1918 through the war of independence (or Black and Tan war) in 1920–1 to the immediate aftermath of the civil war in 1923. The play stresses the Alcock family's personal suffering with the first scene closing melodramatically with the news of the death of the family's favourite and only remaining son, Ulick. But the key issue of the play is how the Alcocks as an Anglo-Irish and Irish Protestant family, will relate to Ireland's newly independent majority nationalist population. Through the character of Vandaleur O'Neill, the option of assimilation is firmly rejected. Having discarded his opportunity of an English public school education, O'Neill, a neighbour and cousin of the Alcocks, is shown as a likeable bumpkin, but also as destructively irresponsible. According to Kate, it is O'Neill's misguided attempt at assimilation that 'has tumbled the big houses into ruins or into the hands of the big graziers or into the hands of the Roman Catholic Church' (Robinson 1982: 154).

In this context, what is proposed instead is a compromise form of assimilation in which Kate will maintain her distance from Ireland's indigenous culture, but at the same time will participate philanthropically in various aspects of it. But in Act II, in the midst

of the war of independence against the British, Kate realizes that she
will always remain an outsider and feels that she has no alternative
except to emigrate: 'There's something deeper, something that none
of us can put into words, something instinctive, this "them" and "us"
feeling' (Robinson 1982: 167). The play's third act engages with
the period in 1922–3 in which many of the homes of prominent
pro-Treaty supporters and senators were burnt down in response to
Cumann na nGaedheal's extra-legal policy of summary executions.
The play's *grand seigneur*, St Leger Alcock, writes a letter to the *grand
seigneur* of the state, the President of the Executive Council, W. T.
Cosgrave, pleading for the life of a local republican who has been
sentenced to death. St Leger procrastinates in the hope that
delivering the letter in person will make its contents more effective,
but he delays too long, the republican youth is executed, and
Ballydonal House is burnt down in retaliation. The play's final act
then addresses itself directly to the immediate social and political
consequences of this cycle of political trauma. Whereas St Leger and
his wife decide that their only remaining option is to emigrate to
England, Kate decides to stay on in Ireland and rebuild the family
home. She announces her decision to her immediate family and to
the local Church of Ireland rector in the following terms:

KATE: . . . now I don't want to give up the 'they' and 'us', I glory in
it. I was wrong, we were all wrong, in trying to find a common
platform, in pretending we weren't different from every Pat and
Mick in the village. Do you remember that grey filly we had long
ago that I christened 'Pearl' and Michael always called it 'Perr'l'
so we all called it 'Perr'l' not to seem to criticise Michael's
pronunciation? That's a trifling example, but it's the sort of
democratic snobbishness we went in for. We were ashamed of
everything, ashamed of our birth, ashamed of our good
education, ashamed of our religion, ashamed that we dined in
the evenings and that we dressed for dinner. . . .
(Robinson 1982: 195)

Kate's suggestion is that Ballydonal House must be rebuilt because
now it has a clear political role within the new state: that of declaring
a hierarchical class structure to be solidly intact. Kate Alcock's *aperçu*
is her rejection of what she describes as the 'democratic snobbishness'
of equality and assimilation. For her, the role of the former
Ascendancy in contemporary Ireland is to glory in their *corps d'élite*
status and not to reconcile themselves to the coarsening effects of

democracy. For AE this produced 'a liberating thrill' (quoted in Brown 1985: 120), but the fact that Robinson's play draws sentimental attention to the vulnerability of the Protestant Ascendancy minority must also have added considerably to the enthusiasm of the play's predominantly nationalist and Catholic audience. The myth of this beleaguered ex-unionist minority as the heroic purveyor of cultural value in Ireland now served a profoundly important role for Ireland's emerging bourgeois élite. It mystified as 'tradition' the notion of inherited wealth and naturalized and gave prestige to the idea of a social hierarchy in Irish society. Moreover, in suggesting an alignment between the interests of the Irish Free State élite and that of the ex-unionist Anglo-Irish minority, Robinson's *The Big House* also articulated Cumann na nGaedheal's own increasing reliance in the late 1920s on social élites (Regan 1999: 311–12).

MacNamara's *The Master* presents a more overt show of support for the government as against the now formidable electoral force of Fianna Fáil republicanism. Performed in March 1928, and in the wake of the 1927 general election, *The Master* is concerned with the dynamics and motivation of political allegiance within an Irish rural setting. James Quinn has been sacked from his position as schoolteacher, but despite the good reason for Quinn's dismissal (Quinn is a drunkard), the local people organize a boycott of the school in support of his reinstatement. The community's action is directed against the female replacement teacher and is motivated by their discovery that Quinn's dismissal will result in his eviction from the schoolteacher's house. The focus of the action is concentrated on Quinn's son, John, who supports the boycott until he recognizes the injustice of the crowd's attack on a 'defenceless girl'. John, and the audience, learn a lesson: never trust the ignorance of the mob. Having learnt this lesson, John now becomes 'one of the makers of the new Ireland' (MacNamara 1928: 71). As with many pro-government newspaper articles in the late 1920s or the realist paintings of Seán Keating, the conflict between Fianna Fáil and Cumann na nGaedheal is portrayed here as a universal tension between Free State modernizer and republican recidivist.

An even more extreme version of this narrative occurs in Johnston's first Abbey Theatre play *The Moon in the Yellow River* (1931). Here Johnston's advocacy of capital punishment for anti-state activity reflects the fraught political context in the run-up to the draconian Public Safety Act of October 1931 and the March 1932 general election. Performed on 27 April 1931, *The Moon in the Yellow River* links two prominent features of the Cumann na nGaedheal administration: the Shannon Hydro Electricity scheme of 1925 and its policy of summary executions and reprisals. For Johnston's play the admirable modernization programme represented by the new electricity scheme can be achieved only if the state is willing to execute those who are irrevocably opposed to such modernization. Consistently naturalistic, the setting of *The Moon in the Yellow River* – a former British Army barracks now converted into a domestic residence – reflects on Ireland's transition from colony to independent modern state. The owner of the house is Dobelle, an anti-romantic Catholic intellectual ('We may believe in faeries, but we trade in pigs' (Johnston 1960: 24)) whose sister, Columba, is an eccentric republican activist (Johnston 1960: 27). A hydro-electric power station is under construction in the area under the supervision of a German engineer, Tausch, who is a passionate believer in the modernizing power of technology (Johnston 1960: 34). The conflict arises when the local IRA detachment, under the command of its urbane piano-playing IRA leader Blake, attacks the power station on the basis that it is an instrument of the government to which the IRA is opposed. Political idealism in Ireland, of the kind represented by Blake and Columba, is a danger because (according to Dobelle) it 'has a disconcerting tradition of action' (Johnston 1960: 28). The immediate threat to the power station is averted, however, by the arrival of Free State troops, but when Blake makes it clear that the republican threat will continue even after they have gone, the Free State officer, Lanigan, shoots Blake dead at point blank range. After this unexpected conclusion to Act II (the shooting takes place just after Blake has finished a piano recital) the remaining act concerns Dobelle's argument that the killing of Blake was a necessary action in order to preserve the integrity of the state and its vitally important programme of democracy and modernization. One element of this argument is Dobelle's scathing attack on Catholic social teaching, which argues that it is better to preserve the life of an unborn infant rather than to protect and save the life of the mother. Because this is deemed to be right (according to the moral standards of 1930s Ireland) whereas killing a person for the sake of progress is considered to be wrong, Dobelle claims that he is 'against right and believes in wrong' (Johnston 1960: 74). 'The birth of a nation is no immaculate conception' (Johnston 1960: 81), and progress and modernization must be protected even if that means killing people. 'At present it wins favour with the claque that hailed the apotheosis of O'Casey under police guard', groaned the theatre critic for the Sinn Féin weekly newspaper *An Phoblacht*, 'one felt sorry for the Abbey players striving to make these marionettes live' (*An Phoblacht*, 2 May 1931: 3).

The Abbey Theatre's performance of Johnston's *The Moon in the Yellow River* marks an extraordinary end to the NTS's first decade after Irish political independence. Although the Abbey Theatre in the early 1930s still had a broadly nationalist reputation, performances of plays by O'Casey, Robinson and now Johnston, meant that this was a nationalism that was also resolutely opposed to the anti-Treaty position of Fianna Fáil and Sinn Féin. The fact that the Cumann na nGaedheal party went on to lose the 1932 and 1933 general elections to Fianna Fáil meant, however, that the idea of the NTS as a forum for national consensus soon became the focus of renewed controversy and debate.

5

FIANNA FÁIL AND
'THE NATION'S PRESTIGE',
1932–48

The Irish theatre must be an independent theatre, and it
must justify its claim to independence by its power to define
its ideals. . . . Until these ideals are re-defined the mob
will insolently present its own 'sodden enthusiasms' as
ultimatums to the theatre, and the theatre will not be able
to reply. We are come to a sorry pass when a hotel-keeper
from Connemara, or a publican from Mayo, can rise in our
Dáil and dictate to the artist what he may do, or must do.
That is the artist kneeling in the gutter to beg pennies of a
fool.

(Seán O'Faolain, 21 September 1938)

And this theatre is kept by a Government which poor Pearse
died to bring into being: Have we gone stark, staring mad?
(Fr. M. H. Gaffney, OP, 13 September 1935)

One of the Abbey Theatre's most popular plays in the 1930s and
1940s was Lennox Robinson's comedy, *Drama at Inish*. First
performed in February 1933 (a few weeks after Fianna Fáil's
momentous electoral victory), Robinson's play appears to herald a
new cultural epoch, one in which the NTS forgoes its previous
role of rebarbative social criticism and opts instead for comedy and
popular appeal. Indeed, the narrative action of *Drama at Inish* is
marked by a theatrical self-consciousness that suggests the playwright's awareness of this very significance. A travelling theatre
group, presided over by the ostentatiously Robinsonesque figure of
Hector de la Mare, arrives as cultural missionaries at an Irish seaside
town. Invited there by a committee of local worthies (a Monsignor,
a Member of the Dáil, and the proprietor of the main hotel), it is
hoped that the theatre's aura of cultural prestige will restore the
town's ailing tourist industry. The experiment is a disaster. The

townspeople of Inish react to the performances of Ibsen, Chekhov and Tolstoy first with literal-minded astonishment and then with lugubrious despair. It is a situation of farcical naïveté, reminiscent of Yeats's anecdotal account of the republican demonstrator against *The Plough and the Stars* so zealously worried about Mollser's tuberculosis that he interrupted his protest in order to wrap her in a blanket (Yeats 1954: 711). Far from improving Inish's social and cultural life, the actors' performances have the effect of making matters far worse. What quickly becomes apparent is that for this apparently homogeneous community to exist its many unsavoury truths must be left concealed. By the time of the play's conclusion, the community has eschewed the European theatre *tout court* and has welcomed, with great relief, the return of its annual circus.

At one level, *Drama at Inish* is a comic exploitation of the gap between what Raymond Williams views as the two meanings of 'culture': 'culture' as a society's aesthetic artifacts and 'culture' as its lived experience (Williams 1993: 6). At another level, Robinson's comedy exposes the perceived disparity between the sophistication of the Abbey Theatre's metropolitan audience and what is presented as an almost pre-modern ingenuousness widespread in the Irish provinces. In the case of the latter, theatrical illusion is regularly misrecognized as reality and 'culture', in so far as it can be said to exist at all, is regarded exclusively in mercenary terms. No doubt the impression that Robinson's play is so strongly weighted in favour of sophistication helps to account for its popularity: a spectator's enjoyment of the play – whether in Dublin, Skibbereen or Castlebar – demonstrates, as it were, his or her intrinsic sophistication. At another level, however, *Drama at Inish* declares the impossibility of a theatre of social critique in the context of the petit-bourgeois and increasingly self-confident nationalist world of post-independence Ireland. In this respect, Robinson's metatheatrical narrative has been interpreted as a response both to the anti-intellectualism sanctioned by the 1929 Censorship of Publications Act and to the dramatist's own position as a member of a beleaguered Protestant minority. 'As a Protestant, acutely conscious of the dwindling power of Protestants in the new Free State', writes Christopher Murray, 'Robinson was not advocating opposition. As an amused observer he understood that the sensible attitude was to accept what history had delivered' (Murray 1997: 117–18). Terence Brown, who also views the 1930s as combining 'a deep reverence for the Irish past' with 'an almost Stalinist antagonism to modernism' (Brown 1985: 147), similarly argues that the unadventurous character of Abbey Theatre plays in the 1930s and 1940s is to be interpreted as 'a prudent response' to 'a prevailing conservatism' (Brown 1991: 172). Robinson's *Drama at Inish* seems both to forecast and diagnose the beginning of a decline.

This argument is a familiar one. It conforms to the general view that the cultural politics of Ireland in the 1930s and 1940s is the product of a depressing mix of triumphalist Roman Catholic ideology and the populist nationalism of Fianna Fáil. Within this frame (so dominant that one commmentator has referred to it as a 'conditioned reflex' of 'demonization' (Fallon 1998:3)), the Abbey Theatre is presented as one of the outstanding institutional victims, noticeably declining from the heydays of Sean O'Casey and Denis Johnston in the decade after independence to what is often presented as the later, small-minded, and Gaelic-speaking obsession of Ernest Blythe in the 1940s. And whereas the Abbey Theatre's relationship with the Cumann na nGaedheal government in the 1920s is considered as generally benign – in so far as it was the Cumann na nGaedheal administration in 1925 that granted the NTS its first subsidy – its relationship with the Fianna Fáil government of the 1930s is characterized as depressingly adversarial. This line of interpretation also dominates the theatre and cultural commentary of the period. As early as 1944 the *Irish Times* went so far as to attribute the crumbling standards of Ireland's national theatre institution to what it considered to be the theatre's recent and mistaken policy of performing plays in the Irish language. Peter Kavanagh's landmark study, *The Story of the Abbey Theatre*, published in 1950, advances a similar contention: by the early 1940s the Abbey had became 'swamped by the rabble' with the country's Fianna Fáil Taoiseach, Eamon de Valera, as 'now the Abbey's virtual leader' (Kavanagh 1950: 183). For Kavanagh, as for the *Irish Times*, Yeats's death in 1939 and the appointment of Blythe as managing director in 1941 mark an especially dismal stage in the national theatre's artistic decline.

Robinson's *Drama at Inish*, one might then conclude, constitutes the last laugh of Ireland's *ancien régime* in the face of the increasing hostility of populist nationalism. There is no doubt, moreover, that both the NTS in general and Lennox Robinson in particular were acutely aware of the new political dispensation and of the mutual, hostile suspicion that existed between the Abbey Theatre and Fianna Fáil. Indeed, in several respects the Abbey Theatre's tour of the United States in the autumn of 1932 was deliberately provocative. In the politically charged atmosphere of the time, when Fianna Fáil's retention of power was by no means assured, the repertoire of plays performed (these included Synge's still controversial *The Playboy of the Western World* and *The Shadow of the Glen*, O'Casey's critique of anti-Treaty nationalism in *Juno and the Paycock* and Paul Vincent Carroll's anti-clerical *Things that are Caesar's*) appeared to many in the United States as the Abbey Theatre, once again, proclaiming its pro-Treaty and anti-majoritarian tendencies. Irish-Americans, and particularly those Irish-Americans sympathetic to Fianna Fáil whose donations had helped launch in 1931 the pro-Fianna Fáil newspaper the *Irish Press*, were incensed at what they regarded as this blatant display of cultural partisanship. Among the many who wrote in complaint to the Irish government were two congressmen and a meeting of Fianna Fáil Inc. in New York: each bewailed the 'humiliating' representation of Ireland by the Abbey players and the Irish government's apparent sanction for these performances.[1] Not only had the phrase 'By Special Arrangement with the Irish Free State Government' been inserted in each of the tour's theatre programmes, they pointed out, but the Irish Consul in Washington had travelled especially to New York to host an official welcoming reception (NA: S 6284A).

Antagonism between the Abbey Theatre and the nascent Fianna Fáil administration had been growing for some time. Just one month earlier, in the midst of the celebrations of de Valera's 1933 electoral victory (the first occasion in the history of the state when a political party won an overall Dáil majority) Yeats described the Abbey Theatre on tour as 'ambassadors of Irish taste' on a mission to substitute cultural for political links between Ireland and the United States (quoted in the *Irish Press*, 31 January 1933: 2). Yeats's words were interpreted by the *Irish Press* as a calculated barb at Fianna Fáil's extensive Irish-American support.[2] Such comments were flagrantly incorrect in relation to any weakening of Irish-American support for Fianna Fáil, the newspaper bullishly asserted, and the Abbey Theatre's tour of the United States was to be denounced for its humiliating representations of Ireland. Now more than ever, it argued, the time had arrived for Yeats, the Abbey Theatre, and the recently established Academy of Letters to address their responsibilities to the majority, Catholic population (*Irish Press*, 31 January 1933: 6).

Matters came to a head in February 1933. Two weeks after the first performance of *Drama at Inish*, the Secretary of the Department of Finance wrote to Lennox Robinson in Robinson's capacity as manager of the Abbey. The Secretary expressed concern regarding complaints about the Abbey Theatre's tour of the United States by 'representative Irish societies and influential individuals in the

United States', and then announced that the Minister of Finance had 'consented' to the appointment of Professor William Magennis as the government's representative on the Abbey's board of directors (J. J. McElligott to Abbey Theatre, 27 February 1933: NA S 8208). Magennis, Professor of Metaphysics at University College, Dublin, who was to become a prominent member of the Censorship Board, was also a supporter of the government-appointed Committee of Inquiry on Evil Literature (1926). The minister's 'consent' therefore amounted to a broadside. With a characteristic mixture of rhetoric and hauteur, Yeats responded by dismissing the American protests as philistine and insignificant, and by refusing outright to admit Magennis as a director. Henceforth, Yeats declared pre-emptively, all further government financial assistance was eschewed (Letter, 1 March 1933: NA S 8208). Finally, in a separate letter to de Valera, Robinson announced that the theatre intended to publish its full correspondence with the Department of Finance (NLI: ACC 3961 nfc 98 vol (5) 1932–36). Like the townspeople of Robinson's Inish, the Fianna Fáil government was to be exposed as crass, self-interested and philistine.

The animosity of this exchange is unsurprising. Both the 1932 and 1933 general elections took place within an atmosphere of press hostility against Fianna Fáil (Dwyer 1991: 159–60), rumours of an impending military *coup d'état*, and Cumann na nGaedheal's insistence that de Valera was 'the shadow of a gunman' and that Fianna Fáil was a dangerously revolutionary party (see Keogh 1986: 134–59). From a pro-Treaty and ex-unionist position, the accelerating fortunes of Fianna Fáil in the early 1930s were a matter of grave concern: even, in some cases, a matter of trauma and alarm. And yet, in fact, Fianna Fáil's actual assumption of power was most notable for its uneventful conservatism. Constrained initially as much by the party's lack of an absolute majority as by fears concerning a possible coup by Cumann na nGaedheal's allies in the Army Comrades' Association (see Regan 1999: 324–40), de Valera moved immediately to provide reassurances that there would be no victimization of Treaty supporters within the public service. He even went so far as to appoint a former Cumann na nGaedheal member (James Geoghegan) as his new Minister for Justice (Lee 1989: 176; Dwyer 1991: 161).

Moreover, while to some extent Fianna Fáil's policies of industrial protection and import substitution may be seen as a rigorous implementation of the core Sinn Féin philosophy abandoned in the 1920s by the pro-Treaty Cumann na nGaedheal, the practical effect of such policies was to promote the fortunes of Ireland's native bourgeoisie (see Foster 1988: 543; Dunphy 1995: 160). Most important of all, Fianna Fáil allowed the civil service to remain intact, thereby indicating the party's willingness to reform and redirect, rather than to alter fundamentally, the economic policies of the state. In this respect, Fianna Fáil's treatment of the state as an 'essentially neutral instrument' was a crucial indicator of its attitude to government (Dunphy 1995: 146).

A further important way in which Fianna Fáil was able to provide reassurance to those anxious about the party's revolutionary past was in its attitude to the rise of populist Roman Catholicism. The 1929 centenary celebrations of Catholic Emancipation served as one of the first occasions in Ireland's history in which the full panoply of the state was seen to endorse a majoritarian public life, and this was even more in evidence in the much larger and more extravagant spectacle of the Eucharistic Congress in June 1932. Quite apart from their religious significance for the Irish Free State's majority Roman Catholic population, both of these events had a powerful nationalist appeal. The Eucharistic Congress, in particular, was a spectacular enactment of Ireland's newly post-colonial civic culture (see Ó Tuathaigh 1996: 35), now untrammelled by the former Union-Jack bunting, British military ceremonial and top-hatted presence of the Irish peerage. This was street theatre on a monumental scale: a declaration of Ireland's newly and uncompromisingly independent national status to a sympathetic audience of visiting international dignitaries. Unsurprisingly, therefore, Fianna Fáil now embraced the Eucharistic Congress as a valuable opportunity for popular legitimation and continuity. Notwithstanding the Church's previous condemnations of the anti-Treaty forces, Fianna Fáil as the 'people's party' viewed the congress as a chance both to celebrate what it described as 'the august resurrection of a nation' (quoted in Dunphy 1995: 209), and to leave no shadow of a doubt as to the cabinet's firm allegiance to Catholicism.

The problem for the NTS within this new dispensation was not so much the politics or economic policies of Fianna Fáil, but the party's rhetoric and core ideology. Despite – indeed, because of – the smoothness of the political and economic transition, Fianna Fáil's assumption of power in 1932 and in particular its achievement of an absolute majority in January 1933 was characterized by a major ideological shift. In rhetoric and in symbolism the new government emphasized a democratizing and republican self-identity as the badge of Ireland's political independence. Insisting that his government would not willingly assent 'to any form or symbol' that was inconsistent with Ireland's status as a sovereign nation (quoted in Dwyer 1991: 193), de Valera created an impression of a radical shift in the cultural register of the state. From the cabinet's eschewal of formal wear on state occasions (demonstrated most splendidly when the Papal Legate arriving at Dun Laoghaire mistook de Valera and his cabinet ministers for a phalanx of Garda detectives (Keogh 1995: 95–6)) to de Valera's abolition of the oath of allegiance and his replacement of James MacNeill with Donal Ó Buachalla as Governor-General (Lee 1989: 177), Fianna Fáil's ideology was one that emphasized the democratic accountability of the state and of Ireland's major cultural and educational institutions.[3] 'If you want to be part of the Irish nation,' de Valera lectured the still Union-Jack-flying Trinity College, 'the basis of your pride must be achievements for the Irish nation . . . we want Trinity men not to have their hearts and minds centred upon another country' (quoted in McDowell 1997: 172). Within this context, then, the Abbey Theatre appeared to many as an ideal, and long overdue, target for ideological critique. Its prominently Protestant- and Ascendancy-related directorate, its political associations and alignments with the personnel and policies of Cumann na nGaedheal in the early and mid-1920s, not to mention the controversial anti-republican polemics of plays such as Sean O'Casey's *The Plough and the Stars* and Denis Johnston's *Moon in the Yellow River*, meant that from a Roman Catholic and anti-Treaty nationalist point of view, the Abbey Theatre was a public institution badly in need of reform. Even without the disquieting letter from the Secretary of the Department of Finance in February 1933, the NTS directorate had good reason to be apprehensive.

And yet what is so remarkable about the overall relationship between Fianna Fáil and the Abbey Theatre in the 1930s and 1940s is that there is a striking *lack* of conflict. Given this relationship's inauspicious beginnings with the Abbey Theatre's controversial tour of the United States in 1932–3, Yeats's pointed remarks on the desired future direction of Irish–American relations, and the combative attitude of the Department of Finance, this is indeed all the more notable. What transpires from the fraught exchanges between the Abbey and the government in early 1933, however, is not the cultural and political battle that that correspondence seems so clearly to augur, but rather a hastily arranged meeting between Yeats and de Valera in which de Valera appears to capitulate. De Valera merely emphasizes the need for the Abbey Theatre repertoire to show greater sensitivity in future in relation to Irish-America while, for his part, Yeats reports to his friend Olivia Shakespear that he had been inspired by de Valera's 'simplicity and honesty' and urges her not to believe what she might read in the English papers about the Fianna Fáil leader (Yeats 1954: 806). Furthermore, in the immediate aftermath of the 1932–3 protests concerning the Abbey Players' tour of 'objectionable' and 'humiliating' Irish plays in the United States, the Fianna Fáil leader went out of his way to emphasize the theatre's prestigious inheritance by describing the Abbey in a radio broadcast as 'the finest school of acting of the present day' (quoted in Dwyer 1991: 182). Despite temporarily reducing the Abbey Theatre's subsidy for the financial years of 1933–4 and 1934–5 and publicly urging the NTS directorate to consider more sensitively the feelings of Irish-Americans, the Fianna Fáil administration was meticulous in avoiding any direct confrontation. Even the thorny issue of the government nominee on the board of directors was resolved by elaborate behind-the-scenes negotiations that led to the appointment of Dr Richard Hayes, a candidate agreeable to both parties (Hunt 1979: 146). And when further difficulties arose in the spring of 1934 with the NTS's announcement of the repertoire for its next (1934–5) tour of the United States, the government's objections were again mild. De Valera wrote to Robinson objecting to the choice of the three Dublin plays of Sean O'Casey on the basis that their performance would 'certainly arouse shame and resentment among Irish exiles' and requesting that the government's non-sponsorship of the tour be made clear in all theatre programmes (Letter, 17 April 1934; NA S 8208). Robinson responds solicitously: he readily agrees to the programme disclaimer and concludes, 'the Directors deeply appreciate your friendly attitude in the whole matter' (Letter, 28 April 1934; NA S 8208). Apart from repeating this objection in a public statement in the Dáil (18 April), de Valera made no further attempt to force the Abbey Theatre to alter its tour repertoire. And, in response to another letter of protest regarding the Abbey's tour repertoire of plays, de Valera's private secretary defends both the NTS's artistic autonomy and the continuation of the government subsidy 'enabling the National Theatre Society, Limited to carry on the valuable work which it commenced thirty years ago' (Letter, 19 October 1934: NA S 8208). Yeats also, it would appear, did not wish to press the conflict with Fianna Fáil any further and, in September 1934, he lost no time in correcting a report in the *Sunday Times* which implied the existence of an on-going disagreement between the Abbey Theatre and the government. 'We are on friendly terms with the Irish Government,' Yeats wrote, 'Mr de Valera has not "demanded" the withdrawal of any play by Synge or by O'Casey from our American repertory, nor have I "insisted" on their presence there' (quoted in Yeats 1975: 500).

Notwithstanding the strenuous objections of some Dáil back-benchers, the implacable hostility of influential and widely distributed periodicals such as the *Standard* and the *Catholic Bulletin* and the regular protests of the *Irish Press*, de Valera himself appeared sanguine in relation to Yeats's minimalist assurance: from henceforth all theatre programmes for United States tours would contain notices disclaiming the direct support of the government. It was not so much that de Valera had been snubbed in his dealings with the Abbey Theatre as was claimed angrily by an editorial in the *Irish Press* (9 May 1934: 6), or that the NTS had won a bout in an on-going war with Fianna Fáil as has been claimed by some theatre historians (Kavanagh 1950: 160; Hunt 1979: 146), but that both Yeats and de Valera had managed these early controversies to their mutual advantage. If for the new Fianna Fáil administration, the Abbey Theatre posed a problem, it was an established national institution nevertheless. And while Yeats's reference in early 1933 to the Abbey Players as 'ambassadors of good taste' may well have been patronizing, it was also a telling reminder to Fianna Fáil that the Irish theatre of Gregory, Synge and O'Casey offered the country an internationally recognized cultural prestige which would assist, far more than it would hinder, Ireland's on-going campaign for a fuller and more autonomous form of national statehood. True, the Abbey Theatre's existence as a 'national' theatre partly funded by government subsidy and yet performing plays that tended to be strikingly one-sided in their critique of majoritarian orthodoxies was, sometimes, a source of irritation and ideological embarrassment. (How, it was frequently asked in articles in the *Irish Monthly*, the *Standard* and the *Catholic Bulletin*, could Fianna Fáil reconcile its support for such an institution and at the same time claim to exist as the democratic voice of the people?) At the same time, however, the Abbey Theatre remained an important feature of Irish public life. It emphasized both Ireland's cultural autonomy and the bourgeois normality of the Irish state. De Valera's awareness of the overriding importance of both (an awareness no doubt assisted by the advice of his parliamentary secretary, P. J. Little[4]) is the most likely explanation for his accommodation with Yeats.

But this does not mark the full extent of the NTS's response to Fianna Fáil protests in the 1930s. In the Dublin programme of the Abbey Theatre's repertoire from 1932–5 there is, for example, a notable absence of plays hostile to the politics of Irish republicanism and a marked decrease in plays that are mordantly satirical of contemporary bourgeois Irish life. Social commentary tends to be restricted to mildly satirical comedies of provincial and rural life such as Robinson's *Drama at Inish* (1933) and *Church Street* (1934), George Shiels's farcical treatment of Protestant/Catholic antagonism in *Grogan and the Ferret* (1933), or Rutherford Mayne's sympathetic treatment of the work of the Irish Land Commission and the plight of Irish landlordism in *Bridgehead* (1934). If one reason for the extraordinary popularity of Robinson's *Drama at Inish* was its flattering metatheatrical joke about provincial Irish audiences preferring light comedy to European modernism, such preferences were also the deliberately chosen *modus vivendi* for the Abbey Theatre itself. What this suggests is that it was not just an endemic Roman Catholic '*nostalgie du divan*' in 1930s Ireland that prevented the growth or development of an indigenous modernist theatre (Brown 1995: 28–9), but also the strategic and sentimental interests of Ireland's former social élite.

Regardless of the placatory tones of de Valera and Yeats themselves and the Fianna Fáil executive's generally non-antagonistic attitude towards the NTS, the question of the Abbey Theatre's national accountability remained an important issue of public debate. For the high circulation *Irish Press*, for example, the Abbey Theatre's determination to proceed with productions of O'Casey's Dublin trilogy for their 1934–5 tour of the United States, in spite of de Valera's protests, was nothing short of an insult, whereas for the *Irish Times* the proposed repertoire demonstrated spirited resolve. Clearly what was at stake in the controversy was not merely a disagreement concerning O'Casey's literary merits. What was contested was whether the term 'democracy', now a key word in Fianna Fáil rhetoric (see Lee 1989: 180) could be interpreted as egalitarian meritocracy or as representative accountability. For the *Irish Press*, the idea that a national institution, partly funded by the state, should so disregard 'the elected leader of the people' was a scandalous dereliction of duty (*Irish Press*, 9 May 1934: 6). For the *Irish Times*, annoyed by the government's abolition of special Dáil representation for the universities (a system which especially favoured the predominantly Protestant and ex-unionist Trinity College), the notion of democracy as representative accountability was an opportunistic concession to populism. From this latter perspective, for a national theatre to alter its repertoire merely to suit the wishes of majority opinion was philistinism gone rampant.

'The Government talks glibly about "culture"', the *Irish Times* complained, 'but fears the judgment of educated opinion' (*Irish Times*, 9 May 1934: 6). Thus Fianna Fáil pushing the country towards 'mob rule' underlined a distinction between democracy as the high-minded expression of 'the world's greatest thinkers and statesmen' and the Fianna Fáil version of democracy in which 'the man of intellect and education matter no more and no less than those of the corner boy' (*Irish Times*, 9 May 1934: 6).

But the trenchant rhetoric of contemporary newspaper editorials camouflages a cultural debate in the 1930s that was considerably more complicated than any simple 'culture versus philistinism' opposition. Throughout this period many nationalist intellectuals argue the need for a more representative Irish culture. Thus, Daniel Corkery's *Synge and Anglo-Irish Literature* (1931) attempts to define the nature of an Irish national literary culture in majoritarian terms. In so doing, however, Corkery's proposal ran athwart the fundamental values of English literary modernism and of the Irish literary revival itself. To those schooled in a belief in artistic autonomy and an association of literary prestige with minority critique, that is, Corkery's epiphany at an All-Ireland hurling final is a bizarre solecism.

> I recall being in Thurles at a hurling match for the championship of Ireland. There were 30,000 onlookers. They were as typical of this nation as any of the great crowds that assemble of Saturday afternoons in England to witness Association football matches are typical of the English nation. It was while I looked around on that great crowd I first became acutely conscious that as a nation we were without self-expression in literary form. The life of this people I looked upon – there were all sorts of individuals present, from bishops to tramps off the road – was not being explored in a natural way by any except one or two writers of any standing.
>
> (Corkery 1931: 12–13)

Corkery's argument was that Irish literary expression was asymmetrical in relation to Ireland's majority culture because Anglo-Irish literature (or Irish literature in English) was written in English (not Irish) and because it was out of touch with the pieties of Roman Catholicism. He noted that much Anglo-Irish literature was written for a foreign audience and from a position distanced from the majority indigenous population. It was not so much that Anglo-Irish writers were to be condemned as individuals, but that the 'system' and the critical values of literature itself gave rise to a pattern of endemic distortion (Corkery 1931: 39). For many of the country's Catholic intellectuals, Corkery's thesis had an important appeal. It attempted to address the way in which Ireland's recent literary expression took an overwhelmingly oppositional stance in relation to the country's majority opinion. Corkery's book also reflects a general unease about modernist cultural practices in general: a sense that the cult of aesthetic autonomy was a subterfuge for an irresponsible lack of social accountability.[5]

As far as the Abbey Theatre is concerned, however, the radical nature of Corkery's theory lay in its challenge to one of the NTS's long-standing first principles: that a national theatre's prestige is inextricably linked to the ability of its dramatic narratives to offer a criticism of majority orthodoxies from a minority position. Corkery argued that so pervasive and widely accepted was this assumption that even the plays of Catholic dramatists, such as T. C. Murray or Padraic Colum, were distanced from the majority culture of their upbringing and so portrayed obsessively 'the crassness [of an Irish] upbringing' (Corkery 1939: 15). While one implication of Corkery's argument was the need for a redefinition of literary and cultural prestige in a post-colonial context, Corkery opted for the less radical choice of advocating a national literature primarily concerned with the expression of more authentic and 'hidden' values: Irishness as an adherence to the pieties of land, nationalism and the dominant religion. Because these values are presented in such a way that the terms 'Irish' and 'Roman Catholic' are regarded as virtual synonyms, Corkery's work gained a contemporary reputation, even among his supporters, as right wing and exclusive (see *Irish Press*, 2 March 1937: 8).

These were serious weaknesses. Nevertheless, as an alternative theory of national literature, Corkery's *Synge and Anglo-Irish Literature* drew widespread public attention to the cultural asymmetries at the Abbey Theatre and helped promote a debate about the account-ability of cultural institutions in general. Thus, Aodh de Blacam, writing in a 1935 issue of the *Irish Monthly*, acknowledges Ireland's debt to the early work of the Abbey Theatre in stirring national pride and in promoting 'high and consistent standards in literature,' but then goes on to argue that the Abbey is out of tune with modern Irish life. It is not just a question of the clichéd nature of the NTS's peasant play tradition (' "Kiltartenese" ' as a 'tedious mannerism fit only to be caricatured by Jimmy O'Dea'), but the more fundamental issue that in the case of the Abbey Theatre writers 'the most tremendous things in Irish life' hardly ever appear (de Blacam 1935: 192). For de Blacam, what was to be lamented in particular was the preoccupation with disillusionment (de Blacam 1935: 93), an eschewal of a 'popular art . . . [that] share[s] the unity of the race' (de Blacam 1935: 195) and a marked lack of sympathy with the religious beliefs of the majority (de Blacam 1935: 196). And in a statement that would have confirmed the worst fears of Yeats, Synge and Gregory 30 years earlier, de Blacam concluded that what was most needed in Ireland's national theatre was not ' "art for art's sake" but [religious] orthodoxy' (de Blacam 1935: 198).

For Corkery and de Blacam the notable absence in the NTS repertoire of plays polemically critical of contemporary Irish nationalism were minor concessions indeed. For them, Robinson's *Drama at Inish* may well have announced a transition from social criticism and analysis to rural comedy and the celebration of a generalized ethnicity, but there still remained a persistent, and often (no doubt) inadvertent, Ascendancy perspective. Although Robinson's *Church Street* (1934), for example, celebrates provincial Ireland in so far as it makes much of the claim that Knock, County Mayo, is as legitimate a subject for serious drama as anywhere else, the thematic core of the play is predictable enough. As in all of Robinson's post-independence plays, the preoccupation here is with the social plight of the Protestant middle classes. *Church Street* shows how the local Mayo community is replete with hidden tragedy, but reveals that by far the most intense suffering is that experienced by the Protestant characters: the Pettigrew sisters who live in penury and semi-starvation in their large house because their investments have been squandered by the local (Roman Catholic) bank manager. Yet another example of Protestant long-suffering is Sallie Long, the Church of Ireland rector's daughter, who has been made pregnant by a medical student whose (again Roman Catholic) religious scruples prevent him from marrying her. In Mayne's *Bridgehead* (1934) this cultural asymmetry is even more overt. Mayne's play deals with the work of the Land Commission in dividing up large estates and distributing them among Ireland's extensive former tenant and small farmer population. What *Bridgehead* sets out to show is that for such a project to be successful emotional allegiances are of less importance than the overall strategic goal of land redistribution. What takes place in the theatre, however, is that the human cost of this achievement is portrayed in such moving and pathetic terms that the project itself is called into question. And while the representatives of the Land Commission and the former Ascendancy are portrayed as sensitive, hard-working and well-educated, the small-farmer population is shown as universally greedy, crass, and hypocritical. For the *Irish Times*, *Bridgehead* was 'just the kind of play we need at present' (*Irish Times*, 6 August 1935: 8), but for the *Irish Press* Mayne's sympathy is so clearly with 'the old order' that it 'would have presented a better balance were one decent small farmer or landless man portrayed (*Irish Press*, 19 June 1934: 2).

But it was not just the opponents of the NTS who believed that its repertoire fell short of the standards required of a national theatre. For advocates of the Abbey Theatre tradition such as Seán O'Faolain, the national theatre's main weakness now lay in its reluctance to attack key nationalist orthodoxies with anything like its former combative vigour. In an open letter to Yeats (published in the *Irish Times* in March 1935) O'Faolain argued that the Abbey Theatre was unworthy of its role as a national theatre because it was not sufficiently searching in its critique of Ireland's new acquisitiveness and chauvinism. O'Faoláin insisted that the proper function of a national theatre should be educational and modernizing and that, to this end, it should be concerned with probing the nation's conscience: 'It can reveal Ireland to herself, the new Ireland, if it has the courage to take risks' (*Irish Times*, 2 March 1935: 7). Eulogizing plays such as Robinson's *Patriots* (1912), Padraic Colum's *Thomas Muskerry* (1910) and T. C. Murray's *Maurice Harte* (1912), O'Faolain went on to condemn the Abbey Theatre for not assisting sufficiently those contemporary writers who wanted to criticize the nationalist and religious orthodoxies of modern Ireland (*Irish Times*, 2 March 1935: 7). In a subsequent letter to the *Irish Times*, Michael Farrell (the future author of 'The Country Theatre' series in *The Bell*) was even more direct. Farrell argued that what was required of the NTS was a direct assault on national orthodoxies similar to the iconoclasm of Denis Johnston's *The Moon in the Yellow River* (*Irish Times*, 16 March 1935: 6).

One point of agreement between those who supported the Abbey Theatre and those whose opposition to it seemed implacable was the national theatre's relationship to majority Irish culture and, in particular, to Irish Catholicism. And while there is a certain predictability to Catholic periodicals such as the *Irish Monthly*, the *Catholic Bulletin*, *The Standard* and *The Leader*, at least in terms of their attacks on what was seen as the theatre's overwhelmingly negative relationship to Ireland's majority religion, it is more surprising to find these views expressed by Abbey Theatre participants and supporters like Paul Vincent Carroll, Brinsley MacNamara and Seán O'Faoláin. Carroll, for example, described himself (mistakenly) in 1931 as the Abbey Theatre's 'first Catholic dramatist' (quoted in Sitzmann 1975: 147–8) and in 1935 MacNamara (also mistakenly) referred to himself as 'the one Catholic director on the Board' (*Irish Times*, 4 September 1935: 2). Even Seán O'Faoláin, by now a stalwart opponent of nationalist and Catholic orthodoxies and undoubtedly the most formidable of those who believed that the NTS should have a more rebarbative social role, hinted that by the 1930s the Abbey Theatre had become the domain of a Protestant coterie. O'Faolain argued that whereas the Abbey Theatre's famous conflicts with the political authorities in Ireland all involved a defence of Protestant writers, the theatre was now manifestly neglecting iconoclastic *Catholic* dramatists. O'Faolain repeated this point in 1942 when he accused Yeats of having ignored the new generation of poets, nearly all Catholics 'either by conviction or by atavism' whose life was being made impossible by the Catholic Church (quoted in Fallon 1998: 53).

The relationship between the Abbey Theatre and the Fianna Fáil government may have been smooth, but the Abbey's relationship with Irish intellectual life in general in the 1930s was increasingly embattled. To the mounting accusation that NTS artistic standards had declined, the Abbey Theatre responded by expanding its repertoire to include more European plays and by broadening the scope of productions to include some limited modernist and avant-garde techniques. 'We have got to make a fresh start', Yeats is reported to have declared in late 1934 and, in an apparent contra-diction of his 1919 essay in which he applauded the realism of the 'National School' dramatists (Yeats 1962: 244–59), Yeats had an English director, Brandon Peake, brought specially to the Abbey to conduct modernist and experimental productions. To the more fundamental criticism that the NTS was not nationally accountable, Yeats and his fellow directors responded more hesitantly: first, by promoting the idea of an Abbey Theatre Advisory Committee and, second, in April 1935, by appointing three new directors: John Weldon (Brinsley MacNamara), Ernest Blythe and F. R. Higgins (see Kavanagh 1950: 206). A widely held belief now existed that changes in the Abbey Theatre's repertoire were imminent.

Arthur Shields's expressionistic production of O'Casey's previously rejected *The Silver Tassie* seemed to advertise this much-heralded policy change. Performed during the August Horse Show week and coinciding with the modernization of the theatre's vestibule and the abolition of its 'no smoking' rule, this production appeared to initiate a bold and more experimental artistic policy. But, instead the problem of the national representativeness of the Abbey Theatre became an issue of public debate. As a play that satirized British militarism in the First World War, the thematic emphasis of *The Silver Tassie* was, at least from an Irish nationalist perspective of the 1930s, hardly controversial. In the early 1930s British Legion 'poppy days' were boycotted by the Fianna Fáil government, and the First World War commemorative marches, with their prominent display of Union Jacks and British Army regalia and the singing of 'God Save the King', were registered by nationalists as provocative and insulting. In November 1935 an alternative Remembrance Day celebration organized by republicans marched through Dublin (Hanley 1999: 6). Nor was there anything especially problematic about O'Casey's satiric method: a dramaturgical montage that juxtaposes the heroization of the protagonist as a football champion in Act I with the expressionistic nightmare of his experience on the war front in Act II. What was considered objectionable, however, was O'Casey's attempted ventriloquism of elements of Irish Catholic culture. What was objected to in particular was the play's use of key elements of Catholic religious iconography – from the plainsong chants of the Mass to the black-robed Virgin and dismembered crucifix in Act II – as a means of parodying the glamorization of war.

Press reaction was predictably divided. The *Irish Times* found O'Casey's treatment of religion merely 'ironical' and was mildly enthusiastic about the play, whereas for the *Irish Press*, the *Evening Herald* and the high-circulation Catholic periodical *The Standard*, O'Casey's play was insolently and gratuitously blasphemous of Catholic religious practices. And whereas the *Irish Times* paid detailed attention to the play's impressive 'society' audience (this included the Earl and Countess of Longford, the editor of the *Irish Times*, R. M. Smylie, and ex-Cumann na nGaedheal ministers Ernest Blythe and Desmond FitzGerald), *The Standard* denounced this 'distinguished' audience for making no effort at protest. In an editorial, *The Standard* drew attention to the Abbey Theatre's lack of accountability and called for immediate government intervention so that 'never again will it dare to outrage the sacred ideals which are the proudest possession of our Catholic nation' (*The Standard*, 16 August 1935: 2). The controversy quickly gathered momentum. The National Council for the Federation of the Catholic Young Men's Societies (CYMS) of Ireland and the Galway branch of the CYMS sent a message to de Valera protesting against the performance of *The Silver Tassie* and arguing that the government should introduce theatre censorship forthwith (*Irish Press*, 3 September 1935: 2). In an editorial entitled 'The Nation's Prestige', the *Irish Times* responded to Catholic outrage against *The Silver Tassie* by suggesting that such objections amounted to organized intolerance.

> Any work which does not show Ireland as a land of saints and scholars, any play which ventures to attack or to satirise an aspect of Irish life, is condemned at once as a treacherous onslaught on the national prestige. Synge's 'Playboy' may be permitted in Dublin, but it should not be shown in America in case foreigners might form a bad impression of Irish peasants. Mr. O'Casey's 'The Plough and the Stars' should not be played in Horse Show Week; for the English visitors might learn how horrible the Dublin slums are. This attitude is quite as much responsible for popular resentment as is the feeling that the decencies have been outraged, and it is entirely unhealthy. In Ireland, at the moment, there are a dislike of blunt truths and a fear of criticism which are quite as bad as the excesses that are condemned.
>
> (*Irish Times*, 28 August 1935: 6)

The dispute worsened when the NTS's managing director, F. R. Higgins, publicly stated his agreement with the *Irish Times* and added that 'attacks on the Abbey Theatre are often made by people who invoke culture without knowing what it implies' (*Irish Times*, 29 August 1935: 7).

Objected to in the 1935 production of *The Silver Tassie* was not just O'Casey's parody of Roman Catholic religious practices, but the perceived condescension, anti-Catholicism and anti-nationalism of the Abbey Theatre as an institution. As the *Irish Times* correctly observed, the majority of the protesters against the play directed their resentment not at specific features of O'Casey's play in production, but at 'the Irish theatre movement as a whole' (*Irish Times*, 28 August 1935: 6). For Dr J. Murphy, Professor of English at University College Galway, for example, Shields's production was an instance of the Abbey Theatre once again flouting its position as a national theatre by cocking a snook not simply at Irish Catholicism, but at the social and cultural life of the majority (*The Standard*, 30 August 1935: 3). That Murphy, an academic not known for zealous pro-clericalism,[6] should on this occasion support a CYMS motion condemning the Abbey Theatre gives some indication of the intensity of the issue. The *Irish Times* described the controversy as no more than a 'contretemps' (3 September 1935: 6), but by early September, *The Standard* had raised its condemnatory rhetoric to even greater heights: the Abbey Theatre was 'a plague spot in our midst' with directors 'not of our faith' whose 'end is destruction' (6 September 1935: 8). This impression of a widespread popular grievance against the Abbey Theatre was exacerbated when Brinsley MacNamara resigned his directorship in protest against the production of *The Silver Tassie*. In a full page advertisement in the *Irish Independent*, MacNamara drew attention to his position as 'the one Catholic director present at the time' (see *Irish Press*, 4 September 1935: 1) and argued that he had accepted the proposal to stage O'Casey's *The Silver Tassie* with great reluctance (and then only as a way of avoiding a production of O'Casey's far more objectionable *Within the Gates*). He now stated that the reason for his resignation was the failure of the other Abbey Theatre directors to support him. Although he does not spell it out, MacNamara's statement hints that what was taking place at the Abbey Theatre was a disgraceful indulgence in pre-independence sectarian cultural politics in which a largely Protestant executive compelled their Roman Catholic subordinates to act against their religious beliefs. For many commentators, therefore, the blasphemy of *The Silver Tassie* was inseparable from the Abbey Theatre's historical disdain towards Ireland's majority Catholic culture.

It is all the more remarkable in this context that Fianna Fáil did not intervene in the controversy. Despite the ferocity of attacks on the Abbey Theatre in the aftermath of *The Silver Tassie* production ('And this theatre is kept by a government which poor Pearse died to bring into being: have we gone stark, staring mad?' (Fr. Gaffney, OP, quoted in the *Irish Press*, 13 September 1935: 2)) de Valera and the Fianna Fáil cabinet resisted considerable popular, clerical and parliamentary demands for sanctions to be introduced. Not only this but within the same year the Fianna Fáil government agreed to increase the NTS subsidy to £1000. In response to letters of complaint from outside Ireland, moreover, de Valera continued to defend the Abbey Theatre's autonomy and artistic reputation as a national institution.

> No doubt, the Government could dissociate itself from the Theatre by withdrawing the subsidy, but it has to consider what the net result of such a course would be. The Abbey Theatre is the only theatre in Dublin of which the principal

aim is the development of a distinctively Irish school of drama. It has succeeded in a great measure. With few exceptions (for which, however, a great deal of attention has been concentrated), its plays are unobjectionable, while some are of high artistic value. If the Theatre were to disappear in consequence of the withdrawal of the subsidy, the city and the country generally would have to depend for dramatic entertainment, almost exclusively on imported plays, produced for the greater part by foreign players. That would, in the opinion of the Government[,] cause both moral and cultural loss to the nation, and it is not proposed to take any action which might have such a result.

(NA: S 8208, Letter, 18 February 1936)

If, as Peter Kavanagh has argued, the Abbey Theatre was forced to abandon its conscience under Fianna Fáil (Kavanagh 1950: 182–3), it is difficult to see how this can be attributed to direct political pressure. Moreover, O'Faolain's view that the Abbey Theatre in the 1930s should have adopted a role mordantly satirical of the contemporary state was disingenuous to the extent to which it ignored the way in which the Abbey Theatre had always avoided any such position. To evoke Robinson's *Patriots*, Colum's *Thomas Muskerry* and Murray's *Thomas Harte* as ideal theatrical models for the 1930s or for *The Bell* to wax eloquent in the early 1940s about 'the palmy and piping days of Redmondite Ireland' (M. Farrell in *The Bell*, February 1942: 388) is to miss the point entirely. Plays such as these were written and performed by the NTS at a time when the then British state was actively concerned with the rehabilitation of the Irish Parliamentary Party and with the marginalization of Sinn Féin and the non-constitutional tactics of the United Irish League. True, Colum, Murray and Robinson sharply criticized traditional nationalist orthodoxies in Redmondite Ireland, but they did so from positions that coincided (happily enough for the Abbey) with political attitudes that were then in the ascendant. Furthermore, the Abbey Theatre's pro-state orientation continues both in the volatile pre-independence period of 1916–22 and also in the first decade of Irish independence. In the period 1922–32 the Abbey Theatre's controversial attacks on nationalist orthodoxies in the Dublin plays of Sean O'Casey or in Denis Johnston's *Moon in the Yellow River*, for example, take place within the context of what is an increasingly explicit state support for the theatre. And opposing anti-Treaty republicanism was exactly what the Cumman na nGaedheal executive was doing as well. The changes that take place in the mid-1930s at the Abbey Theatre, and which are so decried by O'Faolain and Kavanagh, were merely a continuation of the NTS's already well-established ideological adaptability. To this extent, the 1935 production of *The Silver Tassie* was a temporary, albeit spectacular, miscalculation.

The immediate effect of *The Silver Tassie* controversy was a further polarization of views concerning the role of Ireland's national theatre. MacNamara's replacement by Frank O'Connor on the Abbey directorate and heated exchanges regarding the play in the autumn and winter of 1935 coincide with another discernible shift in the thematic emphasis of the NTS. With productions of Paul Vincent Carroll's *Shadow and Substance* (January 1937), Lennox Robinson's *Killycreggs at Twilight* (April 1937), Seán O'Faolain's *She Had To Do Something* (December 1937) and of Hugh Hunt and Frank O'Connor's *The Invincibles* (October 1937) and *Moses' Rock* (February 1938), the Abbey Theatre appeared to resume a more combative role in relation to nationalist majority views. Carroll's *Shadow and Substance*, for example, was an unsparing attack on populist Catholicism and its alliance with *nouveau riche* respectability. Carroll's protagonist, an erudite, European-educated priest condemns the 'holy hooliganism' (Carroll 1948: 186) of the Catholic Action movement and flinches at what he regards as the unspeakable vulgarity of popular oleographs of the Virgin Mary, his football-playing curates and the vast majority of the local population. Carroll's play constitutes a vigorous rebuttal, in other words, of the 'violent emotionalism' (Carroll 1948: 152) of the CYMS which, two years earlier, had been so mobilized against *The Silver Tassie*.

The treatment of contemporary Irish society in Robinson's *Killycreggs at Twilight* is broadly similar. Performed in April 1937, within a few weeks of the twenty-first commemorative celebrations of the 1916 Rising, *Killycreggs at Twilight* deals not with the glorious birth of the nation, but with the declining fortunes of a minority. The play's focus is on the vulnerable status of Irish Protestants for whom the big house, and its uncertain and potentially tragic future, is shown as exercising totemic significance. The De Lury estate, 'Killycreggs', then, is a metonym for Ireland's ex-unionist minority and its special difficulties in accommodating to the egalitarian market economy that is contemporary Ireland. Unlike Kate Alcock in *The Big House*, the protagonist of *Killycreggs at Twilight*, Judith de Lury, opts for assimilation by deciding to marry a local Catholic hotel owner, change her religion, and sell the ancestral big house.

JUDITH: There's no room in Ireland now for places like Killycreggs, for de Lurys and their like lounging and fishing and shooting. I wish we'd been burned out in the Troubles; I wish all our sort had been burned out. I wouldn't have behaved like that fool-girl in the play, *The Big House*. I would never have rebuilt Killycreggs, I'd have thanked God to be quit of it.

(Robinson 1939b: 83)

Despite the forcefulness of this speech, *Killycreggs at Twilight* is not a rebuttal to the sentimentalism of Robinson's earlier *The Big House* (*pace* Murray 1997: 118), but rather a reinforcement and a continuation of it. Judith's pragmatic plan to assimilate with the majority is counterbalanced by her nephew Loftus who, with the support of the play's other major characters, insists that Judith is attempting to do something 'outside nature' (Robinson 1939b: 92). In his wish to maintain and preserve the de Lury estate, Loftus declares that the dead generations of the family are speaking through him. And in the play's important final scene, Loftus's point of view (that the family home must be retained by the family at all costs) is accepted as being of equal validity to Judith's decision to marry a Catholic local. Despite the atmosphere of uncertainty and foreboding which pervades the final scene, Robinson's play is fully consistent with the sentimentalism of his earlier 1926 box office success. It is, in any case, a far cry from the apparent timidity of *Drama at Inish*.

A similarly robust opposition to nationalist orthodoxies is evident in Hunt and O'Connor's play, *The Invincibles*, performed in October 1937. Dealing with the famous 1882 assassination of the British Chief Secretary and his assistant in Dublin's Phoenix Park, what was so different and so difficult about Hunt and O'Connor's rendition of this event was not only the implication that this was a bloodthirsty criminal act, but the play's suggestion that it arose as a direct result of the excesses of nationalist rhetoric. The year 1937 concluded with a performance of O'Faolain's *She Had To Do Something* with its overt attack on state censorship and the brutal philistinism of local Catholic vigilance committees. In a post-production speech about the play, O'Faoláin resolutely defended the NTS's record of controversy and described Cathleen Ni Houlihan as a pernicious influence on Irish social life: 'She has been so long out of business as a Queen that she has developed the habit of the court intriguer, against whom all thought is held to be subversive' (*Irish Times*, 28 December 1937: 8).

This is also a period that witnesses Teresa Deevy's extraordinary powerful critiques of the coercive norms of Irish patriarchy. Deevy's version of the NTS's stock peasant setting in *King of Spain's Daughter* (1935) and *Katie Roche* (1936) offers not comic diversion or rural intrigue, but the problematic figure of the unruly female. Set in 1930s Ireland, the protagonist of *King of Spain's Daughter*, Annie Kinsella, is described by the stage directions as an idealized peasant girl: 'she wears a dark shawl, a red dress, black shoes and stockings – all very neat. Her hair is bright gold' (Deevy 1939: 126). Yet Deevy's portrayal of rural Ireland is anything but idealized. The play shows Annie caught up in a brutalized patriarchal regime in which her father beats her with a stick for not bringing him his dinner on time, and in which her flirtations with local men are constantly threatened by vengeful invigilation. To quell and punish Annie's disconcertingly active sexual desire, Annie's father forces her to choose between five years indentured servitude in a local factory or marriage to a man that she does not love. Annie accepts the marriage proposal – 'What else is there for me?' (Deevy 1939: 135) – and her future husband announces that not only does he have money in savings for their future, but that he will evict forthwith his two unmarried sisters so as to make way for Annie as his new wife. But instead of celebrating her impending marriage, Annie goes into deep mourning; instead of relief that her future husband will empty his house in readiness for her, she threatens to call off the marriage if his sisters are evicted ('What would I do without a woman to talk to?' (Deevy 1939: 135)). And instead of being delighted with the news of her future spouse's savings, she views these as proof that he will have complete control over her (Deevy 1939: 141). Deevy's *Katie Roche* performed by the NTS in March 1936, is similarly concerned. Katie Roche is the daughter of an unmarried couple (in this way, she is herself a product of unlicensed female desire) but Katie now works as a house-keeper in a respectable middle-class rural home. The play begins with Katie looking forward to her last dance before entering a convent – 'so what else can I do?' (Deevy 1939: 10) – in order to save her soul. But the way in which Katie speaks of the convent makes it clear that for her it is a terrible institutional punishment. When an older man, Stanislaus Gregg, proposes marriage to her and Katie accepts the proposal, it is clear that this course of action is by no means a solution either. Even after marriage, Katie appears physically unable to stop her philandering and Stanislaus accuses her of not taking seriously her role as wife and behaving instead as if she were in theatricals (Deevy 1939: 63). The play ends with Stanislaus taking Katie away from the community that she loves in order to control her and Katie accepting resignedly, and sorrowfully, that this may be the only solution.

Deevy's plays constitute a forceful exposure of the lack of sexual, employment and institutional options for women in 1930s Ireland. But their theatrical power is also related to their departure from the strict naturalism and social and political polemics that was so regularly adopted by Deevy's NTS contemporaries. The implausible sexual flamboyance of Deevy's main characters, for example, as well as the grotesquerie of some of the conformist characters (such as the religiously devout, Margaret Drybone in *Katie Roche*) give her plays an element of fantasy that removes them from the much more familiar and controversial terrain of the Abbey Theatre repertoire: national verisimilitude. Politics in Deevy's plays are considered more laterally – that is, through the exploration and exposure of ideologies of gender – rather than overtly or satirically as in those Irish dramatic exemplars, Colum, Murray and Robinson, that were singled out for praise by O'Faolain. Ironically, fantasy allowed Deevy's plays to achieve an unprecedented level of social critique. For what is described in *King of Spain's Daughter* and *Katie Roche* is, of course, transparently theatrical, but nonetheless it relates closely to a familiar ideological climate in 1930s Ireland. This was a situation in which the 1935 Dance Halls Act gave sweeping moral vigilante powers to local Catholic clergy as well as to Catholic Action groups (Whyte 1980: 50), and in which, for example, a jail sentence was imposed on a young woman (but not on the man) for kissing and embracing in public (*Irish Times*, 22 October 1937: 5).

The Fianna Fáil government may not have liked any of these plays (and particularly the political biases of O'Faolain and Robinson) but it took no action against them. In fact, this phase of theatrical activity at the Abbey Theatre coincides with an increase in the government's subsidy to the NTS as well as friendly overtures from the Department of Finance. On 5 May 1937, for example, following an earlier meeting with the Abbey directorate, the Minister for Finance circulated the cabinet with a memorandum concerning the 'establishment of a national theatre on comprehensive lines'. The document points out that the Abbey Directorate and the Department of Finance were in agreement concerning the desirability of building a new national theatre complex large enough to accommodate the Gate and An Comhar Drámuíochta (NA: S 9863A). Despite the public rhetoric of Frank O'Connor and F. R. Higgins, therefore, such unanimity implies a desire on the part of the NTS directorate to consolidate its relationship with the Fianna Fáil government. Just as importantly, it also suggests recognition of an agreed need to revitalize the status of the Abbey Theatre as a national institution. In so far as the plan did not succeed this was due to a combination of wartime austerity and inter-theatre rivalry between the Abbey and An Comhar Drámuíochta (as to which was the more senior institution and thus deserving of the larger stage (see NA: S 9863A)), and not because of political obstruction from the government. This lack of friction between the Abbey and the government in the late 1930s may also be explained in terms of changes within Fianna Fáil itself. The increasing dominance of middle-class elements within Fianna Fáil's political support base (Dunphy 1995: 215) and the government's security crackdown against the IRA following the County Cork killing of a retired Royal Navy officer in March 1936, contributed to this official composure (see Dunphy 1995: 209–10).

What the newly combative stance of the Abbey Theatre did produce, however, was a number of critical articles on nationalism, literary representation and theatre. Foremost among these is Gabriel Fallon's theatre column in the *Irish Monthly* which regularly assails the Abbey Theatre's portrayal of majority beliefs in Ireland. In 1938, for example, Fallon complains about 'the literary dictatorship of a coterie' and argues that 'Ireland, as yet, *has no national theatre*' (Fallon 1938: 634). For Fallon, therefore, Robinson's *Drama at Inish* is no lighthearted commentary on the inappropriateness of European modernism for Ireland's provincial audiences, but rather 'small . . . mean . . . full of acerbity and . . . lacking in the chivalrous dimensions of dramatic art' (Fallon 1936: 620). Another nationalist cultural periodical, *Ireland Today* argues that the Abbey Theatre was never part of the nationalist political movement. Its theatre critic, John Dowling, contends that NTS's reputation arose chiefly because Yeats had been temporarily involved in militant nationalist actions in the 1890s and that this disguised the extent to which the Irish literary revival 'was a purely literary adventure having its origins in a class the majority of whom would have dropped it like a hot coal if they had suspected in it a living spark of nationality' (Dowling 1937: 36). Dowling argues that both the Abbey Theatre as an institution and its repertoire of plays is primarily concerned with celebrating the *demise* of political, separatist nationalism.

'They shall be remembered for ever' intoned Mr Yeats, and instead of proceeding, as any sensible people would, to tear the Abbey brick from brick, we went away glowing with pride in that comfortably distant past which we felt was a little too gallant and futile for the twentieth century.

(Dowling 1937: 37)

Dowling illustrates his argument by discussing Yeats's most nationalist play, *Cathleen Ni Houlihan*, and by concluding that it is not the inspiringly militant play that it is sometimes considered by nationalists, but rather a portrayal of Irish insurrection as quixotic and sentimental.

This debate concerning literature and national representation reached its widest audience when, in April 1937, the *Irish Press* published a series of seven articles on 'The Future of Irish Literature'. The series was initiated by the paper's literary editor, M. J. MacManus, who remarked on the country's disproportionate ratio of English to Irish books, and predicted a demise of literature from the 'ascendancy tradition' and its replacement with an Irish writing that would be 'more and more a literature of the people' (*Irish Press*, 2 March 1937: 8). Three of the contributors – Francis McManus, Aodh de Blacam and Daniel Corkery – attacked what they saw as the blatant unrepresentativeness of contemporary Irish writing and its misplaced valorization of artistic freedom. T. C. Murray argued that because of Irish literature's obsession with sexual problems and with a generally negative portrayal of Irish social life it was hardly surprising that such a literature should 'awaken no recognition' in the Irish public and 'an attitude of hostility and anger' (*Irish Press*, 13 April 1937: 8). O'Faolain and O'Connor lamented the philistinism of Ireland's literary censorship while for Francis MacManus, there was an urgent need to establish a popular Irish literature immersed in Catholicism (*Irish Press*, 7 April 1937: 8).

In all of this, the Abbey Theatre was unmoved. For O'Faolain and O'Connor, the NTS was an ideological project inherently opposed to the philistinism of the Irish 'mob'. And, as if to prove the point, the NTS went ahead with 1938 revivals of Johnston's controversial *The Moon in the Yellow River*, Carroll's *Shadow and Substance* and O'Connor and Hunt's *The Invincibles*, as well as a series of celebrity lectures and productions that defended the autonomy of literature against political influence.

Throughout the 1940s, the Abbey Theatre's claim to national status was asserted very broadly in two ways: first, through the performance of plays that address contemporary social and economic issues so as to underline the urgent need for Ireland's modernization and, second, through an increasing emphasis on plays written in the Irish language. In the case of the former, a selection of plays such as George Shiels's *The Rugged Path* (1940), *The Summit* (1941) and *The Fort Field* (1942), Paul Vincent Carroll's *The Wise Have Not Spoken* (1944) and Joseph Tomelty's *The End House* (1944) portray as tragic, but also as inevitable, a range of issues related to contemporary social and political deprivation.

In Shiels's plays this theme is so prominent that it is often intrusively tendentious. *The Rugged Path*, by far the longest running play at the Abbey in the 1940s, has the theme of good citizenship – or, more accurately, the stark need for it in rural Ireland – as its major preoccupation. Both this play, and Shiels's later companion piece, *The Summit* (1941), are concerned with the desirability of a new atmosphere of citizenship in independent Ireland, and the need to abandon Ireland's pre-independence demonization of 'informers.' Both plays emphasize the need for pro- and anti-Treaty forces to unite with the Gardaí in their opposition to violence and intimidation. Although not stated to be in the IRA, the play's Dolis family, as small almost landless farmers with a reputation for lawlessness, land grievance and intimidation, bear a close resemblance to those militant republicans in the 1940s disenchanted with the constitutionalism of Fianna Fáil. By the end of both plays, the audience and the main characters acknowledge that in giving information to the Gardaí and in rejecting a traditional demonization of informers, they are moving beyond Ireland's civil war political divisions. A further homily of social advancement takes place in Shiels's *The Fort Field*. The narrative here shows government engineers arriving in a rural community with a plan to demolish a local earthen 'fairy fort' (or *rath*) so as to build an aerodrome and thus contribute to Ireland's slow-growing economic progress. Strongly opposed by the superstitious villagers who believe that the fort is part of a pre-Christian sanctuary, the villagers are shown overcoming their entrenched opposition to the extent that by the end of the play they are prepared to assist in the fort's destruction themselves (see Hogan 1964: 26–7). Carroll's *The Wise Have Not Spoken* offers another picture of contemporary malaise, portraying an Ireland dominated by the banks and with a political atmosphere almost as oppressive as the former pre-independence regime. Despite this, however, Carroll's play leaves little doubt that militant opposition to the state is futile and destructive and that the only solution lies in emigration. Again in Joseph Tomelty's *The End House* performed by the NTS on 28 August 1944, the play's sympathetic treatment of the plight of Catholic nationalist communities in Northern Ireland, is balanced by its exposure of the futility and danger of Irish republicanism.

Within the context of the NTS's preoccupation with social and cultural modernization and the need, in particular, to reject the militant republicanism of the IRA, the task of identifying the Abbey Theatre as distinctively Irish and 'national' was left increasingly to the theatre's association with Irish-language drama. For the primary driving force for this policy, the former Cumann na nGaedheal minister Ernest Blythe, Irish language revival was viewed as an important means of restoring to the Abbey its pre-Treaty nationalist purpose.

> In the days before the Anglo-Irish Treaty of 1921, the Abbey Theatre was always in the main current of the national movement, but in recent years it has slipped a little into the slack water at the side. The work we are now undertaking for the Irish language will bring us back into the full stream of national life and effort, and will link to the theatre the enthusiasm and support of those who today, in a new field, carry on the work of the Young Irelanders, of the Fenians, of the Land Leaguers, of the early Gaelic Leaguers, of the men of Easter Week.
>
> (quoted in Robinson 1939: 191–2)

In the context of the intensely unresolved nature of the national theatre debate in the late 1930s, then, Blythe's campaign to establish the NTS as an Irish-speaking institution offered not so much a compelling philosophy for Ireland's national theatre, as the only credible philosophy available. And while it is certainly true that the unexpected death of F. R. Higgins, in January 1941 and his replacement as managing director by Blythe opened the way for a major change of direction in Abbey Theatre policy, the theatre's much-lamented Gaelicization in the 1940s was not due solely to Blythe's cultural agenda. Even without the combined effect of Yeats's death and O'Connor's controversial dismissal from the board of directors in 1939, it is doubtful (*pace* McHugh 1951: 471) whether the NTS could have maintained its policy of rebarbative social criticism for much longer. The outbreak of the Second World War and Ireland's declaration of an emergency contributed to an ideological climate in which fomenting of controversy was now dangerously inimical to the more urgent need for national unity and consensus.

6

IRISH THEATRE AND MODERNIZATION, 1948–68

I went down to the Queens
In me scarlet jeans
And showed Mr Blythe . . . me gold fáinne;
Before he could be cross
I let him hear me blas
And now I'm in *Diarmuid and Gráinne*.
                    (extract from *Further Follies*,
                    quoted in Swift 1985: 171)

A [cultural] revival might easily prove to be one of our best safeguards in time of national emergency, a way to future national unity and a very desirable and valuable invisible export.
                    (Patrick J. Little, quoted in Kennedy n.d.: 56)

In early November 1947, two well-known Dublin intellectuals, the playwright and lecturer Roger McHugh and the poet Valentine Iremonger, staged a public walkout from an Abbey Theatre production of Sean O'Casey's *The Plough and the Stars*. Their protest arose not because of an impression of O'Casey's representation of the 1916 rebellion as objectionably unpatriotic, but because of the poor quality of the play's acting and production (*Irish Times*, 10 November 1947: 4). Unlike O'Casey's 1926 protesters, McHugh and Iremonger's protest was bathed in the warm light of public approval. The *Irish Times* praised this resolute stand against Ernest Blythe's 'nonchalant sacrifice of the Abbey's traditional artistic integrity on the altar of the Irish language' and argued that the decline in standards in the NTS was due to Blythe's policy of hiring actors exclusively on the basis of their knowledge of the Irish language (*Irish Times*, 10 November 1947: 4). Other media organs less prone to attack Blythe or the Fianna Fáil government's Irish language policy (such as the influential nationalist weekly newspaper *The Leader* and the liberal Catholic periodical *The Irish Monthly*) also applauded the theatre walkout as entirely necessary and legitimate. For *The Leader* it exposed the extent to which the Abbey Theatre had lost its national character (*The Leader*, 22 November 1947: 8), while for *The Irish Monthly* the incident revealed the theatre directorate's lack of public accountability (Fallon 1948: 91). In walking out of *The Plough and the Stars*, McHugh and Iremonger demonstrated a widely held view that the Abbey Theatre was now suffocating under the weight of a bureaucratic theatre management (see *Irish Times*, 11 November 1947: 2). And while not everyone agreed with the *Irish Times*'s view that the declining standards of the NTS were due to Blythe's rigid Irish-language policy, it was generally accepted that the repertoire and production standards at the Abbey had become calcified (see, for example, *Irish Independent*, 12 November 1947: 6; *Irish Times*, 10 November 1947: 5; Fallon 1948: 88–92). A former Irish language producer at the Abbey, Liam Ó Laoghaire, claimed that the problem was that the NTS had degenerated into a commercial theatre, and that it had failed to effect a transition between the formidable literary standards of its founders and the modernity of contemporary popular culture. There was a jarring discrepancy, he argued, between the portraits of Yeats and Gregory gathering dust in the foyer, and the photograph of Bing Crosby on the mantelpiece of the green room (*Irish Times*, 11 November 1947: 2). Having lost touch with its 'thinking audience', the NTS was no longer worthy of its status as a national institution.

This relatively minor incident in the theatre history of the period belongs to a wider context of disenchantment with the Fianna Fáil government and with the Irish state and its institutions. In 1944 the publication of two long-awaited reports on Irish society (Bishop Browne's *Report of the Commission on Vocational Organization* and Bishop Dignan's *Social Security: Outlines of a Scheme of National Health Insurance*) contributed to a perception of the Irish state as unresponsive to the needs and requirements of its citizens. Both of these documents attracted far-reaching public interest since, inspired by Pope Pius XI's 1931 encyclical *Quadragesimo Anno*, both were concerned with formulating proposals that would model Irish society and its governance according to Roman Catholic social principles (Whyte 1980: 96). Dignan's conclusion that Ireland's existing social services were reminiscent of the Poor Law of British times and Browne's view that good government should involve close co-operation with locally appointed vocational bodies amounted, in each case, to damning indictments not only of a decade of Fianna Fáil in government but of the authority and institutions of the post-colonial Irish state itself (Lee 1989: 275). The coming to power of Fianna Fáil in 1932–3 had been closely associated with a popular demand that the government of the new Irish state should reflect the democratic wishes of the majority. But now, fifteen years later, there was a pressing demand to transform the apparatuses of the state so as to make *them* more democratically accountable. In short, a serious rift had developed between two conflicting philosophies of government: a Catholic-Church-supported belief in vocationalism, and a belief in a more traditional, bureaucratic and centralized form of political authority (Whyte 1980: 117). By late 1947, this 'crisis of legitimacy' (Raymond 1983: 117) was exacerbated by a sharp downward pressure on wages, continuing high rates of emigration (Dunphy 1995: 246–7), de Valera's 1946 decision to shelve the 1944 reports of Browne and Dignan (Whyte 1980: 109) and an impression of Fianna Fáil as arrogant and insensible to public opinion. In 1946, for example, the year immediately prior to McHugh and Iremonger's Abbey Theatre protest, there occurred the extraordinary spectacle of uniformed Gardaí baton-charging Ireland's primary or 'national' school teachers during their strike protest at an All-Ireland football final at Croke Park (MacDermott 1998: 36). Events such as these bore witness to an extensive fracturing of Fianna Fáil's national consensus. By the mid- to late 1940s, in other words, it was not only oppositional old-reliables such as Seán O'Faolain and the *Irish Times* that questioned the authority and legitimacy of government policy, but a sizeable swathe of nationalist Roman Catholic Ireland as well (Whyte 1980: 301). The atmosphere of national egalitarianism that had maintained Fianna Fáil in power in the 1930s and 1940s was now rapidly dissipating. So too was the prestigious status of the Abbey Theatre as a national institution.

A further and particular threat to Fianna Fáil's republican ideology was the prison conditions controversy of May 1946. The controversy began following an inquest into the death by hunger strike of IRA volunteer, Seán McCaughey. McCaughey had been sentenced to death in 1941 and then had this sentence commuted to penal servitude for life. In April 1946, as the Military Court under which he had been condemned had ended, McCaughey gave notice that he would hunger strike in order to achieve his release (MacEoin 1997: 534). The government refused to relent, and he died on 11 May 1946. From the subsequent inquest, it emerged that McCaughey had not been allowed sunlight or fresh air during his time in Maryborough (now Portlaoise) prison and that for a period of twenty months he had been prohibited from speaking or associating with other prisoners (Farrell 1986: 14; MacEoin 1997: 539). The prison doctor admitted that he would not have kept a dog in such conditions (*Irish Times*, 13 May 1946: 7). Two years earlier, Seán O'Faolain's publication of *I Did Penal Servitude*, an anonymous account of life as a prisoner in contemporary Ireland previously serialized in *The Bell*, caused some soul searching for Ireland's liberal intelligentsia ('this book . . . strikes at our conscience. To read it is to be ashamed' (O'Faolain 1945: v)), but the impact of the McCaughey inquest in 1946 had an even more shocking and far-reaching effect. Not only did its exposure of the harsh conditions of Irish prisons reinforce an impression of a callous state apparatus, but the controversy renewed questions about the political credentials of Fianna Fáil. Prisoner mistreatment had been especially pronounced in relation to republicans and, under successive Fianna Fáil administrations in the 1940s, incarcerated republicans faced a draconian prison regime that included long periods of solitary confinement and, in rare but notorious instances, flogging with the cat o' nine tails and execution by hanging. By the time of the McCaughey inquest even the *Irish Times*, traditionally a supporter of a tough law and order policy, admitted that Ireland was 'clinging to nineteenth-century ideas of crime and punishment' and that there was an urgent need for reform (*Irish Times*, 31 May 1946: 5). That de Valera's first public response to the McCaughey inquest was to sack one of the McCaughey family's barristers, Noel Hartnett, from his job at Radio Éireann (Ireland's national radio station), simply added to the impression that Fianna Fáil was behaving with an arrogance and a disdain that was antithetical to its former republicanism. In response to 'clamant demand' the Labour Party published a pamphlet, 'Prisons and Prisoners in Ireland', which called on the government to implement immediate prison reforms, civil rights advocates like Owen Sheehy-Skeffington and Seán O'Faolain became publicly involved in the issue, and a new political party, Clann na Poblachta ('children' or 'family of the republic') campaigned successfully on the once Fianna Fáil slogan of 'Release the Prisoners' (Coogan 1970: 259).[1] By February 1948, there was a new Irish government in power: an unlikely coalition of Fine Gael, Labour and the republican and socialist-oriented Clann na Poblachta.

Iremonger and McHugh's theatre walk out from the Abbey Theatre was not exclusively, therefore, a matter of theatre aesthetics.

It was itself a staged event that condensed wider public misgivings about the nationalist credentials of Fianna Fáil in government as well as the nature and direction of the Irish state as a whole. In demonstrating the failure of the Abbey to command their allegiance, belief or respect, McHugh and Iremonger's urbane public leave-taking was a flat refusal of the 'national' status of one of Ireland's most prestigious cultural institutions. By walking out, that is, they strikingly refuted the Abbey Theatre's primary ideological function as a national theatre: a cultural site, that is, in which the nation state is manifested and reaffirmed in terms of the living consensus of the theatrical experience itself. To this extent, Iremonger and McHugh's spectacle of refusal was like an élite version of a 1946 action by striking turf cutters who demonstrated against the recently elected Fianna Fáil president, Seán T. O'Kelly, by disrupting his speech at the 1916 memorial ceremonies at Arbour Hill (Ní Bheacháin 1997: 48). Blythe's dismissal of the walkout as a publicity stunt ('a piece of impudent self-advertisement' (quoted in NLI: ACC 3691 nfc vol 13 1947–8)) was inaccurate: publicity was precisely the issue. The depressing production standards of the Abbey Theatre now dramatized the condition of the nation in general. Nor was Blythe unaware of the incident's political significance. When Iremonger next returned to the Abbey a year later (this time in his capacity as Personal Secretary to the new Minister for Foreign Affairs and Clann na Poblachta leader, Seán MacBride) only the minister was admitted. Because of the 1947 protest and despite Iremonger's political elevation, Blythe had Iremonger and McHugh banned from the theatre for a further six months (see Abbey Theatre Minute Book: NLI ACC 3961 nfc vol (13) 1947–8).

Iremonger and McHugh's flamboyant national theatre protest coincides with a period of European history in which 'national culture' assumes a new political importance. As in Britain with the establishment of the Arts Council of Great Britain in 1945, the National Theatre Act of 1949, and the Festival of Britain in 1951 (Minihan 1977: 235–8), the arts in Ireland are viewed as an increasingly valuable way of mediating the relationship between the state and the individual (see Lacy 1995: 42, 54). But this was, conspicuously, not happening at the Abbey Theatre. As early as 1945, senior Fianna Fáil policy makers recognized the need for a change. In planning for a programme of post-war development, Erskine Childers and Patrick J. Little, for example, argued for the establishment of an Irish arts council which, they claimed, would do much to stimulate national morale and would also, in Little's phrase, prevent politics from 'going to seed' in the post-war period (Kennedy n.d.: 55–6). Without the government's stimulus and support of Irish culture, argued Childers, there was a danger of 'a certain apathy that shows itself in a destructive rather than a constructive form of nationalism' (Kennedy n.d.: 57). By December 1945 the cabinet had approved in principle an ambitious project for building a new national theatre (NA: S 9863A). Now, more than ever, the field of culture, and, in particular, Ireland's national theatre, was being thought of as a potentially important domain of the state. Even if the Fianna Fáil government and subsequent administrations were slow to follow through on the commitment financially, this broadly Keynesian emphasis on an ever closer identification between state policy and the arts (Lacy 1995) is one of several overlapping features both of the Fianna Fáil administration of the 1940s and 1950s and of the inter-party or coalition governments of 1948–51 and 1954–7 (see Girvan 1989: 170). It is a linkage that is further evident in Fianna Fáil's 1947 proposals for the setting up of a Cultural Relations Committee, in the inter-party government's establishment of this Committee as a branch of the Department of Foreign Affairs in February 1949 (Kennedy n.d.: 60), in the 1951 establishment of the Arts Council of Ireland (An Chomhairle Éalaíon), and in Taoiseach John A. Costello's 1949 Dáil speech on the arts in which the connection between art and Irish industry is insisted upon at length (Dáil Report, 20 July 1949: column 1371, quoted in Arnold 1982: 281). As well as improve its production standards, therefore, there was considerable pressure for the Abbey Theatre to show itself as more relevant to state policy. It is within this context that *The Leader* argues that the Abbey Theatre is not properly a national theatre because it is not adequately accountable to the state (*The Leader*, 13 August 1949: 17), and a 1951 government memorandum asserts that Ireland has 'one small national theatre, with an inadequate subsidy,' but 'no state theatre' (NA: S 151120 A).

But Ireland's post-war modernization was not a matter of simple policy changes or of government-sponsored initiative. It also entailed a process of extensive cultural readjustment and, in particular, a renovation of the country's nationalist ideology in a manner that both appropriated and contained the threat posed by militant republicanism. The Fianna Fáil Minister for Justice, Gerry Boland, may well have believed his 1946 statement that the IRA was dead and that he had killed it (Foley 1992: 206), but there still existed a fear (shared by both of Ireland's main political parties) that Ireland's security and financial stability were threatened by the IRA's unrelenting opposition to partition. By the late 1940s, there is every indication that Blythe and the NTS directorate (Lennox Robinson, Richard Hayes and Roibeárd Ó Faracháin) held a similar set of concerns. The repertoire of plays performed at the Abbey from 1949 to the mid- to late 1950s suggest a period of self-conscious renewal with a strong thematic emphasis on national self-examination in the light of new (post-war) economic exigencies. Bryan MacMahon's *The Bugle in the Blood* (1949), Seamus Byrne's *Design for a Headstone* (1950), Louis D'Alton's *This Other Eden* (1953), Walter Macken's *Twilight of a Warrior* (1957), Hugh Leonard's *A Leap in the Dark* (1957) and John Purcell O'Donovan's *The Less We are Together* (1957) all show the motivating forces of militant republicanism as dangerously anachronistic and as urgently in need of revision. Popular support for IRA republicanism (as manifest in the massive IRA funerals of Seán McCaughey in 1946 and Seán South in 1957) is portrayed as a pernicious recidivism. MacMahon's *Bugle in the Blood*, for example, was first performed at the Abbey on 14 March 1949, and with the popular graffiti 'Release the Prisoners' prominently displayed in the background, the play's action evokes not only McCaughey's hunger strike and death in May 1948, but also the campaigns by Clann na Poblachta and Sinn Féin in the 1940s for the release of the remaining republican prisoners. Set in nationalist 'Southern Ireland', the play's action concentrates on the suffering inflicted on the Trimble household, and in particular on the daughter of the family, Evelyn, by republican militancy. The eldest son of the household, Andy, embarks on a hunger strike, and dies when the authorities refuse to relent. After the subsequent funeral, Andy's brother is transformed into a republican activist and, as a result, takes up a gun to kill a policeman (formerly his sister's lover) and then is killed himself as a result. Spontaneous political action of this sort is portrayed both as internecine and as inevitable. 'Are we to go on', asks Evelyn, 'generation after generation, with black diamonds on our sleeves [in this] . . . green lunatic land where every child is born with a bugle in the blood' (MacMahon 1949: 71), before then lamenting the inexorability of her young son being similarly infected. As with George Shiels's long-running *The Rugged Path* (1940) or Macken's later *Twilight of a Warrior* (in which this theme is rendered more plangently), MacMahon's play urges the spectator to reconsider traditional nationalist attitudes. MacMahon's particular object is to have the spectator view the proper legacy of republicanism not as a militant or revolutionary movement, but as an expression of an exclusively state-oriented politics. Had he lived, the executed republican leader, Pádraig Pearse, would now be a legislator, insists the boys' father:

JOE: Be logical! Be logical, man! Look! When Pádraig Pearse was alive and speechifyin' out of him he was a great hero entirely. But people like you forget that if he had lived to be the first President of the Irish Republic he'd have to prosecute you and me for gaffing a salmon illegally or for riding at night without a light on our bicycles. The short and the long of it is that there is no substitute for law and order.

(MacMahon 1949: 14)

The play's narrative works in a similar way to Joe Trimble's speech: that is, it appeals to the objectivity of the Abbey Theatre audience so as to arraign republican militancy as emotional and thus underline the importance of state authority. Seamus Byrne's *Design for a Headstone* (1950) has a similar purpose. It, also, addresses the controversial subject of republican hunger strikes in the late 1940s through its grim Irish prison setting 'prior to 1950' (Byrne 1956: 7). The play's narrative concentrates on the decision of a senior IRA man, Conor Egan, to undertake a hunger strike in protest against not being granted political status. As the play's action unfolds, however, the audience discovers that Egan's protest is motivated not by politics at all, but by what is portrayed as his hapless personal inadequacy: an unwillingness to challenge his wife. She does not want him to take part in a planned escape (Byrne 1956: 24), and his undertaking a hunger strike is presented (absurdly) as the only way that he can think of avoiding this. Like O'Casey's Dublin trilogy, political commitment, and most especially the kind of anti-state political activity demanded by the IRA, is exposed as a subterfuge for domestic and/or sexual failure. For Abbey Theatre audiences, Byrne's realistic portrayal of life in the republican wing of an Irish prison was innovative and starkly contemporary, but its overall effect was to render anodyne the threat of republican political agency by depicting the struggle in the prisons exclusively as an issue of leadership and gender authority.

There is a similar emphasis in Louis d'Alton's play *This Other Eden*. First performed in June 1953, this was one of the Abbey Theatre's most popular productions with a performance run of twenty-four consecutive weeks (O'Neill 1999: 20). It is set in 'a small town in southern Ireland' and features a committee of local worthies who are assembled together in order to decide how their community might best commemorate a local republican hero murdered by the British during the war of independence. The committee includes a narrow-minded local businessman, John McRoarty (helpfully described by the stage directions as 'a National School product as his speech and manner betray, and therefore entirely uneducated' (D'Alton 1970: 4)), Devereaux, an ex-National school teacher (according to the stage directions, 'a man of first-class ability whose life has been wasted in a backwater like Ballymorgan' (D'Alton 1970: 6)) and Clannery, a nationalist fanatic of the old school and a recidivist *par excellence*. Clannery refers to the post-war trend of British investment in Ireland as 'the new plantation of Ireland' (D'Alton 1970: 11) and 'this new invasion' (D'Alton 1970: 13) and is fiercely opposed to all things English. Included also among D'Alton's dramatis personae, however, is a younger and more sophisticated generation of characters: Maire (McRoarty's anglophile daughter), Roger Crispin (an English speculator) and Conor Heaphy who (it is later revealed) is in fact the illegitimate son of the nationalist hero. How, in this context, should Ireland's republican past be remembered and commemorated? Like an updated version of Shaw's *John Bull's Other Island, This Other Eden* responds to this question by inverting the predictable answers. Instead of a mechanical celebration of nationalist glory, Ireland's political heritage must be viewed more sceptically. From such a perspective, even emigration may be considered not so much as a national scourge, but as an opportunity for young people to escape Ireland's stultifying social conditions. According to Maire, the problem with Ireland is that it exists in a miasma of self-delusion (D'Alton 1970: 35) and so emigration is necessary for the purpose of self-discovery and freedom. Indeed, in the context of Ireland's atmosphere of stringent censorship and moral rectitude, D'Alton implies that there is no other alternative (D'Alton 1970: 36–7). The real nationalist hero, declares Devereaux, is the person who challenges the shibboleths and orthodoxies of a community (D'Alton 1970: 68). By the end of the play the nationalism of McRoarty and Clannery appears embarrassingly strident and outdated.

Walter Macken's *Twilight of a Warrior* also deals with the problematic legacy of Ireland's celebrated republican past. Macken's narrative suggests that the dichotomies that nourish nationalism are destructive and inappropriate to a modern Ireland. Its protagonist, Dacey Adam, is a nationalist hero celebrated in ballads for his exploits against the British during the war of independence, and now a respectable politician and businessman. The play is set in his well-off and comfortably furnished home and deals with the tension between him and a young man (Abel Martin) who wants to marry his daughter (Elva). Dacey's attitude to everyone, including his own family, is adversarial and antagonistic. Any social encounter is transformed into a battle for supremacy. The issue in relation to Abel is complicated by the fact that Abel comes from an area in the west of Ireland (Tobreena) where Dacey fought a famous battle against the British, but which he now regards ambivalently. On the one hand, he thinks of Tobreena as a backward rural place unfit for the likes of his daughter; on the other, Dacey remembers Tobreena as the place in which he was rescued from death by Mary Ann, a woman with whom he also fell in love. Nevertheless, Dacey's ambition in the play is to prevent Abel from marrying his daughter Elva, and his final strategy for achieving this is to tell Abel that he is his son from his union with Mary Ann. But the truth, Abel reveals, is actually quite different: Abel's father was one of Dacey's old enemies, a British soldier who came to live with Mary Ann in Tobreena. Mary Ann did not live alone for years hoping that Dacey would return. In fact, she fell in love with a British soldier and lived happily with him before he died. The old dichotomies and nationalist oppositions (the very concept of war itself) are now redundant. The republican heroism of the past, that made Dacey a hero and his brother (who fought for the British in the First World War) an alcoholic, is now gone. With the shock of this illumination, Dacey collapses.

Even in the case of plays that are less overtly political, like M. J. Molloy's *The Wood of the Whispering* (1953), this sceptical view of national pieties is greatly in evidence. The play tracks the reason for social desolation in the west of Ireland to a psychic paralysis that prevents marriage and causes a massive haemorrhaging of the community. Set in a wood and populated by a bizarre collection of celibates, *The Wood of the Whispering* employs an expressionist setting and dramaturgy to deal with the theme of rural depopulation. The characters include an eccentric bachelor named Sanbatch, and Sadie, a spinster who has been struck mute by the trauma of childlessness. Sanbatch is terrified that he will be sent to the county home, but assumes as his mission the idea of regenerating the community. He attempts to organize marriages as he knows that this is the only way that the community will be saved. The problem, Sanbatch remarks, is an endemic sexual frustration.

SANBATCH: [T]he young priest was talking to me about it [the suicide of Sanbatch's friend Brehony] and about the insane. 'A lot are in the asylum from leading a bad life', he said. 'Father', I ses, 'there's more in the asylum for want of a married life.'

(Molloy 1998: 135).

What is wrong with rural Ireland, Molloy's play suggests, is the stultifying effect of emigration and the engrained conventions of celibacy that give rise to it. Innovative and theatrically exciting, Molloy's expressionistic treatment of this theme renders this all-pervasive atmosphere of social prohibition as the play's own logic as well: 'The Wood of the Whispering they do call this wood on account of all the courting couples that used to be in it some years ago before all the lads and the girls went foreign' (Molloy 1998: 132).

These Abbey Theatre plays of the 1950s exist in striking contrast to the oleaginous conformity of Frank Carney's much performed *The Righteous are Bold* (1946). Whereas Carney's play celebrates the wholesome integrity of a Catholic west of Ireland peasant household, and portrays the secular and individualistic ideology of a returned emigrant from England as a form of satanic possession, MacMahon, Byrne, D'Alton and Macken all urge the need for a reassessment of nationalist verities, and, in particular a reassessment of Ireland's antagonistic relationship with Britain. NTS plays of the late 1940s and early 1950s thus form part of a deliberate anti-utopian and counter-revolutionary strategy 'aimed at limiting the development of republican idealism by deliberately limiting what could be imagined of the future' (Morash 2000: 75).[2] As Morash correctly observes, there was a close relationship between the anti-republican tendentiousness of the NTS repertoire in this period and Blythe's own strenuous and ongoing insistence that anti-partitionism should be an exclusively cultural and ontological project (Blythe 1997: 38; Morash 2000: 76).

This is a point that Blythe himself freely acknowledged. Writing in 1965, he described the constructive influence of the Abbey Theatre in this period as its marketing of Irish culture for international audiences ('a national economic asset in virtue of its considerable importance as a tourist attraction' (Blythe [1965]: n.p.)) and its exposure of republican anti-partitionism as unrealistic. The former aspect – generating tourist revenue – became an increasingly important function from the early 1950s. In 1953, the recently established Irish Tourist Association promoted the idea of a national cultural festival (An Tóstal or 'the pageant') as a way of achieving 'a rapid expansion of tourist traffic' (Kennedy n.d.: 112). In 1954 (the year of the Abbey Theatre's Golden Jubilee Celebrations) the

Department of Foreign Affairs printed a 12 page special on the Abbey Theatre in its weekly bulletin, *Éire-Ireland* (NA: S 14751C) while the often astringent *Irish Times* now praised the NTS as 'our national theatre' and 'a magnet that draws visitors to our shores from every quarter of the world' (*Irish Times*, 25, 27, 28 December 1954: 5).

That there is a strong *parti-pris* element to the plays performed at the Abbey Theatre in this period is consistent, therefore, with the post-war reorientation of Irish economic life towards increased exports, European state co-operation and (through the offices of the newly founded Industrial Development Association) Ireland's active encouragement of inward capital investment. This drive towards a free market economy was accelerated by the country's participation in the post-war European Recovery Plan (or Marshall Aid) in 1948 and by its withdrawal from the British Commonwealth in 1949. By the early 1950s, the vocabulary and politics of economics had begun to replace Ireland's more traditional rhetoric of a nationalist 32-county autonomy (Breen *et al.* 1990: 4). As with the all-party Anti-Partition League of 1949 which campaigned for a constitutional end to the border, or with Blythe's insistence on an exclusively constitutional solution to partition in the *Leader* (see Inglis 1962: 170–1), the Abbey Theatre plays of the 1950s expose not only a concern with a depoliticization of Irish republican militancy, but also a compelling need for an adjustment of nationalist ideology to the exigencies of foreign capital. Indeed, with British capital as the most substantial investment in Ireland and two-thirds of Irish exports destined for Britain (Rottman and O'Connell in Litton 1982: 63), the time for a radical redefinition of Ireland's relationship with other countries, and with Britain in particular, was now long overdue.

But it would be an error to conclude that Abbey Theatre plays were written to a formula or that they were strictly and exclusively concerned with advocating a new secular orthodoxy. The modernization agenda of the NTS was not unproblematic. While the anti-republican tendentiousness of its 1950s plays does have much in common with Shiel's earlier *The Rugged Path* and *The Summit*, what marks the plays by D'Alton, Byrne, MacMahon and Macken as different is their strong emphasis on issues related to personal choice and the apparently inevitable conflict between the desire of the individual and the traditional rulings of Irish Catholicism. In *Design for a Headstone* and *This Other Eden*, for example, there is an impression that Ireland's existential development is hindered not only by sanctimonious nationalism, but by the overbearing influence of

Catholic social dogma. As a character in Byrne's *Design for a Headstone* puts it, contemporary Ireland consists of 'church and state, moving hand in hand, to crush the soul of a single man' (Byrne 1956: 72–3). Indeed, it was exactly this perspective that led to a minor disruption of an early performance of Byrne's play by protesting members of the Catholic action group *Maria Duce* (Hogan 1967: 97).

Moreover, accelerating ideological changes in 1950s Ireland are especially evident in the controversies, and in some cases the marked *lack* of controversy, in relation to particular theatre productions. When Cyril Cusack advertised his production of Sean O'Casey's *The Bishop's Bonfire* at the Gaiety Theatre in 1955, for example, the announcement was met, predictably enough, by a barrage of criticism from *The Standard*. In weekly articles, editorials, and on its letters pages, *The Standard* roundly condemned the impending production as an offence: 'This is not art; this is not drama. This is but crude vulgar abuse which will ring as harshly in the ears of decent Protestants, as in those of conscientious Catholics' (*The Standard*, 4 March 1955: 1). And yet, despite even the eloquence of the church's *éminence grise*, Alfred O'Rahilly, nationalist Catholic Ireland (or at least the Dublin theatre-going part of it) remained extraordinarily unpersuaded. True, no Irish reviewer could find O'Casey's play anything but slipshod and confused, but it was also reported that over 2,000 people lined the streets outside the theatre prior to the performance and that 1,200 people had to be turned away (*Irish Press*, 1 March 1955: 1). The production was extended by two weeks in order to meet the unprecedented audience demand (Brown 1985: 229). Even the *Irish Press* (which might have been expected to be sympathetic to the point of view advocated by *The Standard*) urged its readers to attend the O'Casey play so that they could judge just how bad it was for themselves (*Irish Press*, 7 March 1955: 4). To this extent, Cusack's production of *The Bishop's Bonfire* was not quite a '*succès de scandale*' or 'blow struck for artistic freedom' (*pace* Brown 1985: 229), but rather a sign of the increasing popular force of Ireland's modernization process. Audiences flocked to O'Casey's play not because it was regarded as nationally representative, but because it proclaimed a new and dissenting resistance to the traditional paternalistic role of Irish Catholicism.

There is a similar change evident in the theatrical productions that took place at Dublin's Pike Theatre in Herbert Street. Unlike Blythe's mostly tendentious and formally conservative programme of plays at the Abbey, the Pike repertoire evokes an entirely different cultural agenda. Founded by Alan Simpson and Carolyn Swift in 1953, the

Pike was a *théâtre de pôche* that modelled itself not so much on the consensual ideology of nationalism, but on the more adversarial stance of a modernizing élite. To this extent, the Pike belonged to the 'new wave' of theatrical experimentation that was then taking place in London and Paris. Like the English Stage Company at the Royal Court theatre or Roger Blin's productions of Anouilh and Beckett at the Théâtre de Babylon in Paris, the Pike was self-consciously avant-garde. Moreover, in terms of organization, aesthetic philosophy and style of presentation, the Pike pitted itself deliberately in opposition to the NTS. Nominally, it was a theatre club, open not to a representative sample of the nation's *populus*, but to members only. And, with its small 50-seater auditorium, its regular expressionistic designs by the painter Pauline Bewick, and its repertoire of high modernism and facetious revue, the social and cultural atmosphere at the Pike was one of radical exclusivity: 'a revolutionary force of small means [designed to] . . . stir up the theatrical lethargy of post-war Ireland' (Simpson 1962: 1). Its late-night revues, annual 'follies', and productions of Ionesco and Beckett, displayed an exciting and often provocative disregard for Ireland's prevailing moral and aesthetic conventions. There were regular attacks on the GAA (Gaelic Athletic Association) and on the moral pronouncements of the Catholic hierarchy such as Bishop Browne's 1957 diatribe against bikini wearing at the Galway seaside: 'You can't undress to kill/On the beach at Salthill/But you can in Cannes' (Swift 1985: 229). Typical scenes from *The Follies of Herbert Lane* also included satires of M. J. Molloy, a spoof of the well-known Abbey Theatre and Irish-speaking actress Siobhán McKenna, and a sketch 'implying that, despite Irish independence, England still controlled the Irish economy' (Swift 1985: 117–18). There was irreverent *double entendre*, acerbic political and cultural commentary, jibes at Blythe's Irish-language policy at the Abbey, and mink bikinis. Rapturing in the libidinous physicality of theatrical performance – at times, facetious and at times cutting-edge – the Pike marked out the theatre as possessing a transgressive power vital to Ireland's modernization. Not only was the Pike unconcerned with representing national consensus, it was also opposed to it. This was an anti-national theatre with a mission.

Just as importantly, the Pike Theatre was a cultural phenomenon that celebrated the arrival of a new, urban, liberal élite. In terms of its performances and the experience of club membership, that is, the Pike proclaimed the existence of a new generation: educated cosmopolitans for whom the shibboleths of nationality and religion were no longer valid. To this extent, the Pike's flaunting of aesthetic autonomy in 1950s Ireland has a particular political importance. In the state as well as in the theatre, autonomy was being conceived of as no longer a question of national representativeness, of political, 32-county independence, or indeed of politics at all, but as an experience that related increasingly to a private world of desire. The Pike's propensity for risqué sexual remarks and social critique cocked a snook at the norms of Roman Catholic Ireland in much the same way that, in Britain, Anthony Crossland put forward a vision of socialism as personal pleasure (Louvre 1992: 45–50).

Brendan Behan's *The Quare Fellow*, premièred in November 1954, illustrates some of the achievements, and limitations, of the Pike's modernizing agenda. As a relentless exposure of the inhumanity of capital punishment Behan's play assaults the cosy middle-class consensus underlying the contemporary Irish state. In a quasi-Brechtian fashion, the play 'alienates' this consensus by revealing the extent to which an execution, a sporting event at the national stadium (Croke Park), and a theatre performance all possess an underlying similarity.

WARDER REGAN [*almost shouts*]. I think the whole show should be put on in Croke Park; after all, it's at the public expense and they let it go on. They should have something more for their money than a bit of paper stuck up on the gate.

(Behan 1956: 76)

Regan's reference to the 'whole show' and to 'the public expense' is disquieting to the extent that this state-ordained punishment (the hanging of the quare fellow) is also an integral part of the audience's own entertainment. Indeed, the subversiveness of Behan's approach can be gauged by the awkwardness with which the play was transferred to the Abbey Theatre: here the prompt copy of the performed 1956 version shows extensive cutting especially in relation to Regan's scathing critiques of capital punishment in Act I (NLI: ms 29,083: 28). But by 1954 Irish prison reform and capital punishment were by no means the explosive political issues that they had been in the late 1940s. *The Quare Fellow*, a play that Behan began writing at the time of McCaughey's hunger strike and death in 1947, was in the mid 1950s a work long after the political outcry of 1947–8 as well as O'Faolain's *I Did Penal Servitude* and Byrne's *Design for a Headstone*. Moreover, Behan's play does not address itself to the more controversial issue of republican hunger striking and, even in the uncut and published version, it does not outline the possibility of any alternative to incarceration and state punishment. The best that can be hoped for, Behan's play suggests, is a reform of the prison system so as to render it more responsive to the needs and sensitivities of the individual. The formidable Victorian setting of the play and the stark display in the opening scene of the word 'Silence' (Behan 1956: 1) does indeed convey to the audience an immediate and forceful impression of the prison's inhumanity. But the experience of Behan's narrative action urges merely a renovation of this system so as to take account of a new emphasis on the individual. In addition, it is the *inevitability* of the capitalist organization of Irish society that is so emphatically asserted in the scene at the ending of the play: the three prisoners dividing the property of the executed 'quare fella' as 'shares' to be exploited for profit on the prison's open market (Behan 1956: 86). In short, Behan's attack on the hypocrisy and inhumanity of the contemporary Irish state as evident in the continuing practice of capital punishment, is moderated considerably by the play's simultaneous suggestion that this kind of inhumanity and hypocrisy is, simply, an indelible feature of the prisoners' life as well.

The Pike Theatre's newfound importance was also related to its position as a key venue for the Dublin Theatre Festival. For the Fianna Fáil Minister for Industry and Commerce, Seán Lemass, the Dublin Theatre Festival was a vital part of the country's overall economic modernization. He described tourism as 'export business of the highest value' (quoted in *Irish Press*, 13 May 1957: 5) and embarked on an ambitious programme of economic reform. Lemass gave priority to assisting Ireland's export capability, amended legislation which had hitherto prevented the use of large amounts of foreign capital (Tobin 1984: 5), and commissioned and promoted a report by the civil servant and economist T. K. Whitaker which argued for the benefits of multinational capital investment. As one commentator puts it, 'by summer 1957 even the *Sunday Press* editorial and letter pages carried items in favour of foreign capital' (Bew *et al.* 1989: 83). The Pike Theatre, then, was an integral element of this broader modernization agenda. Thus in 1957, the Pike's extensive repertoire of avant-garde plays made it a semi-establishment institution (much to its founders' amazement and pleasure). 'The Public Relations Department of the Tourist Board were constantly on the telephone', writes Simpson, 'begging seats for this or that distinguished foreign journalist. . . . For the first time in my life I was learning the pleasures of official V.I.P. treatment' (Simpson 1962: 139).

The problem was that this took place within a broader context of conflict between the country's accelerating agenda of economic liberalization and the substantial opposition to this from important elements within the Catholic hierarchy. In particular, Archbishop John Charles McQuaid and Bishops Browne and Lucey fiercely opposed any change to paternalistic vehicles of state ideology such as the Censorship Board, as well as any expansion of the state into what they regarded as the exclusively private areas of individual morality, healthcare and Irish family life. Since the church-inspired collapse of Noel Browne's 'mother and child scheme' in 1951 (see Whyte 1980: 199–226), there were numerous controversial incidents in which church and state were brought into direct conflict with each other. In 1955, for example, the Minister for Agriculture had been forced to withdraw his proposal for a single institute of agriculture because of Dr Lucey's criticism of the plan as 'out-and-out statism' and thus a wholly unreasonable obstacle to the church's proper influence on education (Whyte 1980: 310). Later on in the same year, Archbishop McQuaid requested that an international soccer match between Ireland and Yugoslavia be cancelled on the basis that Yugoslavia was a communist country and had a record of anti-Catholic persecution. On this occasion, however, the government refused McQuaid's request and the football match went ahead with a substantial attendance. Swift's remark that 'people who had never been to a football match in their lives turned out to show their independence' (Swift 1985: 238) may be an exaggeration *post facto*, but the incident was, nevertheless, a sign of the changed times. As well as showing the ubiquity and omnipotence of Roman Catholic power in 1950s Ireland, it also suggests the limits within which it was increasingly constrained (Whyte 1980: 318). Another striking example of the ideological tensions of the period was the much publicized boycott of Protestant businesses in Fethard-on-Sea in County Wexford in May 1957. The boycott took place following a dispute concerning the education of the children of a mixed (Catholic/Protestant) couple, and led to a direct clash between some of the Catholic hierarchy and the Fianna Fáil Taoiseach, Eamon de Valera. De Valera's description of the boycott as 'ill-conceived' and Bishop Browne's view that the boycott was entirely justified ('a peaceful and moderate protest' (quoted in Whyte 1980: 323)) illustrates the extent to which the state was prepared to clash publicly with the Catholic Church.

This was the immediate cultural context for the controversy concerning the Pike Theatre's European première of Tennessee Williams' *The Rose Tattoo* in 1957. According to the Pike Theatre's co-founder, Carolyn Swift, Williams's play was chosen as the Pike's contribution to the first Dublin Theatre Festival because 'the play has a theme of religion versus primitive superstition and should appeal particularly to an Irish audience' (TCD: Pike Archive, ms. 10813/ 383/14). This statement suggests little doubt that the production was intended as provocative. With Williams's strong neo-Freudian emphasis on female desire (oriented exclusively around male sexuality) and the play's persistent comparisons between sexual orgasm and religious ecstasy, it could hardly have been otherwise. Nevertheless, the theatre was taken aback when, following an anonymous complaint from a member of the public concerning the alleged dropping of a contraceptive on stage (Anna Manahan, quoted in Hickey and Smith 1972: 131), Alan Simpson was arrested on a summary warrant and charged with producing 'for gain an indecent and profane performance' (*Irish Press*, 24 May 1957: 1). Recently released government files from the Office of the Attorney-General, however, indicate that the case against Simpson and the Pike Theatre had been pursued by elements within the Department of Justice and its indefatigable secretary, Peter Berry, even before the play's opening performance (see NA: AG 2000/10/535 and 536 (SR 18/31)). On 9 May 1957, three days prior to the Dublin première of *The Rose Tattoo*, Berry wrote to the Attorney-General stating that the Minister of Justice had been approached by a member of the Dáil regarding the possibility of bringing a prosecution of the Pike on the basis of indecent theatrical performances, and enquiring of the Attorney-General about the legal options available (NA: AG 2000/10/535).

Clearly organized by some elements within Fianna Fáil, Simpson's arrest, and the extensive publicity that it received, had a devastating effect on the Pike's activities. Membership declined from 3,000 to 300 (Swift 1985: 281), and the Pike was forced to abandon its plans to move to the much larger Gate Theatre in the city centre (Swift, letter to the editor, *Irish Times*, 6 January 2000: 15). Although the case against Simpson was dropped eventually (following a refusal by the Gardaí to reveal who had given them their instructions) the fact that costs amounting to £2,500 were not awarded meant that Simpson and Swift were forced to establish the Rose Tattoo Appeal Fund in a time-consuming and debilitating effort to raise funds (see Mulhare *et al.* 1958: 185). And while the failure of the case against Simpson was indeed 'a turning point' in Irish theatre history in so far as it encouraged those who wished to challenge Catholic orthodoxies and made the Gardaí less inclined to proceed against theatre productions (Brown 1985: 230), it also reveals the depth of the cultural conflict that was then taking place. Indeed, what is so notice-able about *The Rose Tattoo* controversy is not only the assiduity with which elements within the political establishment pursued the case against Simpson, but also the extent of Simpson's popular support. Two days after Simpson's arrest crowds of supporters, variously described as numbering 100 and 500, took to the street outside the Pike in a demonstration of solidarity (see press cuttings in TCD: ms. 10813/391/20). And support for Simpson's position included not just well-known liberal intellectuals like the Trinity College don, Senator Professor W. B. Stanford, but also serving members of the Irish army (Simpson was an Irish army captain), various members of the public and a group of staff members from a tyre factory in Cork (TCD: ms. 10813/402/12). In many ways, therefore, the arrest of Simpson was itself a dramatization of the ideological battle that was taking place in the 1950s: between an expansionist state agenda (championed by politicians like Lemass and senior civil servants like Whitaker) and the defensive reactions of dominant elements within the Catholic church. That the *Bulletin of the Department of Foreign Affairs* contained an advertisement for *The Rose Tattoo* at the same time that the Attorney-General instituted proceedings against the play was not so much a contradiction, but rather evidence of the erratic and sometimes uncoordinated nature of the state's post-war expansion.

There was another theatre controversy in 1958. Within the context of a campaign by Archbishop McQuaid against the government-led liberalization of the Censorship Board, difficulties arose in relation to the choice of two plays for that year's Dublin Theatre Festival. In late 1957, the Festival had published a list of 25 plays for performance that included Sean O'Casey's flagrantly anti-clerical, *The Drums of Father Ned*, as well as a dramatization of James Joyce's *Ulysses* by a Northern Ireland dramatist Alan McClellend. The problem arose when the Secretary of the Festival's organizing body, the Dublin Tóstal Council, requested permission (either naïvely or disingenuously) from McQuaid for an inaugural mass (DDA: Letter, 21 October 1957, McQuaid Papers, Arts and Culture Box, Tóstal File). The Archbishop responded by letter saying that permission would not be granted if the Tóstal Council approved of the productions of Joyce's *Ulysses* as well as the O'Casey play. He also added, by way of conclusion, that '*The Rose Tattoo* ought to have been a lesson to the Tóstal' (DDA: McQuaid to Fr. Tuohy, 13 November 1957; Arts and Culture Box, McQuaid Papers). The Tóstal Council gyrated with panic and confusion. First, it announced that the production of both plays was to be rescinded, then it declared that they were to go ahead as planned, and then, finally, it stated that both controversial productions had been cancelled (*Irish Times*, 15 February 1958: 1+7). For the Church's part, however, much more was at stake than a matter of the two productions. What was at issue, and now publicly contested, was the pace and extent of liberalization in Ireland and the prestige and political status that the Church had hitherto been accorded. When the Dublin Jesuit principal refused permission for the staging of a play by Samuel Beckett in Dublin's St Francis Xavier Hall (DDA: McQuaid Papers, Tóstal File, Secretary to Archbishop, 14 January 1958) the situation quickly escalated. Beckett responded angrily by refusing any further performance of his plays in Dublin (Swift 1985: 296) and, in April 1958, that year's festival was cancelled in its entirety (*Irish Times*, 28 April 1958: 1). By the end of the year, the Dublin Theatre Festival had learnt its lesson and an October performance of J. P. Donleavy's *The Ginger Man* at the Gaiety was cancelled at once due to complaints from McQuaid. Now contrite, the Dublin Theatre Festival invited Archbishop McQuaid to become a patron, McQuaid declined magnanimously, and the 1959 festival opened with a traditional celebratory mass (DDA: McQuaid Papers, Tóstal File, Arts and Culture Box, Letter, 4 December 1958).

The debacle of the 1958 Dublin Theatre Festival may have ended in a triumph for the public authority of the city's Roman Catholic hierarchy, but the victory was short-lived. The year 1958 also coincided with the publication of T. K. Whitaker's momentous government report, the 'Programme for Economic Expansion'. This gave accelerated momentum to Ireland's economic and social modernization process (Raymond 1983: 114–17) – against which the Church had little chance of any long-term success. By declaring so forthrightly that the state's primary economic objective was export-based and that this objective would be achieved mainly by means of foreign investment (Lee 1989: 344), Whitaker's report was not a sudden statement of doctrine, but the culmination of an economic modernization process that had been in train for well over a decade (Raymond 1983: 114). Nevertheless, the Whitaker Report is considered as a watershed in twentieth-century Irish society partly because it focuses attention on a major ideological shift (see Bew *et al.* 1989: 102; Lee 1989: 344). In conjunction with other factors such as Ireland's membership of the World Bank in August 1957, Lemass's rapprochement with Terence O'Neill's Stormont government in Northern Ireland and the signing of the Anglo-Irish Free Trade Agreement in 1965 (Lee 1989: 367–8), the implementation of Whitaker's recommendations led to a period of unprecedented economic growth. By 1964, the level of unemployment had dropped by over 30 per cent and the purchasing power of wages had risen by over 20 per cent (Tobin 1984: 95); and between 1960 and 1969 over 350 manufacturing enterprises were established, many of which were multinational corporations (Tobin 1984: 5). The impact of the Whitaker report on Ireland's economic growth in the late 1950s and 1960s – 'faster and more sustained than at any previous period in Irish history' (Walsh 1979: 33) – coincided, therefore, with a further massive expansion of the state in the areas of economic and social planning. But the gradual dismantling of the paternalistic state apparatuses of the 1940s and their replacement in the early 1960s by an 'effective consensus for an activist and "social democratic" state' (Bew *et al.* 1989: 111) did not mean that the state had diminished in power, merely that its mechanisms for the implementation of social policy were beginning to change. Just as economic planning in Ireland after 1958 tends to be 'coordinative' rather than directive in so far as the former focuses 'its economic power towards certain strategic points' and so manipulates the economy rather than controls it directly (Raymond 1983: 115), so there was now a much greater emphasis on personal pleasure and on individual consumption as the basis for political agency.

Keynesian principles were now installed as the main items on Ireland's developmental and modernization agenda (Breen 1990: 5). Broadly speaking, then, the legitimacy of the state tended to be viewed increasingly in terms of its responsiveness to the requirements of the individual rather than as a reflection of any dominant philosophy or ideological position. These changes are evident in the repertoire of plays at the Abbey Theatre to the extent that the plays performed there tend to reflect a widening gulf between traditional nationalist views associated with the foundation of the state and a contemporary world for whom such views are no longer relevant. Macken's *Twilight of a Warrior* is one example: here, as has been briefly discussed, Adam Dacey's disillusionment with post-revolutionary Ireland and his nostalgia for the republican idealism of Mary Ann in Tobreena is shown to be so ill-founded that he collapses with a fatal heart-attack when he hears the news that Mary Ann had lived happily with one of Dacey's former Black and Tan opponents. John O'Donovan's satirical farce, *The Less We are Together* (1957) is another instance as it too calls attention to what it sees as the unreality of the traditional nationalist aspiration for a 32-county Ireland. Set in a farcical version of Ireland's political future, O'Donovan's play has the 'Rest in Peace' party winning the 1982 general election. An ambitious but sickly Taoiseach presides over a cabinet dominated by women, but the principal satirical target of the play is the cross-party consensus that existed in 1950s Ireland concerning the need for Irish unity (see Foley 1992: 209). The Taoiseach's plan to resolve partition is to have Ireland rejoin the British Commonwealth so that 'instead of asking the Six Counties to come in with us, we go in with the Six Counties' (O'Donovan n.d.: 25). The play's splendid denouement has Britain reject Ireland's offer as too expensive. In a world dominated by economics, O'Donovan implies, nationalist aspirations and rhetoric are grossly irrelevant.

But the unprecedented flourishing of the Irish theatre in the 1960s arises partly because of the way in which the inadequacy or inappropriateness of traditional nationalist verities is rendered not satirically (as in Macken and O'Donovan), but as an existential trauma. Irish drama's 'second renaissance' (Murray 1998: 162) occurs not simply because of a blessing of talent from younger writers like Brian Friel, John B. Keane, Thomas Kilroy, Tom Murphy and Hugh Leonard, but because of a fundamental shift away from the Abbey Theatre's more tendentious dramatic methods of the 1950s. Friel's *The Enemy Within* is a case in point. Here, the primary dramatic tension is between loyalty to Ireland, experienced as a compelling and atavistic pull, and loyalty to a more transcendent sense of self. Performed by the NTS in August 1962, *The Enemy Within* focuses on the life of the Derry contemplative monk, St Columba, not so much in terms of historical biography, but in terms of an imaginative account of Columba as 'private man' (Friel 1979: 7). In the preface to the play, Friel draws attention to the implied analogy between sixth-century Ireland and the contemporary preoccupation with partition and national unity, but also insists that the play 'is neither a history nor a biography but an imaginative account' (Friel 1979: 7). Friel's Columba is depicted as kind, reflective and paternalistic; revered by his small community of monks, but still susceptible to the lure of tribal and family loyalties in his native Tirconnail (the modern County Donegal). In the first act of the play, Columba succumbs to his family's request that he return to Ireland so as to lead his kinsmen in battle against a tribal adversary and in the process alienates a character named Oswald, a recent English arrival to the community. In the second act, Columba resists a second request to return but at the cost of having his family reject him. And at this moment Oswald (the emphatically English novice who is also portrayed as a potential modernizer for the island community) returns to the monastery. Friel's play suggests that the authenticity of the private self, presented here in Christian terms, must resist traditional loyalties to Ireland as mediated by family and kinship bonds and that this leads to national regeneration. Here, an important theme of Abbey Theatre plays in the 1950s – a sharp movement away from loyalty to a traditional Irish nationalism – is given an existential rather than simply a polemical valence.

The new form of community that is envisaged at the end of *The Enemy Within*, in other words, is one closely similar to Lemass's vision for 1960s Ireland: prepared to relinquish its traditional nationalist animosity towards England in order to embrace the rejuvenating power of international capitalism. To this extent, Friel's earliest Abbey Theatre play articulates a narrative with strong resonances for the post-Whitaker Ireland of the 1960s. Privacy, or the authenticity of the spontaneous self, is offered as a fundamental principle for a reinvigorated form of national community. In presenting this amalgam of Christian liberal existentialism in opposition to the familiar and more traditional loyalties of territory and nationhood, *The Enemy Within* offers a substantial renovation of the anti-republican critique of plays like Bryan McMahon's *Bugle in the Blood*, Macken's *Twilight of a Warrior*, or John McDonnell's 1961 satire about Ireland's partition *All the King's Horses*.

Blythe's failure to grasp this point may well explain why so many of Friel's and Murphy's plays did not receive their first productions at the NTS. His view of the Abbey Theatre as exercising a 'constructive influence on public affairs' by virtue of its 'satirical treatments of the Northern Ireland problem . . . and ventilation of issues to do with Church authority' (Blythe 1965: n.p.) indicates Blythe's more tendentious approach to the national question. *Philadelphia, Here I Come!* (Gaiety Theatre, Dublin, 1964), *The Loves of Cass McGuire* (Abbey Theatre, 1966), and *The Mundy Scheme* (Olympia Theatre, Dublin, 1969) return again and again to Friel's view of the destructive relationship between traditional features of an Irish nationalist identity and the homogenizing effects of an all-pervasive multinational capitalism. Portrayed throughout as a matter of tragic or farcical inevitability, every attempt to maintain an insular or nationalist independence is shown to lead directly to its opposite: either the anonymity of emigration or an exacerbation of economic dependency. An acceptance of the unstoppable nature of Ireland's modernization is coupled to a nostalgia for a pre-modern Ireland of the past. This was an extremely successful formula. *Philadelphia, Here I Come!*, was first performed as part of the Dublin Theatre Festival in September 1964, and then transferred to New York in

1966 where it became the longest-running Irish play on Broadway (Farquharson 1997: 98). Like John B. Keane's popular musical, *Many Young Men of Twenty* (1961), Friel's play deals with the emotional topic of emigration, but at a historical moment when emigration figures entered a sharp decline. Whereas *Many Young Men of Twenty* is an overtly sentimental and tendentious attack on the inability or unwillingness of Irish governments to redress this problem (Keane 1961: 43–4), Friel's play adopts an altogether different approach. Friel's protagonist, Gar O'Donnell, is shown as having been left behind in the modernization programme not so much for social and economic reasons, but because of personal ineptitude. Gar does not belong to that pre-1958 category of small farmers and rural unskilled labourers from the west of Ireland that had been so marginalized by Whitaker's programme of economic regeneration (Breen *et al.* 1990: 7; Tobin 1984: 95–102). Instead Gar belongs to a rural, middle-class setting with his father occupying the roles of shopkeeper and a local County Donegal county councillor. Gar himself attended university in Dublin but dropped out after a year of dissipation. Indeed, by far the most important reason for his decision to emigrate is not so much the bleak social conditions or the dismal employment prospects experienced by many in the western counties in this period (Tobin 1984: 102), but rather his frustrated sexual desire. Gar's (oedipal) trauma is evident in his hapless and fateful succumbing to his Aunt Lizzie's invitation to live in her home in the United States largely because of his perception of her as a substitute for his deceased mother (Friel 1965: 64). Not only is the Donegal of *Philadelphia, Here I Come!* absurdly out of place in a world increasingly dominated by the idioms of Anglo-American popular culture, but the audience is shown that there is no public language in which Gar can express his private world of desire. The tragic irony of the play, and one that Friel was to exploit and develop in *The Loves of Cass McGuire* and in many of his later plays, is that the changes necessary for personal fulfilment (in this case, emigration) entail a fundamental loss of plenitude. Identity can be realized only through its loss.

This point is further illustrated by the play's portrayal of rural Ireland. A realization or fulfilment of desire entails, above all, a complete submission of the self to the play of international market forces; thus, Ireland can become modern only by abandoning the essential markers of its distinctiveness. The inadequacy of traditional, rural, County Donegal – whether in the form of S. B. O'Donnell, 'a responsible respectable citizen' (Friel 1965: 21), Senator Doogan, the schoolteacher, or the Canon – is presented less as a political or economic problem than as a form of personal crisis. But as Nicholas Grene so astutely points out, Friel's play also affirms the absolute rightness of Gar's decision to emigrate (Grene 2000: 205). Here, the familiar dramatis personae of a T. C. Murray or Lennox Robinson play (the local politician, the parish priest and the national schoolteacher) are confronted by a more experimental and quasi-expressionistic use of dramaturgy adopted from contemporary United States dramatists like Thornton Wilder, Arthur Miller and Tennessee Williams. To this extent, the extraordinary box office success of *Philadelphia, Here I Come!* is to be attributed, at least partly, to what Grene describes its 'acceptably middle-brow deviation from naturalism' (Grene 2000: 202).

Tom Murphy's *A Whistle in the Dark* (1961) also deals with the one major social and political issue which Whitaker's reforms did little to change: emigration from Ireland's western seaboard counties. Rejected by the Abbey and first performed at the Olympia Theatre in Dublin in 1962, the stage action of *A Whistle in the Dark* implies that what motivates emigration from Ireland is not so much economics, but the enduring psychic hold of stereotypes of Irish national identity (see O'Toole 1987: 171–2). The play is set in the interior of a house occupied by an Irish immigrant family living in Coventry and centres on the owner of the house, Michael Carney, and his changing relationships with his English wife Betty and his extended family from Ireland: his father (Dada), brothers (Iggy, Harry, Hugo and Des) and the family hanger-on (Mush). From the beginning, Dada and his retinue behave like drunken and belligerent thugs, violently disrupting the domestic order of the house by smashing furniture and threatening and harassing Betty. Michael's family 'business' is prostitution and racketeering; as recreation, the family conduct on-going drunken brawls with English working-class gangs as well as more vicious attacks on other immigrant or minority communities. While Michael starts the play by attempting to reassure Betty that his family is reformable and by laughing himself at stereotypes of the Irish, the unfolding action shows Michael's domestic and bourgeois aspirations – his desire to settle down and 'fit into' English society – as steadily eroded by the family's disruptive tribalism. The specific conflict between Michael and his family concerns Michael's efforts to convince his younger brother Des to return to Ireland so as to avail himself of the new meritocratic opportunities there. Whereas Michael conceives of this prospect as offering a kind of bourgeois plenitude ('just something, respectable, to be at home' (Murphy 1989: 27)) the other members of the Carney family have an entirely different view. For them, especially for Dada and Harry, Des staying on in Ireland means that he would be forced to succumb to an inevitable position of subordination. They consider emigration as essential not for economic reasons, but because Ireland is associated with a pervasive, but poorly understood feeling of dependency. Des has left a good job in Ireland because he is tired of being told what to do (Murphy 1989: 37), and Harry's memory of schooling is one of sadistic humiliation. For the Carneys, Ireland is associated not with the plenitude of a home, but with an anonymous middle-class 'them' that insists on their subordination.

Murphy's linkage of an Ireland obsessed by class distinctions with an addictive and tribal violence becomes clearer as the play proceeds. In Act I, for example, Harry describes his favourite weapon, a metal knuckle-duster made from an ass's shoe as 'a souvenir from Ireland' (Murphy 1989: 28), and in Act II he replies in a stage Irish accent to Michael's reiterated question about the purpose of their violence. The Carneys celebrate their gang-fight victory over the Mulryans as a tribal and nationalist victory, with Dada describing his sons as 'champions of England! Great Irishmen!'; Mush recites a ballad that compares his brother Iggy to the twelfth-century Irish hero, Brian Boru (Murphy 1989: 77–8), and Dada sings about the need for nationalist solidarity in the face of the English colonial oppressors.

> But those homes were destroyed and our land confiscated,
> The hand of the tyrant brought plunder and woe;
> The fires are now dead and our hearths desolated,
> In our once happy homes in the County Mayo.
> (*Chorus*)
> So, boys, stick together in all kinds of weather,
> Don't show the white feather wherever you go;
> Be each as a brother and love one another,
> Like stout-hearted men from the County Mayo.
>
> (Murphy 1985: 79)

The occasion of this ballad (a gang fight victory over another Irish immigrant family) exposes Irish national identity as a contradiction. It is associated both with an enervating experience of dependency and with the 'pride' that the family claim to be fighting for. Thus, the Carneys demonstrate their identity as Irish by attacking another Irish immigrant family; Michael proves his patriarchal authority by alienating Betty, and shows that he belongs to his family by killing his brother. The relentless irony of the play is that in order to achieve an 'Irish' nationalist identity, the Carney family has to emigrate to England and act out this colonialist and self-destructive stereotype. The killing of Des is the play's concluding irony. Michael, the character who in the opening scene of the play was at pains to emphasize his distance from stereotypes of Irish identity becomes, in the play's final moments, an apparent living proof of the power of the stereotype and of its recurrence. In Murphy's formulation, therefore, the stereotype of the 'Paddy' is shown to emerge from a preoccupation with *nationalist* identity rather than with any specifically colonialist intention.

That so few of the major plays of Friel or Murphy were premièred at the Abbey in the 1960s was not simply a result of Ernest Blythe's nationalist conservatism (O'Toole 1987: 7). More important than Blythe's undoubtedly formidable personal opinions was these plays' preoccupation with existentialist crises, a preoccupation that hardly conjugated at all with the traditional idea of the NTS as expressing a social consensus. Blythe tended to think of the Abbey Theatre as dedicated to the enactment of key *issues* relating to the Irish state, whereas for Murphy, Kilroy and Leonard Friel the emphasis now was on the experience of the individual. Sixteen years after Iremonger and McHugh's walkout, in February 1963, the *Irish Times* lamented (once again) the Abbey Theatre's fall from grace: 'the Abbey Theatre is not a national theatre. It was. To dignify it with that name now humiliates the living no less than it mocks the dead' (*Irish Times*, 20 February 1963: 7).

7

NATIONAL THEATRES IN NORTHERN IRELAND, 1922–72[1]

> The Catholic community gives us most of our best actors and actresses. Derived chiefly from Gaelic stock, its people take naturally to the theatre. Almost every parish has its dramatic society, its talented performers, for whom the heightened traffic of the stage is hardly to be distinguished from the vivid emotional experiences of every-day life.
>
> (Kennedy 1946: 51)

From the establishment of a separate parliament in Belfast in June 1921 to that parliament's setting up of the Council for the Encouragement of Music and the Arts (CEMA) in 1943, no formal relationship existed between the theatre and the state in Northern Ireland. Unlike the contrasting situation south of the border, with the Cumann na nGaedheal government's subsidization of the NTS in 1925 and the tension between the Abbey Theatre and the Fianna Fáil government in the early 1930s, there is no evidence that any of Northern Ireland's uniformly unionist government administrations maintained any similar interest in the theatre or that the theatre was regarded as related to state policy. This is not entirely surprising. Whereas, as we have seen, the Abbey Theatre was associated with a form of cultural nationalism with an intimate and complex relationship with the struggle for Irish statehood, the state in Northern Ireland was oriented towards maintaining a pro-British allegiance. To this end, the professional theatre in Belfast in the 1920s and 1930s continued its long-standing trend of importing most theatre productions from London. In addition, most of the major amateur and semi-professional urban groups, such as the Ulster Group Theatre (1940–59) and the Northern Drama League (1923–39), remained under non-nationalist control.[2] An amateur and mainly rural-based, nationalist theatre tradition did exist in Northern

Ireland (as it did also in the rest of the island), often under clerical supervision (Farrell 1941: 87–8). Local theatre groups such as the Omagh Players performed second-hand Abbey Theatre plays or, in much rarer instances, performed published work like Louis Lynch's 1936 play, *Heritage*.[3] But as far as professional theatre was concerned, theatre managements in Northern Ireland maintained an unwritten policy of avoiding plays that dealt directly with issues relevant to nationalist and republican politics. In so far as such plays existed, that is, the main theatres in Northern Ireland excluded from their repertories drama dealing with issues such as religious discrimination or sectarian violence. The only exception was the tendency to portray such issues as farcical absurdity – all the more laughable because so entirely unrelated to the structures or apparatuses of the state (as in Gerald MacNamara's much revived *Thompson in Tir na nOg* (1918)). And while it is true that Northern Ireland dramatists such as Rutherford Mayne and George Shiels did engage with political issues (in plays such as Mayne's *Bridgehead* (1939) and Shiels's *The Rugged Path* (1940)) this is directed more towards production at the Abbey Theatre, and towards a critique of Irish nationalism and the southern Irish state, than to any consideration of unionist ideology or of the political administration in Northern Ireland. One noteworthy exception, Joseph Tomelty's *The End House* (1944), a play that deals with the serious effects of the Special Powers Act on a Catholic community in Belfast, was not performed professionally in Northern Ireland until the early 1990s, despite its successful première at the NTS and Tomelty's established reputation as a skilled dramatist.

This relationship (or the lack of one) between the state, the theatre and Northern Ireland's minority nationalist community is consistent with other aspects of cultural politics in the early decades of the Northern Ireland state. In general, the suppression of socialist, nationalist and republican politics was achieved less by means of direct censorship (despite its extensive provision in the Special Powers Act (1922) and in subsequent legislation (Farrell 1976: 94)) than by unionist control of the principal print and broadcasting media and of the main cultural institutions. In terms of culture and public ceremony, the self-identity of the Northern Ireland state was dominated by an overwhelming unionist political perspective (see McIntosh 1999). Moderate nationalist opinion was confined to newspapers such as the *Irish News*, the *Frontier Sentinel*, and the *Derry Journal*,[4] while that which was regarded as exclusively nationalist culture (such as Irish dancing, language and music) was systematically restricted by the state to the private, often ghettoized, space of the communities themselves (McIntosh 1999: 3).

Yet the relationship between theatre and minority protest in the *later* decades of the Northern Ireland government (circa 1943–72) cannot be so neatly summarized. With the establishment of CEMA in 1943, the Northern Ireland state assumed responsibility for an organization directly concerned with relating 'culture' to 'the people' (*CEMA (Northern Ireland) Annual Report* 1943–4: 2). This begins a process by which the theatre came to be seen as an important site for legitimizing the state's claim to be representative. Modelled on the British version of CEMA (established in 1937), CEMA in Northern Ireland initially functioned as a paternalistic, wartime institution designed to raise patriotic morale. But in the early period, CEMA's policy of importing cultural organizations from Britain, and also (due to wartime restrictions on travel between England and Ireland) from Dublin, was sharply criticized. As David Kennedy puts it in the literary magazine *Rann*, 'the title [of CEMA] does not say where the arts are to be encouraged, and judging by its work one might be pardoned for thinking at times that it exists to encourage English and foreign artists at the expense of the *Ulster* taxpayer' (Kennedy 1953: 42). Earlier articles by Kennedy and Jack Loudan, published in the Belfast-based magazine *Lagan* argued that the existence of CEMA afforded an important opportunity to promote an 'Ulster theatre' and that what was needed in order to do this was a system of state subsidized theatres along the lines of those supported by the Arts Council in Great Britain (Loudan 1946; Kennedy 1946). By the late 1940s CEMA policy in Northern Ireland had altered accordingly. Whereas in 1943 CEMA had launched its activities with its proposal 'to provide for the Province as a whole' the benefits of the many 'excellent musicians and dramatic companies . . . constantly touring in Britain' (*CEMA (Northern Ireland) Annual Report 1943–4*: 2), by 1948–9 it advocated the provision of a permanent professional 'Ulster' theatre in Belfast with a mandate to present 'a number of plays having an Ulster theme and an Ulster setting' (*CEMA (Northern Ireland) Annual Report* 1948–9: 9). This was the informal beginning of Northern Ireland's formal national theatre initiative.

As Northern Ireland's version of a national theatre movement, the campaign for an 'Ulster theatre' also marks the emergence of a cultural movement in Northern Ireland known as 'Ulster regionalism'. The primary ideological goal of Ulster regionalism was the legitimation of the partitioned (six-county) Northern Ireland state by making it appear identical to the ancient (nine-county)

province of Ulster. Unionist politicians, under pressure to demonstrate Northern Ireland's political integrity to a potentially critical
Labour government at Westminster, soon came to appreciate its
benefits. In July 1949, for the first time since the foundation of the
Northern Ireland state, the theatre – more specifically, the 'Ulster
theatre' – appears as an item on the Northern Ireland cabinet agenda.
As a Ministry of Education memorandum records for that year: 'it
is felt that it is in drama rather than in art or music that Northern
Ireland can offer to the United Kingdom as a whole a characteristic
and distinctive contribution' (PRONI: ED 13/1/2034 – Letter
14 January 1949). The Stormont Parliament in Belfast,[5] including
some Nationalist members, expressed general agreement concerning
the need to support the efforts of 'Ulster' drama. And in 1951,
following a formal invitation to contribute to the Festival of Britain,
a parliamentary grant of £9000 was made available to assist in the
formation of an Ulster Theatre Company.

The presence of a representative theatre in Northern Ireland was
regarded as an important cultural asset. Like the Festival of Britain
in Northern Ireland in 1951, and the coronation visit of Queen
Elizabeth in 1953, an Ulster theatre was seen as an indication of
the state's bourgeois stability, an attractive sign of its present and
potential capitalist development and an opportunity to exhibit a
social consensus (McIntosh 1999: 103–4). Indeed, Stormont's
unprecedented enthusiasm for developing a state or regional theatre
in Northern Ireland may also be explained in terms of the unionist
government's incorporation of elements of the post-war cultural
ideology of the British state. Middle-class culture, and especially the
theatre, was regarded as an important means by which a regional
identity might be fostered with the minimum of political dissent.
The view that CEMA should promote a 'national' or regional culture
for Northern Ireland, that is, coincided with the 'nationalization of
culture' which formed an integral part of the expansion and
modernization of the state as promoted by Westminster (Minihan
1977: 235). In Britain T. S. Eliot's 1948 observation that culture had
become 'an instrument of policy . . . something socially desirable
which it is the business of the State to promote' (quoted in Minihan
1977: 215) was more than fully realized by the massive increases in
state funding for the arts (and especially for the theatre) and by the
enthusiastic passing at Westminster of the 1949 National Theatre Act
(Minihan 1977: 235–8). The attractiveness of a state theatre and of
a canon of 'Ulster' drama for a regionalist cultural policy was that it
manifested Northern Ireland's political normality.

But, conversely, there was also an impression (sometimes undisguised) that theatre itself endorsed the naturalness of Northern Ireland's sectarian hierarchy. Thus, David Kennedy's 1946 article takes it for granted that the institutional theatre's intrinsic structures of financial, directorial and authorial control affirm pre-existing social divisions. He argues that while the proper expression of 'the true Ulster accent' lies in the austere authorial voice of Northern Ireland Presbyterianism, the natural medium for this voice is the less inhibited, but also less disciplined, 'Catholic community . . . for whom the heightened traffic of the stage is hardly to be distinguished from the vivid emotional experiences of every-day life' (Kennedy 1946: 51). Kennedy's belief that the one religious community exists, like the constituent elements of the theatre, in harmonious balance with the other ('Ulster dramatists, Ulster audiences and Ulster actors need one another' (Kennedy 1946: 54)) and, at the same time, his call for a serious drama that would analyse sectarian animosities, reveals the fundamental dilemma posed by cultural modernization in Northern Ireland. For an 'Ulster theatre' to function as a national theatre, social problems such as religious discrimination in employment and housing had to be represented. Yet even to acknowledge sectarianism as a problem pointed immediately to the contested nature of the Northern Ireland state.

In Northern Ireland, one could say, nationalizing culture was a process shadowed, and often obstructed, by an extremely awkward problem of definition: what and whose was the nation in question? Whereas in Britain the ideological successes of CEMA and later the Arts Council depended to a large extent on the illusion of their autonomy – what Raymond Williams has described as 'administered consensus by co-option' (Williams 1979: 160) – the sectarian divisions of the Northern Ireland state raised immediate questions of ownership and political control. Indeed, as early as 1941, Michael Farrell, writing in *The Bell*, remarked how, for a Protestant, talk of an Ulster drama 'smacks suspiciously of a National outlook' (Farrell 1941: 88). One way in which this problem was evident in the professional theatre was the insistence by CEMA (at Stormont's behest) on the playing of the British national anthem at *all* theatrical performances and other arts events. The only exception to this policy was art exhibitions. As one CEMA memorandum puts it in relation to a visiting choir from Denmark: 'it was essential that the National Anthem be insisted upon . . . in order to make clear to the foreign visitors the unity between Northern Ireland and Great Britain' (PRONI: AC 3/2; Memo, 12 May 1949). Yet as early as

1944, the issue of the playing of the national anthem had led to vigorous protests from some of the local CEMA area representatives in Newry, Omagh and Armagh, all areas with substantial nationalist majorities (PRONI: AC 3/2, 'Report on Local Committees Visited in Connection with the Playing of the National Anthem', 8 December 1944 in 'Playing of National Anthem' File). And in April of the following year, the secretary of the Newry branch of CEMA announced the resignation of the entire committee because of CEMA's obduracy on this issue (PRONI: AC 3/2, Letter, 25 April 1945). For unionists, the playing of the national anthem at arts events was a statement of allegiance and for this reason it was insisted upon at all performances during the Festival of Britain in Northern Ireland (McIntosh 1999: 110).

For the mainly Catholic nationalist population in Northern Ireland, however, CEMA's national anthem policy remained a potent symbol of alienation. Thus an article in the *Frontier Sentinel* responded to the national anthem controversy by renaming CEMA as the council for the '*Dis*couragement of Music and the Arts' and by stating bluntly that the effect of this policy was the cultural disenfranchisement of nationalists.

> It has been pointed out that in the Six Counties the British National Anthem is regarded by all parties as a party song, that is inseparably associated with Partition, to which a vast section of the population is opposed, and this compulsory rendering at public entertainments could only emphasise its political character and hurt the national feelings of Anti-partitionists who consider that the Ministry's intention is to create an atmosphere still more hostile to the reunification of Ireland. . . . widespread indignation exists at the enforcement of a regulation which virtually bans a third of the population from attending performances.
>
> (PRONI AC 3/2: Newspaper Clippings,
> *Frontier Sentinel,* 23 June 1945)

Similar controversies are recorded in the early 1960s. In each case, the pattern was more or less the same. Nationalists involved in local arts or theatre groups attempt to persuade CEMA to adopt a more moderate or flexible policy on the national anthem so as not to alienate predominantly nationalist audiences. CEMA then considers the request and consults with Stormont; finally, CEMA responds to the local organizers by declaring that no change whatsoever can be allowed. Even in the case of CEMA sponsored performances of sacred music this rule was enforced. In 1953, for example, following an 'embarrassing' moment when the issue of the national anthem was raised in an interview with the representative from the Arts Council of Ireland (An Chomhairle Éalaíon),[6] the General Secretary of CEMA sought advice from the Minister for Health and Local Government, Dame Dehra Parker, and received the following emphatic reply: 'the National Anthem should always be played at the *beginning*' (PRONI: AC 3/2, Letter from Dehra Parker, Minister for Health and Local Government to W. H. N. Downer, General and Financial Secretary, CEMA, 19 August 1953: emphasis in the original). Such an arrangement made it considerably more difficult for refractory nationalists to be absent. Despite strong protests, CEMA's controversial national anthem policy was maintained in full until, and without any formal announcement or apology, it was repealed in 1965 (Bryson and McCartney 1994: 92–3).

For nationalists, then, CEMA's sponsorship of the arts was inseparably linked to the 1921 partition of Ireland and to an array of discriminatory legislation that characterized the injustices of unionist authority. The national anthem rule was not, therefore, an issue of 'lore' or something that affected only a small proportion of the Catholic arts community (*pace* Bryson and McCartney 1994: 92–3). Indeed, as minority protest increased in the 1950s (fuelled in many instances by precisely the legislation that was designed to prohibit it) it became important to Stormont that the theatre remain under strict political control while also appearing to exist 'outside' politics. Cabinet discussions concerning the establishment of a 'national' or state theatre in the mid-1950s reveal considerable division and uncertainty as to how these two conflicting consider- ations might be managed. On 15 August 1956, for example, a Stormont cabinet meeting argues that while the concept of a national theatre is to be supported, there is also a pressing need 'to secure that its control [is] in the right hands' with 'proper control over the type of drama performed' (PRONI: CAB 4/1016: 2–3). Terence O'Neill (Minister of Education) and Dehra Parker (Minister of Health and Local Government) argue that these difficulties might be overcome with the establishment of a governing Trust 'responsible for the general artistic policy and the detailed financial administration of the theatre' (PRONI: CAB 4/1016/12: 1). In their view, unionist control of the theatre would be secured by the composition of the Trust: the Vice-Chancellor of Queen's University, the Lord Mayor of Belfast, three CEMA nominees, one Guild of Supporters' representative and an optional government nominee. The necessity and effectiveness of this scheme is further underlined in a CEMA memorandum submitted to the government by Ritchie McKee, Chairman of the Sub-committee on Theatre in Belfast:

> The question of control is of paramount importance . . . and I do not see any difficulty in arriving at a formula whereby it can be assured that control will always be vested in what may be termed the 'right hands'.
>
> (PRONI: CAB 4/1019: 1)

Another CEMA recommendation was that a state or 'national' theatre in Belfast would not concern itself with avant-garde experimentation (PRONI: 'Theatre in Belfast: Report of Mr McKee's Sub-Committee', PRONI: 2435/2/5). There would be no risk, in other words, that Northern Ireland's state or 'national' theatre might become a platform for nationalist protest or that it might offer – by means of an avant-garde theatre practice – any divergent models of political or social organization. Its exclusive ideological role was the generation of a particular kind of state-oriented consensus. Other members of the cabinet, such as Harry Midgley (Minister of Labour), argued that such an expedient 'would still leave the government too closely associated with the project' and that, therefore, the plan should be abandoned (PRONI: CAB 4/1016: 3). Midgley's argument was that Stormont certainly needed to invigilate any prospective national theatre, but that it should not be seen to do so, either through the medium of CEMA *or* through any appointed Trust. It was this view that prevailed. Following a leak to the press, a number of newspaper articles called for the government to state precisely who would have control of the theatre and how and whether this group would be regarded as representative: 'Who decides membership? What qualifications are necessary to join the apparently select band? To whom are the Council [i.e. the proposed Trust] responsible?' (see the *Belfast Telegraph*, 22 September 1956: 3).[7] The leak clinched the cabinet's decision, forcing the cancellation of an eight-year-old plan to establish an 'Ulster' or state theatre in Belfast.

The struggle to maintain unionist control of CEMA policy and of an 'Ulster theatre' bears close affiliation to the widening gap between Stormont's desire to portray itself as a representative democracy and the coercive exigencies of unionist control. Preventing the politics of minority protest access to the public sphere had always been an important priority for successive Northern Ireland governments, but was all the more urgent in the post-war period. Increasingly in the 1950s minority protest drew attention to the contradictions between Northern Ireland's promotion of itself as a modern democracy and the gerrymandering, discrimination and repression upon which the state appeared so increasingly to depend (see O'Leary and McGarry 1993: 149). In particular, there is an ever-widening fissure between the imposition of draconian security legislation designed to curtail nationalist political protest, and the implementation of reforms relating to the British welfare state (Farrell 1976: 189, 213–14; O'Leary and McGarry 1993: 120–39).[8] In the 1950s, for example, unionist legislation concerning health, education and child benefits coincide with the 1951 Public Order Act, the 1954 Flags and Emblems Act, and the reintroduction of internment in 1956 under the Civil Authorities (Special Powers) Act of 1922. This was a disquieting ideological dilemma. The Northern Ireland government found itself caught between wanting to present itself as a modern, liberal democracy fully compatible with the new liberalism of the post-war British state and the demands of a nationalist minority population whose protests against gerry-mandering and religious discrimination in housing and employment increased markedly following the foundation of the Anti-Partition League in 1945. From the point of view of nationalist protest in this period, the focus remained almost exclusively on what was regarded as the iniquitous effects of partition. But that the ending of partition (and thus of the Northern Ireland state itself) was a nationalist prerequisite to the achievement of their basic civil rights, served merely to confirm a unionist belief in the necessity of repressive measures (see Murray 2000: 396–7). The 1957 statement by the Minister of Education – 'All the minority are traitors and have always been traitors to the government of Northern Ireland' (quoted in Farrell 1976: 221 and in Brewer 1998: 101) – was less a maverick outburst, than a blunt summation of government policy. Stormont parliamentary debates amply confirm this. Repeated protests by members of the Nationalist or Republican Labour Parties concerning discrimination in public employment and the suspension of civil rights were routinely answered according to the same logic: nationalist opposition to the constitution of the Northern Ireland state was, *sui generis*, a subversive and illegitimate activity (*Northern Ireland Hansard 1953* and *1959*: 1822–66). Indeed, the Public Order Act and the Flag and Emblems Act had been designed specifically to curb such *non*-violent forms of political opposition.

The failure of Northern Ireland's national theatre project was intimately related, therefore, to changing political conditions in the 1950s. Despite an economic boom in the post-war years, the permanent unionist administration at Stormont had, in fact, some cause to be anxious. Nationalist and Labour opposition to Ulster regionalism and to Unionist control of the theatre remained strong and was evidenced in particular by a protest that took place in the course of the 1953 PEN conference in Belfast. While several of the official speakers at the conference laid emphasis on the idea of Northern Ireland as a distinctive 'British' region and delegates were circulated with a free copy of a special regionalist issue of the literary magazine *Rann*, a group of Belfast Labour councillors distributed an open letter that argued that Ulster regionalism was merely the other side to the sectarianism and gerrymandering of the Northern Ireland state. The letter complained of the existence of a pervasive unionist censorship in Northern Ireland that prevented the theatre, and literary culture in general, from representing the nature and effects of sectarianism and political discrimination.

> As the Congress is concerned with the difficulties surrounding literary work in small countries, our visitors may be interested in a special aspect of that subject, an aspect which probably has no parallel elsewhere . . . A quiet, but nonetheless powerful censorship prevents the writer for radio or the theatre from dealing with the very tensions that are the most prominent features of life in the area. The political and economic domination by the Unionist Party is taboo as a subject as is the victimization of political opponents. The nearest approach that can be made is on the level of broad farce. Treatment of historical questions, even of several centuries ago, is banned unless it is on an officially approved basis. The dilemma of the 'Ulster' writer will remain as long as the political and economic situation from which it springs endures.
>
> (quoted in O'Malley 1988: 142–3)

The PEN protest had little immediate effect; it provoked no official comment and, like the on-going national anthem controversy, it remained conspicuously absent from the pages of the main Belfast newspapers. Nevertheless, it does indicate the extent to which literary and theatrical culture in Northern Ireland was regarded as a hotly contested arena. To this extent, an 'Ulster theatre' was not just an opportunity for dissolving the contradictions of the Northern Ireland state, but a vehicle for their exposure.

One moment in which the gap between theatrical representation and political control appears especially conspicuous is in a 1958 controversy concerning Tyrone Guthrie's production of Gerald McLarnon's play, *The Bonefire*.[9] The play is set in 1951 in a small town outside of Belfast and features the Twelfth of July celebrations and their engendering of a near-hysterical anti-Catholic hatred. The first part of the play is set on the eve of the twelfth when Orangemen and their supporters first burn effigies of the reigning Pope and then celebrate the victory of King William at the Battle of the Boyne. Within this context, the main narrative action concerns Vanessa, an upper middle-class Protestant, who, despite being engaged to a local Protestant boy (Willy McNulty) has, inexplicably, conducted a passionate sexual relationship with a Catholic (Hanna). When Hanna discovers that Vanessa is now engaged to be married he engineers a fight with Willy in the course of which Willy strikes Hanna and, apparently, blinds him. Willy is sent to prison for assault but, since his victim was a Catholic, he is immediately elevated by the local branch of the Orange Order to the status of hero.

The first impression of McLarnon's narrative is that Hanna is a victim of Protestant anti-Catholic violence. But this impression is soon complicated when the audience discovers that Hanna is not, in fact, blind and that the misapprehension of his blindness has led to a miscarriage of justice in the case of his Protestant attacker. Moreover, the fight between Hanna and Willy took place not because of Protestant/Catholic animosity or political grievance, but because of sexual jealousy. Despite the play's Twelfth of July setting, therefore, there is no mention in the narrative of the political role of anti-Catholicism.

Anti-Catholic sectarianism is presented instead as an irrational and atavistic force similar, in many respects, to the tensions created by sexual rivalry. Vanessa and Hanna's passionate affair is presented as irrational and as inexplicable as the anti-Catholic chants of the Protestant mob. By the end of the play, Vanessa and Hanna agree that the only way that they can maintain their integrity is by killing themselves by leaping into the flames of the bonfire. This suicide attempt is botched when Vanessa's father prevents her leaping into the flames and Hanna is burnt to death. Hanna's death leads to a reconciliation of the sectarian tensions of the play in so far as Willy now runs to help fetch a Catholic priest and the entire group on stage murmur a Catholic prayer of contrition. Despite the many awkwardnesses of the play, and the total absence of any consideration of the relationship between sectarianism and the state, McLarnon's narrative does suggest, very forcefully, that fanatic anti-Catholicism is a dangerous force and must be rejected.

For unionists, McLarnon's play was an outrageous and strident caricature of the hallowed traditions of Ulster loyalism. The *Belfast Telegraph* described *The Bonefire* as 'a vomit of disgust'; CEMA had been involved in funding the Ulster Group Theatre where the play was being performed, and the newspaper considered that it was now inappropriate for CEMA to be so associated. In particular, it argued that McLarnon's play should not be allowed to represent Northern Ireland at the Edinburgh festival (*Belfast Telegraph*, 20 August 1959: 1). Publicly, CEMA stated its removal from the controversy, but a special memorandum sent by its General Secretary, J. Lewis Crosby, to the Minister for Finance sought to reassure the cabinet as a whole that the Ulster Group Theatre had been instructed to maintain entirely separate accounts: one for the ordinary business of the theatre, another for McLarnon's play. On no account, therefore, was *The Bonefire* to be subsidized by public funds. While CEMA did not wish to act as a state censor, the memorandum continues, it retained, nevertheless, a formidable instrument of control: the power to provoke 'the bankruptcy of a theatre under present conditions' by refusing to renew its subsidy against financial loss (PRONI: ED 13/1/2033, Memo 16 October 1958). Whether *The Bonefire* should be sent to the Edinburgh Festival or not was a controversy that only abated when Guthrie himself insisted that any change to the script would result in the immediate removal of his name from the production (*Belfast Telegraph*, 19 August 1958: 4). Guthrie's defiance marks an important change. The previous long-standing consensus in Northern Ireland by which controversial social issues had been silently excluded from the theatre no longer existed. To the contrary, it had now become a matter of artistic integrity that the dramatist *should* be allowed to represent issues as religious discrimination and sectarianism.

It is important, however, not to exaggerate Stormont's hostility to the theatre. *The Bonefire* may have been criticized because of its portrayal of loyalist Protestant organizations, but its première, like many others, amounted to a semi-state occasion attended by the Governor of Northern Ireland, Lord Wakehurst, as well as various cabinet ministers and senior unionist officials (*Belfast Telegraph*, 19 August 1958: 3). Indeed, Lord Wakehurst, who also served as patron of CEMA, took a personal interest in *The Bonefire* and wrote to McKee the next day with a list of points suggesting ways in which McLarnon's play might be improved. Moreover, while withdrawal of CEMA funding constituted a formidable weapon of unionist control, the Council also recognized (at least publicly) the need to develop a more representative funding policy: 'before adequate financial assistance is forthcoming the theatre in Northern Ireland must come to be regarded *by all* as an essential service to the public' (Lewis-Crosby 1959: 23). Criticism of the representation of sectarianism on the stage, then, was less a question of a blanket unionist insistence that the topic should not be dealt with, but a concern that its *politics* should be transcended. This was also, more or less, what *The Bonefire* had achieved. But what was so objectionable about McLarnon's narrative is the intensity with which sectarianism is registered as an irrational atavistic force. The main fault of McLarnon's *The Bonefire*, concluded the *Belfast Telegraph* review, lay in its failure 'to rise above the problem that it states' and thereby not provide its audience with an adequate 'release' (*Belfast Telegraph*, 19 August 1958: 3). Or, as Wakehurst's admonitory note to McKee put it, 'the Ulster situation must not be allowed to get out of hand [in the play]. It gives local colour and framework but no more' (PRONI: D 2435/2/7: Letter from Lord Wakehurst to Ritchie McKee).

In other aspects of the public sphere, the unionist government at Stormont continued to regulate and exclude any expressions of sympathy or solidarity with republican and nationalist political demands (O'Leary and McGarry 1993: 134–5). Analysis of the BBC archives in Belfast indicates that despite liberalization of Northern Ireland broadcasting policy in the period 1948–69, the subject of partition could not be raised as an issue, and religious discrimination was hardly ever discussed (Cathcart 1984: 171–2). In April 1959 a major controversy arose following the showing of the BBC television documentary *Small World* in which the Abbey Theatre actress Siobhán McKenna questioned Stormont's legitimacy and stated her unambiguous support for 'the idealistic young men of the IRA' (*Belfast Telegraph*, 27 April 1959: 7). Outraged that a publicly funded body such as the BBC should be used to ventilate support for an organization committed to the violent destruction of the Northern Ireland state, the Prime Minister (Lord Brookeborough) dispatched a delegation to London headed by Ritchie McKee (now wearing his other hat as national governor of Northern Ireland's BBC). This resulted in a punitive banning of the second instalment of the programme (*Belfast Telegraph*, 2 May 1959: 6) which, it was freely admitted, contained no reference to the IRA, to Northern Ireland, to religious discrimination or to any possible source of nationalist grievance (*Belfast Telegraph*, 1 May 1959: 1). Nevertheless, and despite strong protest from some Labour MPs at Westminster, unionist opinion remained intransigently unanimous: McKee's decision had been the correct response.

Less than one week later, McKee provoked an entirely different reaction when he attempted to apply a similar tactic in relation to the theatre. Acting now in his capacity as Chairman of the Ulster Group Theatre's board of directors, McKee ordered the immediate suppression of Sam Thompson's play *Over the Bridge* on the grounds that any performance of that play was likely to result in civil disturbances. What resulted instead was a major public controversy. Because McKee was also a prominent unionist supporter, the Vice-President of CEMA as well as the head of CEMA's drama sub-committee, his suppression of the Group Theatre production was regarded by many as badly disguised state censorship. Three other Group Theatre directors – James Ellis, Maurice O'Callaghan, and Harold Goldblatt – resigned in protest against McKee's action, and an acrimonious dispute concerning political interference in the arts took place within CEMA. The dispute resulted in a victory for McKee and led to the resignation of the secretary general of CEMA, J. Lewis-Crosby, in October 1959. Thompson himself took the Group Theatre to court in a successful legal action concerning breach of contract, with Thompson arguing that *Over the Bridge* had been formally accepted for production by the Group Theatre's artistic director, James Ellis, in 1958. In the meantime, a special theatre company (Over the Bridge Productions) was established to perform the play at an alternative location. Swamped by offers of production, Thompson had no difficulty in finding a venue, and in January 1960 *Over the Bridge* was produced in a spectacular and lucrative production at the Empire Theatre in Belfast. Directed by James Ellis, this production was one of the most expensive in Northern Ireland's history and attracted a total of 42,000 spectators with an average of 1,200 per performance (Mengel 1986: 310).

That Ellis's production was so popular and that it took place despite initial unionist opposition is the reason why *Over the Bridge* is now widely considered as a *cause célèbre* in the cultural history of the Northern Ireland state. As with Alan Simpson's controversial production of Tennessee Williams's *The Rose Tattoo* in 1957 at the Pike Theatre in Dublin, the 1960 Belfast production of *Over the*

Bridge tends to be regarded as an important turning point in the history of Northern Ireland's cultural modernization. And just as the Simpson production is taken as heralding the liberal era of the Fianna Fáil leader, Seán Lemass, the success of *Over the Bridge* appears to mark the demise of Lord Brookeborough's style of dogmatic unionism and the emergence of the new, progressive face of unionism under Captain Terence O'Neill. More importantly, both productions are viewed as establishing, or re-establishing, the inherent neutrality of theatre as a social and cultural institution. McKee's attempted suppression of *Over the Bridge*, like the attempted criminal prosecution of Alan Simpson, is seen as a recidivist and unusual exception.

Thompson's play addresses the issue of sectarianism by means of a sequence of narrative deferrals. Set in a Belfast shipyard, the action begins with a group of Protestant trade-unionist dockers debating the relationship between the socialist ideals of the movement and what is seen as a Northern Ireland *realpolitik* of anti-Catholic discrimination. Thus a candidate for the position of union organizer, Warren Baxter, maintains that the only reason that he will be elected is because his opponent is a Catholic. This cynical manipulation of sectarian prejudice is opposed by Rabbie White who points to their seventy-year-old colleague, Davy Mitchell, as an exemplar of trade union principles transcending discrimination. But when all three men are confronted by an actual dispute they share the same approach. Even though the dispute centres on the victimization by a loyalist worker (Archie Kerr) of a Roman Catholic (Peter O'Boyle), the three men are unanimous that both Kerr and O'Boyle are equally to blame and that the issue cannot be dealt with through the formal mechanisms of the trade union. It does not occur to them either that O'Boyle is in an absolute minority (he is also the only Catholic character in the play), or that the dispute itself is concerned exclusively with O'Boyle's political identity. Kerr describes O'Boyle as a republican and a 'member of an illegal organisation' (the 1956 outlawing of Sinn Féin meant that the two were often synonymous) whereas O'Boyle's accusation against Kerr is that these are slanders by which Kerr is stirring up sectarian hatred against him.

The fundamental problem of the narrative is that of establishing the political identity of a vulnerable minority. But this is presented as a question whose answer is undecidable. The result is a series of narrative deferrals. Thus when no progress ensues from an attempt to have Kerr and O'Boyle confront each other directly there is no option except for Davy to agree reluctantly to refer the matter to a union branch meeting. The meeting never takes place. It, in turn, is deferred by means of the play's recourse to a related anxiety concerning the political identity of working-class Catholics in Northern Ireland: the spectre of republican violence. Rumoured to be the work of the IRA, a shipyard explosion kills a Protestant worker and results in the routine mass expulsion of all Catholics. This *deus ex machina* effect, and O'Boyle's responding decision to stay at work and not be intimidated, further shifts the audience's attention from a simple case of sectarian discrimination to the more ambiguous and unresolvable question of O'Boyle's political identity. In one scene O'Boyle is described as behaving 'hysterically' and violently losing his temper with the Protestant mob who are demanding his immediate expulsion. In another, and the only scene featuring on-stage physical violence, O'Boyle hurls a hammer at the mob leader. Portrayed as a mixture of petulant and violent obduracy, O'Boyle's militancy results in precisely that which he had earlier been accused of: dividing the trade union membership by means of subversive political protest. This focus on O'Boyle as a disruptive force is increased by its coincidence with Kerr's newfound moderation. Now solicitous of the welfare of all Catholics Kerr joins his colleagues in urging O'Boyle to give in to the mob's demands. When O'Boyle persists in his refusal to accept expulsion, Baxter, White and Kerr argue that they are no longer able to help him. The threat that this poses to the union is indicated by Davy Mitchell's insistence that he has been left with no option but to defy the mob and join O'Boyle in his protest. The result is a brutal offstage attack in the penultimate scene leading to Mitchell's death and O'Boyle's unspecified injury.

Ironically, therefore, O'Boyle's active resistance to sectarian victimization suggests his association with a republican politics which is presented, in turn, as undermining the validity of that resistance. Minority protest regarding sectarian discrimination seems petty or irrelevant in the face of the murder of the elderly Protestant trade unionist; in fact, Mitchell's death is partly a result of that protest. In short, the narrative action of *Over the Bridge* may be said to reinforce what was almost a leitmotif in the unionist rhetoric at Stormont in the 1950s: the discrediting or criminalizing of minority protest by associating it with violence. One instance of this, for example, was the tendency of unionist politicians to use the word 'sectarian' to refer exclusively to nationalist protests *against* political discrimination against Catholics. Moreover, in so far as *Over the Bridge* suggests that religious discrimination is ultimately determined by individual conscience and not by politics, the play reinforces the dominant unionist belief that religious discrimination cannot and should not be legislated against.

But if the narrative action of *Over the Bridge* works to support unionism, why, in that case, did McKee act so precipitously to suppress the play? One reason why this question has not received the critical attention that it deserves is because of the widespread assumption that the rehearsal copy of the play (read by McKee in May 1959) is identical to the (published) version performed in January 1960. This impression was conveyed by early press reports and in subsequent years it has been reinforced by Stewart Parker's introduction to the published text of *Over the Bridge* as well as by an otherwise meticulous study of Thompson by Hagal Mengel (1986). Nevertheless, the rehearsal copy of *Over the Bridge*[10] indicates an important change to the play's final scene. In the rehearsal copy of the play, Mitchell's death is followed by Baxter distancing himself from Davy's trade union position and accepting his foreman's offer of promotion. As a result of this, and of Baxter's failure to show solidarity with Mitchell, he is rejected 'hysterically' by Marian (Mitchell's daughter) to whom he had been engaged:

MARIAN: (*Contemptuously*). Share my bed with you? Bring your brats into the world. I wouldn't let you touch me, you would defile and debase any decency my father taught me. (*Raising her voice.*) You would corrupt me you filthy scoundrel. Get out of my house. (*Warren tries to take hold of her but Marian steps back sobbing.*) Don't touch me, stay away from me.

(BCL: Rehearsal copy of *Over the Bridge*: 63)

The resemblance between Marian's emotionally strident and 'hysterical' language and the earlier depiction of O'Boyle serves – albeit inadvertently – as an unsettling reminder of that which the action as a whole had so far attempted to defer: the worry that the obdurate persistence of anti-sectarian protest might force Protestant social identity into a crisis by foregrounding its privileged relationship to the state. Thompson's initial ending to the play, then, leaves the audience with an unresolved dilemma. While Mitchell's death implies a violent annihilation of identity as one response to anti-sectarian protest, Baxter's rejection by Marian suggests that the only other alternative is a damaging complicity. The disquieting implications of the rehearsal copy's final scene also help to contextualize McKee's actions since the rehearsal manuscript ends with an unresolved crisis of identity that undermines the reassuring effects of the previous narrative. In accord with Louis Althusser's famous comment on Brechtian dramaturgy, the play's initial inconclusiveness functions so as to disrupt the spectator's 'self-recognition' leading to the 'inexhaustible work of criticism in action' (Althusser 1982: 151). Indeed, on several occasions, McKee had made it clear to Thompson that his objection to *Over the Bridge* was to its *theatrical performance*, and not to its publication or to the possible merits of its narrative. To this extent, McKee's banning of the play was politically astute.

That it was political insight – not philistinism or class animosity (*pace* Mengel 1986: 307–8) – that was at the basis of McKee's suppression of the play is further suggested by the fact that this was the one scene that was changed in the course of its subsequent production. Working in conjunction with the play's director, James Ellis, and acting on the advice of Tyrone Guthrie, Thompson agreed to excise the final scene and replace it with the scene that appears in the published version (James Ellis, 9 December 1993; telephone conversation with author). In this *revised* and published version of the play, the focus is on the tragedy of Davy Mitchell's death. Baxter's role is entirely altered. Although he enters drunk, Baxter makes no criticism of Mitchell but, on the contrary, seems to support Marian's position through his scathing attack on the foreman (Thompson 1970: 118). Instead of attacking the uselessness of Mitchell's solidarity with O'Boyle, which, in the earlier version, was what had caused Marian to reject him, Baxter appears obsessed with the group's complicity. The point that he keeps returning to is that when Mitchell went to protest in solidarity with O'Boyle, both he and his trade union colleagues appeared powerless to do anything. This is precisely the issue – trade union complicity in religious discrimination – that Thompson's narrative goes to such extraordinary lengths to evade. But, here in the published and performed version of the play there is again a deferral. At the moment of impending crisis precipitated by Rabbie's violent rejection of Baxter's suggestion of complicity (Thompson 1970: 118–19), confrontation is avoided by the timely appearance of a Protestant clergyman.

BAXTER: A man told me yesterday that he walked away, and so did hundreds of his so-called respectable workmates because they said it was none of their business. None of their business, Rabbie, that's what they said. Then they walked away, and that's what frightens me, [*he sobs quietly*] they walked away! [*Rabbie puts his arm around Warren's shoulder and leads him to one side.*

The Clergyman comes forward and opens his Prayer book. They all bow their heads as he speaks the prayer for the dead. The curtain falls.]

(Thompson 1970: 119)

Thompson's play ends not with the interrogation of sectarianism that its previous narrative seems constantly to anticipate and yet defer, but with an unambiguous instantiation of Protestant loyalist identity within a populist, working-class context. With an on-stage audience bowing in reverence before a Protestant clergyman, the final tableau demonstrates, almost pedantically, the theatre's continuing role in support of unionist political domination. And this would have been even more strikingly obvious if, as with all CEMA-sponsored events and most public performances in Northern Ireland, the play had been accompanied by the playing of the British national anthem. It is hardly surprising, therefore, that Ellis's production in January 1960 was so warmly and unanimously received. What had been achieved by it was no less than that consensus which CEMA had struggled throughout the 1950s to try to establish: an 'Ulster' theatre which could be seen to be representative and yet which clearly and unambiguously supported Viscount Craigavon's famous dictum: 'We are a Protestant Parliament and a Protestant state' (quoted in Phoenix 1994: 376).[11]

The popularity of *Over the Bridge* does not, therefore, signal a transition from a climate of censorship to one of artistic freedom. Rather than denote a new mood of anti-sectarianism in Northern Ireland, Thompson's achievement lies in the appropriation by *Over the Bridge* of some of the principal issues of nationalist protest in Northern Ireland (in particular, anti-Catholic violence and religious discrimination in employment) – and the play's disarticulation of these from their main political expression in republican and nationalist protest. This is a *coup de théâtre* for the state in the sense that the theatre might be said to include nationalist minority interests while simultaneously reaffirming the terms of that minority's exclusion. As far as the continuing hegemony of Ulster unionism was concerned, Thompson's play offered a reassurance. It was a reassurance that was all the more welcome because it occurred in the face of the dramatic rise of the Northern Ireland Labour Party in the period 1958–62 and the growth of an increasingly vocal Catholic middle class (Lee 1989: 413; O'Leary and McGarry 1993: 162; Bew *et al.* 1995: 17, 128–9). The socialist and nationalist threat implicit in the play's treatment of sectarianism and the strong labour emphasis of Thompson's working-class characters, idioms and setting are superseded by the play's portrayal of sectarianism as arising from a Catholic/nationalist grievance, and the serendipitous final scene in which overt support is expressed for an overarching Protestant identity.

But if, from a unionist point of view, the ideological success of *Over the Bridge* depends on the play's association of minority protest with political subversion, this was, in fact, an association which was quickly becoming redundant (see Lee 1989: 414). Thompson's play tends to ignore the extent to which nationalist protest in this period was already switching from a campaign of anti-partitionism to an insistence on the provision of basic civil rights within the Northern Ireland state. The evident failure of the IRA border campaign (1956–62), the effects of the 1944 Education Act (which resulted in better educational opportunities for Catholics in Northern Ireland) and the more conciliatory foreign policy of the Dublin government under Lemass all contributed to the new 'civil rights' emphasis of the early 1960s. From this point on, O'Leary and McGarry remark, 'Catholics began to interact more with state institutions and expect more from them' (O'Leary and McGarry 1993: 157).[12] The history of the Lyric Players Theatre and, in particular, its attempt to establish a broadly-based nationalist cultural institution with state support, provides graphic illustration of the many problems facing such an interaction.

Once again, the problem was that theatre was regarded both as a public space to be contested and as an institution amenable to interaction with the institutions of the state. Set up by Mary and Pearse O'Malley in March 1960 as a non-profit cultural foundation, the Lyric Players Theatre Trust had formerly existed as the Lyric Players Group, a private theatre group housed and funded by the O'Malleys since March 1951. Like National Unity, a precursor of the civil rights movement set up in Belfast in 1959, the Lyric Players Group was associated with a student society at Queen's University Belfast and originated following an impromptu Christmas entertainment organized by the O'Malleys for the University's Newman Society.[13] Through Mary O'Malley, its main director and designer, the Lyric Players Group was influenced both by Austin Clarke's Dublin-based Lyric Theatre Company (1944–52), which specialized in the performance of verse drama, and by the socialist-oriented New Theatre Group in Dublin which concentrated on plays dealing with labour issues. This combination of influences was reflected in the Lyric's formalist commitment to the autonomy of the aesthetic *and* in its view that the theatre might also provide the impetus for an all-Ireland (32 county) cultural movement. As the O'Malleys took pains to point out, the Lyric Players Group was modelled both on the early National Theatre Society at the Abbey Theatre in Dublin and on Belfast's early Ulster Literary Theatre. Four honorary directors had been chosen with this dual focus in mind: Padraic Colum, a poet and dramatist who had earlier been associated with the Abbey; Rutherford Mayne, a former writer for the Ulster Literary Theatre; John Irvine, a (Protestant) poet from Belfast; and Thomas Kinsella, a (Catholic) poet from Dublin. The enterprise was planned deliberately, therefore, so as to include both Roman Catholic and Protestant, nationalist and unionist. Nationalist in so far as it stressed an all-Ireland cultural heritage, the Lyric nevertheless went to considerable lengths to ensure that this could not be interpreted as a threat to the Northern Ireland state or as excluding Protestants.

Despite the broadly socialist and nationalist associations of its founders, the Lyric remained implacably opposed to 'political drama', 'propaganda', or any view that art might be politically determined.

> A propaganda play or a trivial farce or comedy may be thought provoking or entertaining but it will hardly ever be seriously considered as 'art'. . . . The [Lyric's] restriction to poetic drama was quite deliberate. Interpreted widely, however, it did allow us to include all the world classics (if we so desired) and any good contemporary play could be included on the basis of poetic content in the internal structure. It permitted the total exclusion of all bad or trivial plays whether written in prose or verse.
>
> (quoted in O'Malley 1988: 148)

Adopting this aesthetic, however, did not imply a belief that art and politics could, *in practice*, be separated. On the contrary, the claim that the theatre should remain politically neutral functioned strategically for the Lyric Players Theatre as a means of resisting unionist control. Thus when Ernest Blythe, managing director of the Abbey Theatre and former Irish cabinet minister, sent the O'Malleys a memorandum that urged the need for nationalists in Northern Ireland to accept the authority of the state by turning their attention to cultural pursuits such as the theatre,[14] Pearse O'Malley flatly rejected Blythe's injunctions by pointing out the extent to which they ignored the fundamental injustices and coerciveness of the Stormont state (Blythe 1997: 40–4). The Lyric Theatre's assertion of a Yeatsian model of the theatre as existing outside of immediate political concerns functioned to protect its autonomy from what was perceived as an all-pervasive atmosphere of unionist consensus.

But the problem with the Lyric, at least as far as Ulster unionism was concerned, was precisely this claim to political independence. It was unimportant that the Lyric performed exclusively verse or 'poetic' drama, subscribed to an aesthetic that shunned politics, or attracted an audience that was almost exclusively middle class. What was important was that it was a centre of nationalist cultural expression and that by the 1950s it had expanded into a vibrant cultural enterprise. The Lyric Theatre initiative involved a diversity of cultural projects that included paying regular and much acclaimed theatre visits to Dublin, an Irish handicrafts shop in Belfast, a music academy, an art gallery, and an all-Ireland literary magazine, *Threshold*. Fastidiously avoiding any direct criticism of the Northern Ireland state, the third issue of *Threshold* argues that 'a balanced integration of all social factors is necessary for healthy progress' and points to Padraic Colum's essay 'The Nation and the State' as a further exemplification. Colum argues that the conflation of the terms 'nation' and 'state' makes the state appear 'beyond human judgement' and that the terms should now be separated (Colum 1957: 34). Whereas the state is characterized by *power*, the nation is a community formed by a particular environment characterized by *piety*: 'piety towards the past, its traditions, its landscape' (Colum 1957: 34). Colum's point is that the state should acknowledge (and diffuse) its natural enmity towards nationalism by becoming more pluralistic and tolerant: 'our state should be pluralistic, recognising varieties of interest, not fixed in a singleness that rightly takes the image of a stone' (Colum 1957: 37). Stormont and Northern Ireland are not mentioned by name in the article, but the desire for political reform is unambiguous. Indeed, what the Lyric Players Group set out to achieve at a cultural level could be described as the equivalent to the political objectives of the early civil rights movement. This was not at all the destruction of the Northern Ireland state, but rather its reformation in a manner that would allow for equal rights and a proper role within the state for Catholics and nationalists.

The Lyric Players Group may have been unwilling to confront Stormont directly, but the implications of its cultural objectives were none the less clear. What was sought was a pluralist, non-discriminatory state in which nationalist self-expression could freely exist. The decision of the Lyric to become professional in 1960 brought this cultural project to an important new stage. On the one hand, the decision was the practical extension of all that had been achieved by the theatre throughout the 1950s and its corresponding need for better resources. On the other, the decision by the Lyric to become professional meant assuming an openly public role within the state. In the words of the O'Malleys themselves the Lyric Theatre would become 'part of the community' (Mary O'Malley, BBC interview 1966; quoted in O'Malley 1988: 25) and 'an appropriate theatre in a permanent form for Northern Ireland' (NUIG: O'Malley Archive: Letter, August 1982, P. Pearse O'Malley to J. Noel Spiers). Such a role meant engaging directly with the institutions of the Northern Ireland state and, specifically, with CEMA and the Arts Council for Northern Ireland (ACNI). The O'Malleys were both aware that if the Lyric secured CEMA/ACNI funding, the theatre would then come into conflict with the Stormont government policy concerning the obligatory playing of the national anthem. But they also believed that this policy might soon change and that the likelihood of a direct confrontation would not arise (Dr Pearse O'Malley, telephone conversation with author, 19 September 1994). If the Lyric did receive community and ACNI support without any political strings attached, it would mean the success of its attempt to achieve a cultural space free from unionist interference and suppression.

But establishing the Lyric as a cultural project that would serve as a semi-independent public space existing outside of Stormont's political control merely exacerbated unionist suspicions that the Lyric represented a nationalist threat to Northern Ireland's cultural integrity. (Such suspicions may well have been fuelled by Mary O'Malley's role as an outspoken Labour councillor in the 1950s, as an opponent to Ulster regionalism, and as one of the organizers of the 1953 PEN protest.) Nor were these suspicions allayed by the appointment of a Capital Development Trust composed of key members of Northern Ireland's unionist establishment and business community. As late as 1966, and with ACNI support not yet forthcoming, a professional fund-raising advisory group to the Lyric concluded that the greatest difficulty facing the theatre's attempt to become professional lay in 'the erroneous belief that the theatre was in some way linked with politics' (NUIG: O'Malley Archive; Bostok Memorandum, July 1966: 27).

The main difficulties for the Lyric in this period – fund-raising and locating a site on which a permanent theatre might be built –

stemmed, therefore, from the ambiguous relationship of the Lyric to the Northern Ireland state. At one of the earliest meetings of the Lyric trustees in October 1960, this problem arose in a discussion concerning the playing of the (British) national anthem. While the matter was temporarily put to rest with the acceptance of a compromise amendment indicating that the anthem would be played 'at the discretion of the Trustees, at any outside function inside Northern Ireland' (NUIG: O'Malley Archive; Minutes, 28 November 1960) the issue arose again following the eventual granting of an ACNI subsidy in 1968. Mary and Pearse O'Malley opposed any change to the theatre's policy of not playing the British national anthem while other members of the Trust argued that the continuation of such a policy would jeopardize any future financial support for the theatre. A majority vote approved of the playing of the national anthem in certain (ceremonial) circumstances and the anthem was played at the first public performance of the theatre on 28 October 1968. The following day Mary and Pearse O'Malley resigned from the theatre management in protest. (Pearse O'Malley subsequently withdrew his resignation on the under-standing that the national anthem would be restricted to ceremonial protocol only, and that the performance on 28 October may have fallen into this exceptional category.) But in October 1969 a further controversy arose. A fund-raising group composed of local businessmen offered to support the Lyric provided the trustees signed a document requiring them to 'gratefully acknowledge that the funds which have been allocated to it [the Lyric] by the Arts Council were placed at the disposal of the Government of Northern Ireland' and that the national anthem 'was accepted as part of the ceremonial involved on special official and public occasions' (NUIG: O'Malley Archive: Minutes, 6 October 1969). Put simply, the theatre had to articulate, in unambiguous terms, its loyalty and gratitude to the Northern Ireland state. That this demand was made in the midst of widespread protests by the civil rights movement against key aspects of the Stormont administration was not accidental. Three of the trustees, including Pearse O'Malley, refused to sign the statement on the grounds that to do so would be to compromise the theatre's political independence:

> Dr. O'Malley was asked to sign the statement proposed by the potential Fund Raising Committee. . . . Dr. O'Malley again reiterated his point of view which had been made clear at previous meetings. The Trustees could not abdicate their

authority and responsibility to any outside group, no matter how well meaning. When such a group in fact places a condition on their support which could undoubtedly affect the independence of the theatre, the situation did not permit of compromise.

(NUIG: O'Malley Archive; Minutes, 23 October 1969)

O'Malley's refusal to sign led to the resignation of four unionist members of the theatre's seven trustees. The *Belfast Telegraph* (15 November 1969) condemned O'Malley for not resigning himself, whereas the Dublin-based *Sunday Press* (16 November 1969) argued that the incident was indicative of a corrupt political regime. For proponents and opponents alike, O'Malley's actions suggested an analogy between the Lyric and the general objectives of the civil rights movement. Like many nationalist and civil rights leaders of the time, the Lyric may have been willing to co-operate with the state up to a point. But what it was not willing to do, however, was voluntarily endorse traditional practices – symbolic or otherwise – of unionist coercion.

8

NATIONAL THEATRE AND THE POLITICAL CRISIS IN NORTHERN IRELAND, 1968–92

A hoarse Northern voice in the darkness screams accusations
at us, unrehearsed and unrepentant, and the tried and sure
and familiar script suddenly hangs limp in the actor's hand.
(Tomás MacAnna, programme note to Abbey Theatre
production of Brecht's *The Plebians Rehearse the Uprising*,
2 December 1970)

In July 1966, the President of Ireland, the now elderly Eamon de
Valera, conducted the official opening of the newly rebuilt Abbey
Theatre. Among the ensuing ceremonies was the performance of a
composite history of the NTS which included a parody of the 1907
and 1911 protests against *The Playboy of the Western World*, as well
as a lampoon of Cardinal Logue's condemnation of *The Countess
Cathleen* in 1899. That this revue took place apparently much to the
delight of the assembled state dignitaries indicates the extent to
which the cultural role of Ireland's national theatre had now changed
(*Irish Times*, 18 July 1966: 1). Like the occasion in 1968 when the
Abbey Theatre players donated to the Pope (apparently without
irony) a white, leather-bound copy of Synge's *The Playboy of the
Western World* (Kilroy 1971: 97), what was here demonstrated – on
the stage and in the auditorium – was the accelerating momentum of
Irish modernization. Not only had Irish audiences stopped rioting,
they were now laughing at the very idea of such behaviour. With its
championing of Brechtian dramaturgy at the Peacock (Welch 1999:
186), its attempt to establish a working-class theatre project in the
Cabra area of Dublin in 1967, and the strong socialist emphasis
of the newly established Abbey Theatre Playwright's Workshop,
Ireland's national theatre demarcated an ambitious cultural agenda.
Blythe's conception of the NTS as a symbol of national consensus
was now replaced by a range of cultural functions. By the late 1960s,

191

that is, the NTS presented itself not only as a forum for national representation, but as a space for artistic experiment, and as a catalyst for social and political change. Apart from the 1966 visit by the octogenarian de Valera, the newly built Abbey Theatre appeared to have transcended the long years of its nationalist beginnings.

This glimpse of post-nationalist cultural euphoria did not last for long. Political destabilization following the Northern Ireland civil rights marches in 1968–9 not only presented an immediate and serious threat to the nationalist and modernizing ideologies of the Irish state, but had far-reaching implications for the idea of an Irish national theatre. Ireland's traditional nationalist rhetoric that had for years proclaimed its solidarity with the Roman Catholic minority in Northern Ireland (and which in 1968 had been revived by senior Fianna Fáil politicians like George Colley and Kevin Boland) was now rapidly decoupled from the Irish government's attempt to confine the disruptive effects of the crisis to the northern side of the border. Despite the Fianna Fáil government's stated enthusiasm for the goals of the civil rights movement, and Taoiseach Jack Lynch's emotional description of partition as 'a deep throbbing weal across the heart and soul of Ireland' (quoted in Bew *et al.* 1989: 98), it was Lynch's own Fianna Fáil administration that announced support for British government policy in Northern Ireland in October 1970 and that, two months later, declared Ireland's preparedness to reintroduce internment. And, whereas by 1967 the modernization of Ireland in the late 1950s and 1960s had culminated in an unprecedented liberalization of Ireland's literary and film censorship laws (Tobin 1984: 161–2), the early 1970s witnessed the reintroduction of an array of draconian censorship legislation to deal with the effects of the conflict in Northern Ireland. Restrictions such as Section 31 of the Broadcasting Act (described by one commentator as 'more far-reaching than anything since the wartime censorship' (Farrell 1986: 18)) now served as a blanket prohibition of any expression that could be construed as promoting the aims of any organization that used or advocated violence. For practical purposes this meant the IRA and its political wing, Sinn Féin. Along with the Irish government's amendments to the Offences Against the State Act in 1972 and 1974, this legislation soon led to an atmosphere in which support or sympathy for the nationalist minority in Northern Ireland was regarded with suspicion. Representing the nation in the theatre was now an acutely sensitive political issue raising, once again, an awkward problem of definition: what exactly was the nation in question?

The tension between the government's traditional nationalist rhetoric, its liberal ideology of modernization, and its immediate political hostility to nationalist protest in Northern Ireland was strikingly evident at the Peacock Theatre in the 1970s. In September 1970, for example, the NTS's artistic director for the Peacock, Tomás MacAnna, announced that the 1970–1 programme of plays would reflect a policy of 'total involvement' and that 'political satire, historical comment and documentary experiment' would be the season's principal ingredients (*Irish Times*, 7 September 1970: 12). And yet an incident that took place in the course of that season's opening night illustrates the extent that such 'involvement' was circumscribed by a growing anxiety concerning political control. The production in question, a revue entitled *A State of Chassis*, written by Eugene Watters, John D. Stewart and Tómas MacAnna, consisted of a series of sketches that gave an impression of the equal absurdity of civil rights protesters and of loyalist reaction. It satirized, in particular, the Irish republican, civil rights leader and Westminster MP, Bernadette Devlin who had recently been arrested in the course of a 48 hour police siege on Derry's Bogside, an area known in August 1969 as 'Free Derry'. The opening night's performance of *A State of Chassis* was interrupted when two fellow civil rights activists (Eamon McCann of the Derry Labour Party and John Kelly of the Belfast Citizen's Defence Committee) climbed onto the stage and condemned the revue for its caricature of minority politics in Northern Ireland (*Irish Times*, 17 September 1970: 1). As the actors attempted to ignore the interruption and carry on with their performance, the protesters handed them and the audience leaflets calling for the release of all incarcerated civil rights activists. The demonstration in the theatre ended when the voices of the protesters were drowned out by the audience's slow handclap and when, to background applause, McCann and Kelly were physically ejected by MacAnna and a group of spectators.

The most interesting feature of the 1970 protest at the Peacock Theatre, as far as Irish cultural history is concerned, is the intensity with which it was immediately condemned. Describing the protest as a 'riot,' the *Irish Times* and the *Belfast Telegraph* characterized McCann's and Kelly's intervention as an 'ignorant,' 'bigoted' attempt 'to upstage' a legitimate performance. Objected to in particular was the taking control and redefinition of the theatre as itself a space for public protest. For both newspapers, a comment made by one of the protesters (Eamonn McCann), 'Nobody can act here in that it does not mean anything' (quoted in the *Irish Times*, 17 September 1970: 1) implied a repudiation of the role of the institutional theatre as such and it was this, they argued, that now had to be unequivocally rejected. Most commentators agreed. Because of its use of the confrontational and disruptive tactics of political protest and a theatrical 'happening' in order to challenge the consensual, 'distancing' process established by the revue (Friel 1972: 305; Maxwell 1973: 91–2), the physical ejection of the protesters was an action that was heartily approved. Acknowledged by all involved in the controversy (protesters, ejectors and commentators) is a close connection between the aesthetics of the theatre and the politics of the state. Just as what was at issue in the establishment of alternative republican and socialist administrations in 'Free Derry' and the 'No Go' areas of West Belfast from 1970–4 was the legitimacy and authority of a state-oriented and constitutional politics, what was at stake in the widespread opposition to the protest at the Peacock in September 1970, was the issue of the NTS's claim to representativeness.

MacAnna's emphasis on the need for a satiric distancing from the insurrectionary mood of republican nationalists in Northern Ireland may well have coincided with the main direction of government policy, but it was not a view that was wholeheartedly shared by others at the NTS. That the Abbey Theatre's soon-to-be appointed artistic director, Lelia Doolan, publicly supported the protest, whereas MacAnna, of course, did not, indicates the extent of the divisions. Additional evidence of conflicting political agendas is to be found in the controversial removal of the national anthem from performances in 1971, the première of Hugh Leonard's mordantly anti-nationalist farce, *The Patrick Pearse Motel* (March 1971) and, in the same theatre season, a commemorative evening to mark the fiftieth anniversary of the death of the nationalist hunger-striker Terence MacSwiney (October 1970) as well as a (failed) attempt by the Abbey Theatre staff to organize a benefit night 'in aid of the refugees from the North of Ireland' (Abbey Theatre Minute Books 1971: n.p.).[1] MacAnna's use of the phrase 'Brechtian Yeatsian' to describe what he claimed was the NTS's tradition of remaining aloof from political engagement (programme note to Brecht's *The Plebians Rehearse the Uprising*, Abbey Theatre, 2 December 1970) manifests a similar confusion. Those responsible for artistic policy at the Abbey in the early 1970s were now beset with problems very similar to those associated with the failed establishment of a national theatre in Belfast in the 1950s. Policy makers were torn between the need to show that minority protest could be represented in the theatre (and could therefore be assimilated to a politics organized in terms of the state) and concern lest, in the course of any such representation, the theatre itself might be used as a means of protest or as a forum for an alternative politics.

This was part of a wider dilemma. For many nationalist writers and intellectuals there was a growing fissure between a traditional view that literature should remain aloof from political engagement and a strong personal outrage and frustration in relation to the treatment of the minority Catholic population of Northern Ireland. One event in particular that threatened to bring this contradiction to a crisis was the shooting dead of thirteen unarmed civilians by British paratroopers on 30 January 1972. Known as 'Bloody Sunday', this incident took place when British soldiers attempted to disperse an illegal civil rights demonstration which had been held to protest against the Stormont government's introduction of internment in August 1971. Although the Unionist government had banned the demonstration, 20,000 people were nonetheless in attendance. Popular reaction in Ireland to the killings on Bloody Sunday included protest marches organized in most cities and towns across the state, a general strike and the impromptu burning down of the British Embassy in Dublin. In the months following Bloody Sunday, nationalist outrage at what had happened was directed at the official British government tribunal of inquiry conducted by Lord Widgery and then at Widgery's published conclusions. These conclusions exonerated the British Army by claiming that several of the dead civilians may have been carrying weapons, and by arguing that ultimate responsibility for the killings lay not with the soldiers, but with the organizers of the illegal protest march (Widgery 1972: 38–9). That Widgery's findings were promptly contradicted by a group of international lawyers affiliated to the United Nations (see Dash 1972) merely underlined the widespread nationalist view that the Widgery tribunal of inquiry was an elaborate cover-up.

And yet, despite the political effect of Bloody Sunday in galvanizing nationalist outrage at British 'law and order' in Northern Ireland, the killing of the thirteen civilians also inaugurated a reinvigorated counter-insurgency project directed primarily against republicans. Now with the imprimatur of the Irish government (Deane 1992: 12), the key strategy of this policy was that of containing 'the troubles' by criminalizing all forms of extra-constitutional minority protest (see O'Dowd et al. 1982). In Northern Ireland the British government introduced no-jury

'Diplock' courts, and extended the Special Powers Act to include those who advocated membership of an illegal organization. In the Republic of Ireland, the government responded by establishing the juryless Special Criminal Court and by introducing the Offences Against the State (Amendment) Act. Unsurprisingly, literary and theatrical responses to Bloody Sunday, and to the conflict as a whole, were decidedly muted. As early as March 1970, the poet John Montague, writing as guest editor of *Threshold*, complained of 'a monstrous block' in soliciting Irish writers to engage with the conflict in Northern Ireland (NUIG: O'Malley Archive: John Montague to Mary O'Malley, 2 March 1970). Indeed, one of the few literary attacks on the British judicial establishment, Thomas Kinsella's satiric poem 'Butcher's Dozen', received extensive critical opprobrium, because of what was seen as its detrimentally propagandistic (i.e. anti-British) emphasis. It was in this broad cultural and political context that Brian Friel's *The Freedom of the City* was first performed at the Abbey Theatre on 20 February 1973.

Set in February 1970 in the aftermath of a banned civil rights march in Derry, many of the details of *The Freedom of the City* evoke the events that took place on Bloody Sunday and the subsequent Widgery Report: the play's three protesters (Lily, Michael and Skinner) have taken part in a banned civil rights protest and they escape from CS gas and rubber bullets by taking refuge in what they later discover is the Mayor's Parlour in the City Guildhall. Their accidental occupation of the Guildhall, widely regarded as a symbolic bastion of British colonial and unionist values in Northern Ireland, prompts an accumulation of rumour, speculation and exaggerated news reports. Liam O'Kelly, a Radio Telefís Éireann (RTE) journalist, cites 'unconfirmed reports . . . of about fifty armed gunmen' (Friel 1974: 29), a drunken nationalist balladeer alludes to 'a hundred Irish heroes' (Friel 1974: 30), and a British Army Press Officer makes reference to 'a band of terrorists . . . [of] up to forty persons' (Friel 1974: 39). Friel's narrative has the Guildhall surrounded by an array of army and police with Lily, Michael and Skinner largely oblivious to what is taking place outside. The British officer in charge of the military siege orders the three to surrender, but when they do finally emerge, with their hands raised above their heads, they are summarily gunned down. With the exception of the use of tanks (not used in Northern Ireland until 'Operation Motorman' and the ending of the 'no-go' areas of 'Free Derry' and 'Free Belfast' in July 1972) and Friel's inclusion of the 8th Infantry Brigade (Friel 1974: 49), the military operation as it is described in *The Freedom of the City* (Friel 1974: 49) bears close similarity to the military operation of Bloody Sunday (see Widgery 1972: 7).

The outcome of the action – that Lily, Michael and Skinner are shot dead – is known from the beginning: that is, the opening tableau shows the three characters sprawled grotesquely at the front of the stage, photographed, and then quickly receiving the Last Rites from a priest holding a white handkerchief (Friel 1974: 15). In this detail also, Friel's play evokes the audience's recent memory of Bloody Sunday, since one of the best known media images of that day was the photograph of a priest (Fr. Daly) waving a white handkerchief while attending to the wounded and dying. But Friel's emphasis is less on a diegesis of these events, than on an investigation of the manner of their representation. The play is a sequence of flashbacks in the course of a Widgery-like British government inquiry that concludes by exculpating the army and suggesting that the three may have emerged firing from the Guildhall.[2] Instead of concentrating the audience's attention on what might happen to the three civilians, therefore, Friel's play recasts the spectator in the role of adjudicator. The spectator's role is presented as one of assessing and reviewing as evidence a wide range of speculative and 'objective' accounts made by those who remain outside the Guildhall. Encouraged to compare what can be seen and heard to take place in the Mayor's Parlour with the many verbal commentaries and assessments of this action that are made from the outside, this dramaturgical method comes to a head when what the audience can see and hear in the theatre is contradicted by the Judge's conclusions exonerating the army. In the final scene, the spectator witnesses Lily and the others with their hands above their heads – clearly unarmed – and then a fifteen-second burst of gunfire. That the three civilians are innocent appears as obvious as the immediacy and transparency of the spectator's perception.

As with the widespread nationalist perception of the Widgery Tribunal in relation to the events of Bloody Sunday, then, the findings of the inquiry in Friel's play are shown to be consistently at odds with the action that takes place in the Guildhall. The Judge describes his procedures as 'fact-finding' and 'objective' (Friel 1974: 18), states his determination to adhere only to the immediate facts, and refuses to take into consideration the social circumstances of the three ('We are not conducting a social survey' (Friel 1974: 17)). But objectivity, in this case, conceals his willing acceptance of the way things are from the point of view of the authorities, allowing, for example, the blatant lie of the British Commanding Officer ('My lord, they emerged firing from the Guildhall' (Friel 1974: 50)) to pass without question and supporting the assumption that the occupation of the Guildhall was deliberate. Lily, Michael and Skinner are described as either 'callous terrorists' (Friel 1974: 18) or as the perpetrators of a 'misguided scheme' (Friel 1974: 18). But, in both cases, they are assumed to be guilty. Friel's technique of having the shooting take place immediately after the Judge has finished his magisterial-sounding conclusions (Friel 1974: 95–6) reinforces this impression that it is the distortions that are implicit in the Judge's 'law and order' rhetoric that lead directly to the shooting. In each of these respects, *The Freedom of the City* suggests that the presence of the British Army in Northern Ireland, along with the judicial apparatus that supports it, is not at all a solution to the conflict, but rather one of its most baneful ingredients. Indeed, it was this impression of the play that contributed to its reputation as controversially anti-British when it was first performed in London and New York.

Nevertheless, *The Freedom of the City* does not simply attack the fact-finding objectivity upon which Widgery's *Report of the Tribunal* and the play's fictional inquiry both claim to be based. To the contrary, in so far as Friel's play suggests that distortion is inextricably involved in *any* attempt at description or assessment, it works to undermine, rather than to reinforce, the basis of an all-Ireland nationalist consensus. True, much of the play's satire is directed against the British Judge's inquiry, but the arrangement of the dramatic narrative also implies that responsibility for the shooting extends to the entire nationalist community. Thus, for the RTE journalist from Dublin the occupation of the Guildhall is the subject of a sensational news story (O'Kelly describes the incident as the 'fall of the Bastille' (Friel 1974: 29)); for the Catholic Priest, the three civilians are martyrs, and for the nationalist Balladeer the situation in the Guildhall is an excuse for alternately belligerent and maudlin versions of a populist Irish nationalism (Friel 1974: 29–30, 69–70). Priest, Balladeer, Journalist and people on the street are shown as participating in various forms of representation of the incident that are inaccurate and distorting. Even in the case of those accounts that are delivered *after* the three have been killed (as in the case of the Priest's sermons and O'Kelly's funeral commentary), the play's inverted timescale suggests that their cumulative effect is somehow responsible for the shooting that takes place at the end. In short, Friel's play indicates that it is not just the Judge's inquiry that is complicit in the killings of Lily, Michael and Skinner, but the general tendency to stand back from a situation and represent it and, in particular, a contemporary Irish nationalist exploitation of this. The cumulative effect of this tendency, so the movement of the play suggests, is the killing of the three civilians. The fact-finding objectivity of the Judge (or Widgery) cannot be singled out for condemnation or satire because, Friel's play insists, it is just one version of the distorting process of representation in general.

This point is further emphasized in the neo-Brechtian scene in Act II when Lily, Michael and Skinner address the audience directly and describe the final moments before they were killed (Friel 1974: 69–73). Each of the characters' final perceptions are marked by a realization that their previous way of representing things was inadequate: Michael dies trying to articulate the word 'mistake' (Friel 1974: 71), and Skinner dies realizing the inadequacy of his 'defensive flippancy' (Friel 1974: 72). Only in the moments immediately before the shooting are they able to see things accurately:

LILY: I thought I glimpsed a tiny truth: that life had eluded me because never once in my forty-three years had an experience, an event, even a small unimportant happening been isolated, and assessed, and articulated. And the fact that this, my last experience, was defined by this perception, this was the culmination of sorrow. In a way I died of grief.

(Friel 1974: 72)

Lily's mixture of perspicaciousness and regret ('a tidal wave of regret' (Friel 1974: 71)) suggests that she believes that she never experienced her life properly because she has never been able to represent it: 'never once in my forty-three years had an experience, an event, even a small, unimportant happening been isolated, and assessed, and articulated' (Friel 1974: 72). For the audience, however, there is the additional irony that Lily's death has been brought about largely because of the same process that she most needs for herself.

As is typical of Friel's plays in general, irony is deployed as a way of undermining the possibility of a recognizable political or social engagement (see Deane 1985: 168). On the one hand, Lily's description of life in a converted warehouse with a sick husband and eleven children, and the contrast between this and the neo-Gothic extravagance of the unionist Guildhall, underlines the urgent need for radical social and political change. Skinner's 'Freedom of the City' skit (Friel 1974: 52–4, 83–6, 89–91) expresses the same need, with its satire on the complete irrelevance of Derry's unionist political establishment to the lives of the city's Catholic poor. Moreover, the coincidence between Skinner's socialist eloquence ('It's about us – the poor – the majority stirring in our sleep' (Friel 1974: 77)) and the authoritative-sounding statistics and analysis of the sociologist, Dr Dodds, indicates the play's apparent support for a socialist/republican critique remarkably similar to that which was put forward by Bernadette Devlin during her 1971 United States' visit to the imprisoned political activist, Angela Davis. Pointing out that 50 per cent of people in Catholic 'ghettoes' in Northern Ireland were unemployed and that 5 per cent of the population controlled 85 per cent of the wealth, Devlin compared her struggle to that of Davis: 'Her fight is like mine, for the liberation of her own people' (*Irish Times*, 23 February 1971: 9).

On the other hand, however, *The Freedom of the City* suggests that political formulations such as these are fundamentally inadequate because they are always a betrayal of what is seen as the essential complexity of individual experience. Thus, in Michael's case, civil rights idealism masks his desire for middle-class respectability: 'all those people marching along in silence, rich and poor, high and low, doctors, accountants, plumbers, teachers, bricklayers – all shoulder to shoulder' (Friel 1974: 43). Even Skinner, who is presented as the most politically astute of the three and whose perspective most resembles that of well-known Derry-based political activists such as Devlin and McCann, has a tendency to subvert his formulations with facetiousness, as if sensing that there is something about them that is not quite right (Friel 1974: 77–88). But it is Lily, the only female character in the play, who most clearly draws attention to the limitations of any political formulation. Her civil rights formula, 'wan man – wan vote – that's what I want' (Friel 1974: 76), is exposed as a subterfuge for the real reason why she goes on the march: her 'irrational', 'motherly' concern for her Down's Syndrome son Declan. Presented by Friel as the play's embodiment of spontaneous individuality, Lily's hope that her incurable son will be healed undermines the slick political formulae of Skinner and Dodds.

In conclusion, while *The Freedom of the City* does indeed call attention to some of the social conditions afflicting nationalist ghettoes in Derry in the early 1970s prior to British direct rule (1972), and to the way in which Northern Ireland's political and legal apparatus is weighted against this community, the play also suggests that the conflict has arisen not because of social conditions, or because of a resistance to these conditions, but because of a wider existential crisis in which individual freedom and the processes of representation exist in perpetual and tragic opposition to each other. Hence, the play's movement from the public, media-based view of the Northern Ireland crisis in the opening scene (in which the directness and immediacy of representing an event appears as easy and as familiar as the taking of a photograph) to the final tableau in which Lily, Michael and Skinner stare out into the auditorium as if confronting the spectator with their inscrutable individuality.

The final impression of *The Freedom of the City* is not one of political protest, therefore, but of an inevitable and universal complicity between the state and *all* forms of representation. This split between the complex spontaneity of the individual and the fallen world of language and representation underlines the inadequacy of any kind of sociological or political analysis. The sociologist Dodds's direct address to the audience, 'middle-class people, with deference, people like you and me' (Friel 1974: 51), encourages the spectator to share Dodds's position of analytical objectivity, but this is gradually undermined by the audience's developing awareness of the dehumanizing consequences of such objectivity. Moreover, Dodd's sociological perspective (that the Northern Ireland crisis is one version of a more widespread crisis within late capitalism) is further eroded by the fact that Dodds is oblivious to the rest of the actors. The play urges its audience not to trust any political formulation of the conflict. This is an impression that is reinforced by the effect of the final scene, when, immediately before the shooting, the three civilians stand 'across the front of the stage, looking straight out' (Friel 1974: 95) as if confronting the audience with its responsibility for what is about to take place. Any tendency that the audience might have to stand back from the situation on stage and consider the play's action analytically or objectively (let alone stand back and draw political conclusions from the conflict in Northern Ireland) is severely curtailed by its awareness that this is precisely the process that is now being condemned. The audience's 'future orientation' – its desire to make sense of the action by relating it to a particular social context – is shown to exist in violent disjunction not only to the lives of the three civilians in the play, but, by implication, to the spontaneous complexity of the individuals who are actually involved in the crisis. Friel himself cautioned that *The Freedom of the City* was 'not about Bloody Sunday,' and added that the greatest difficulty in relation to the situation in Derry in the early 1970s was the existence of a 'cliché articulation' with 'answers for everything' (quoted in *Hibernia*, 16 February 1973: 18). Rather than mark a regrettable 'narrowing of focus' in Friel's career as a dramatist (O'Toole 1985: 20), *The Freedom of the City*, and especially the correlation that it implies between representation and distortion serves as a demonstration of Friel's own frequent statements concerning the impossibility of representing the crisis in the theatre.

For the NTS in the early 1970s, then, the première of *The Freedom of the City* offered a resolution to the conflicting demands of the state's nationalist and modernizing ideologies. With a dramaturgy that incorporated neo-Brechtian audience address and expressionistic devices towards a parody of a Widgery-like tribunal of inquiry, Friel's play represented the conflict in a manner that gave vent to nationalist disquiet about political injustice in Northern Ireland and yet at the same time undermined the notion of an anti-unionist or anti-British nationalist consensus. Indeed, following the Dublin première of *The Freedom of the City* there was a conspicuous absence of plays relating to the political experience of the Catholic, nationalist population in Northern Ireland. Plays chosen for performance at the NTS theatres instead tended to portray the conflict primarily in terms of a violent assault on the individual as in Wilson John Haire's *The Bloom on the Diamond Stone* (Abbey, 1973), Patrick Galvin's *We do it for Love* (Abbey, 1976), Stewart Parker's *Catchpenny Twist* (Peacock, 1977), Graham Reid's *The Death of Humpty Dumpty* (Peacock, 1979), and *The Closed Door* (Peacock, 1980). 'Far from being successful', complained the critic Jack Holland in 1976, 'a really good play about Belfast would probably have been booed off the Abbey stage, or if a good poet ever committed himself to a work on the Northern troubles, it would in all likelihood be denounced as Republican propaganda' (*Irish Times*, 29 June 1976: 10).

One apparent exception to the tendency not to engage with the circumstances or motivation of nationalist protest and resistance in Northern Ireland is Friel's *Volunteers*, performed at the Abbey Theatre on 5 March 1975. *Volunteers* engages directly with the motivation of a group of republican internees, but in a manner that elaborates on the approach adopted in *The Freedom of the City*. While dealing with issues of immediate political importance in Northern Ireland such as republican militancy, police brutality and internment without trial, the narrative of the play's action and its setting – an archaeological excavation in Dublin – suggests that the political crisis in Northern Ireland is motivated less by issues that are specific to the history of Irish unionism, sectarianism and the British state, than by atavisms for which the whole of Ireland is responsible. Like

Seamus Heaney's *North* (1975), a book of poems that was published in the same year as the performance of *Volunteers* at the Abbey, the main emphasis of *Volunteers* is directed towards revealing Irish history as constructed according to certain recurrent motifs. The audience is left with the impression that the only way of resisting the historical inevitability within which the prisoners appear trapped is to repudiate it altogether. As with Friel's *The Freedom of the City*, however, the difficulty is that *Volunteers* seeks to convince the spectator that history is a narrative construction and open to a plurality of interpretations by means of a sequence of action that is itself predicated on the fixed assumption that the threat of republicanism is invisible, a priori, and immutable. Tautology is pervasive. While portraying republicanism as a dangerous abstraction obsessed with naïve ideas of transcendental identity, the play removes republicanism from the stage action altogether and from any sense of *its* historical context. There is a contradiction between the play's call for the deconstruction of inherited notions of historical 'truth' and the relentless naturalism of its own dramaturgy. Once again, as in the case of *The Freedom of the City*, it is the theatre spectator's inability to do anything, except watch passively the action on stage that serves as the proof that nothing, in fact, *can* be done politically.

Meanwhile, in Northern Ireland, the political role of the Lyric Players Theatre had also changed. Its perception of itself as the 'conscience of the community', its substantial increase in ACNI funding for 1970–2, and the spectacular rise in political protest altered somewhat the Lyric's previously awkward (and sometimes oppositional) relationship to the Northern Ireland state. From the early 1970s, that is, the Lyric Theatre's stance of maintaining 'independence', 'neutrality' and 'objectivity' functioned less as a means of resisting unionist political control, and more as a way of distancing the increasingly militant politics of working-class republicanism.

John Boyd's *The Flats* provides a good example of this. First performed in March 1971, this is one of the earliest attempts to represent the social identity of a Northern Ireland nationalist ghetto.[3] Its opening stage directions – the cyclorama of contemporary Belfast, off-stage singing of a civil rights ballad, and voice-over news report from Radio Free Belfast quickly establish the play's setting as the nationalist 'No-Go' area of 'Free Belfast'. The opening civil rights ballad recalls the Northern Ireland Civil Rights Association (NICRA), at its height in 1968–9 and demanding equal rights for Catholics and a reform of the RUC, and 'Radio Free Belfast' is recognizable as the NICRA radio propaganda campaign established on 17 August 1969 by the Marxist student group, People's Democracy (Deutsch and Magowan 1974: 40). More particularly, the play's title, setting and opening news bulletin recall a series of violent attacks on the Unity Flats, a predominantly nationalist area of Belfast known locally as 'the Flats.'

For contemporary audiences at the Lyric Theatre, that is, the initial civil rights ballad and mention of the threat of an attack on 'the central flats' by a mob from the Shankill Road 'in the summer of 1969' (Boyd 1981: 2) evoked a specific moment and place. As well as the civil rights marches of 1968–9, it called to mind a series of anti-Catholic sectarian attacks that took place in 1969, but also the highly sensitive political issue of Protestant loyalist violence and its relation to the Northern Ireland state. On Saturday, 2 August 1969, for example, a loyalist mob of about 1000 and supported by 200 members of the Shankill Defence Association launched a stoning attack on Unity Flats. All the windows of Unity Flats were smashed, several of the occupants were injured and there was an escalation of rioting for a further three days. Many of the details of the attack as described in Boyd's play closely resemble this incident (Boyd 1981: 4, 12, 14) which led in part to the deployment of British troops in Northern Ireland on 15 August. Other attacks took place on 27 September and 11 October. In the case of the former, loyalist mobs armed with bricks, stones and bottles were confronted by British troops and the RUC on guard outside the Flats and on 11 October loyalist gunmen opened fire, killing one RUC man (the first to be killed since 1962) and wounding several others. The British troops returned fire and shot two loyalists dead. Ironically, this attack was in response to the perceived humiliation of loyalists by the Hunt report: a British government recommendation that the RUC be reorganized and that the B-Specials (a paramilitary police force recruited almost exclusively from Protestant loyalists) should be disbanded (Lee 1989: 430; Munck 1985: 142). The 1969 attacks on the Unity Flats, therefore, were not only instances of Protestant mob sectarianism, but evidence of an emerging estrangement between loyalism and its traditional alliance with Northern Ireland's security apparatus. Despite its highly sensitive political topic, however, the first performances of *The Flats* were received without controversy and the play went on to a revival in the same 1970–1 season and became one of the Lyric's most popular productions.

Boyd's strategy for rendering anodyne the politically sensitive topic of Protestant anti-Catholic sectarianism is not just narrative deferral (as in Thompson's *Over the Bridge*), but straightforward avoidance. In this play, the spectator's attention is concentrated not on the political identity or motives of the attacking mob, but on the various responses to its threat by the mainly Catholic inhabitants of the Flats. There is no mention at all of the Shankill Defence Association, loyalist gunmen or even the RUC. Despite the specificity of the setting and frequent allusions to an impending attack, then, neither the mob nor anybody representing it ever appear on stage. The Protestant mob and its leader are merely heard as voices off, and then only very briefly, in the concluding moments of Act III.

Boyd's dramatic action is generated instead by the conflicting views of the Donnellan family as to how an attack should be dealt with. Act I begins with Joe Donnellan having arranged for his wife Kath and daughter Brid to be evacuated to the country while he and his son Gerard remain to look after the flat. Kath then refuses to leave upon her discovery that the flat has been used to smuggle guns, and that Joe and Gerard are involved with the Citizens' Defence Committee and its clandestine plans for an armed defence of the area. Opposed to all militant resistance, Kath believes that the British Army should be allowed to protect the Flats without interference and that the loyalists should be ignored. Brid and Brid's fiancé Sean support her in this. The central, undisguised concern of the play is thus the question of political authority. Is the British Army or the Citizen's Defence Committee the legitimate authority in the nationalist areas of Belfast?

Boyd's answer is a resounding affirmation of the British army. Throughout *The Flats* the nationalist politics of the Citizens' Defence Committee are presented to the audience as naïve, confused and tautological. Joe, while admitting that the flats need to be protected and that the British Army has done this well in the past (Boyd 1981: 7), also maintains that the presence of the Army is an unwanted foreign interference and that the two communities should be allowed to work out their differences by themselves. He justifies his opposition to the British Army on the basis of 'nearly a thousand years' of Irish history (Boyd 1981: 32), but is only able to explain the relevance of this history by again evoking the presence of the British Army (Boyd 1981: 33). For the nationalists in the play – Gerard, Joe and Malachi – the inexplicability of their demands and, in particular, the inability of Phil and the British captain to understand them, is presented (inanely) as the proof of their legitimacy (Boyd 1981: 62).

From this beginning, Boyd's narrative develops predictably. As with the Dublin plays of Sean O'Casey, nationalism and violence are associated repeatedly to the detriment of the family. Immediately after the Defence Committee's smuggling of guns into the flat in Act II, for example, an '*Irish tune*' (Boyd 1981: 46) is heard before a radio announcement drawing attention to the increasing likelihood of violence and, later on in this Act, a nearby bomb explosion is followed by Adam's exultant waving of the Irish tricolour (Boyd 1981: 62). There is a growing impression of an accumulating atmosphere of excitement and violence inspired by Irish nationalism and Joe's drinking increases steadily according to his involvement with the Defence Committee. Adam, also, is described as 'boozy looking' (Boyd 1981: 10) and as probably a meths drinker (Boyd 1981: 61). More importantly, political imperatives such as Joe's commitment to a revolutionary notion of history and his virulent opposition to the British Army are shown as a clouding of judgement and a way of avoiding his more immediate domestic responsibilities. For the Defence Committee and Radio Free Belfast, women and children are a nuisance to be dispensed with as quickly as possible so that their fighting can continue unimpeded (Boyd 1981: 52, 63, 84). In a scene closely reminiscent of the third act of O'Casey's *Juno and the Paycock*, for example, Kath's living room is stripped bare of its furniture by Joe, Gerard and Adam so that it can be commandeered by the Defence Committee. Finally, as the approaching mob is heard off-stage, Monica, a Protestant and close friend and neighbour of the Donnellans, is shot dead while running for help for her invalid mother.

The futility of republican and nationalist resistance is a point that is laboured extensively. As Sean carries Monica's body on stage, for example, Gerard – now the voice-off of the radio Announcer – makes an energetic appeal for non-sectarian unity:

(*Sean comes in from left. He is carrying Monica. A bullet has entered her forehead. She is dead. Very gently he lays her body down, and turns away in grief.*)

ANNOUNCER: I appeal to you . . . Do not let this happen! I am a student! My family lives in the Flats. No Catholic is an enemy because he is a Catholic. No Protestant is an enemy because he is a Protestant . . . A man's religion is his private concern. Do not be divided by religion . . . Do not be misled by leaders . . . We must unite . . . we must unite as workers . . . we must unite as Irishmen and Irish women . . . we must unite for peace and justice and for a better life. We must unite . . .

(Boyd 1981: 84)

Gerard's use of a rhetoric that closely resembles that of People's Democracy, his description of the Protestant attack on the flats as a 'crime,' and his reiterated appeal for working-class and national unity are exposed as ironic in the light of a stage action which suggests that Monica's death is the immediate and most likely consequence of such 'unity'. Moreover, since Monica is a Protestant, her death will be almost certain to exacerbate the 'crime' of sectarianism that the radio broadcast is so fervently denouncing. People's Democracy, Radio Free Belfast, the Citizens' Defence Committee, and the IRA – in short, a cross-section of the nationalist and republican resistance groups in Northern Ireland – are all shown not to have protected Belfast's working-class or to have brought it together, but rather to have increased the ways in which it is divided. In a scene that resembles the finale of McLarnon's *The Bonefire*, Boyd's play then concludes with a tableau in which Kath recites the Rosary over the Protestant Monica's dead body while Phil, a friendly British soldier, kneels prayerfully on the stage beside her.

As is clear from this summary, the main conflict of *The Flats* is not at all a sectarian or even a political one. This is not a play about antagonisms between the Protestant Shankill Defence Association and Belfast's nationalist Citizens' Defence Committees. On the contrary, *The Flats* evokes the much more familiar conflict of O'Casey's Dublin plays: between the security of the home and a militant Irish republicanism that threatens to undermine it. In so far as it is mentioned at all, sectarianism in Northern Ireland is presented more as an aberration than as a pervasive feature of ordinary life. Religious discrimination is portrayed as a phenomenon restricted to the hooliganism of the Protestant mob, to Joe's vague reminder of the shipyard pogroms of 1920, 1935 and 1942 (Boyd 1981: 36) and, much more harmlessly, to Kath's amusingly anachronistic moral imperatives – her stricture to Sean that 'a single Catholic fella livin' in London is better off with a good Catholic family' (Boyd 1981: 48) and her shocked outrage when the British Army captain enquires whether she and Joe are living together 'without marital status' (Boyd 1981: 54). With the exception of Kath's one remark to the effect that Sean would not get a government job in Northern Ireland because of being a Catholic (a remark which takes Sean himself by surprise) there is no indication in the play that religion in Northern Ireland bears any relation to social conditions. Indeed, Monica, as the play's sole Protestant character, is shown to be just as badly off as her Catholic neighbours. Her unseen invalid mother is by far the worst affected by the crisis: unable to sleep because of her nerves, subjected to anonymous intimidation, and collapsing in the final scene. Furthermore, the play's background cyclorama, in place throughout the three acts, emphasizes the physical identity of Belfast's Protestant and Catholic working-class districts. Even Joe and Gerard, both staunch socialists and republicans, insist that Protestants and Catholics are discriminated against to the same extent (Boyd 1981: 16, 49). In Northern Ireland, Joe remarks, there is 'nothin' for anybody' (Boyd 1981: 49). Protestant anti-Catholicism may be the *sine qua non* of the play, in the sense that it is the issue upon which the action is predicated, but it is, nonetheless, an abstraction, an unexplained and invisible absence.

Boyd's use of an O'Casey-like formula in *The Flats* (the view that domestic security and the security of the state are mutually dependent, and that both are threatened by the emergence of indiscriminate republican paramilitary violence) affirms the legitimacy of the British Army's presence in Northern Ireland and that of a British administered 'law and order.' But the fact that *The Flats* was first performed within the context of a dramatic rise in the Army's use of domestic 'arms searches' directed mainly at the Catholic nationalist neighbourhoods of Belfast and Derry (a staggering 17,262 searches took place in 1971 (Lee 1989: 433)) rendered this meaning decidedly factitious. No doubt opening one's door to an Army search party did make family security and the inviolability of the domestic leap suddenly to mind, but more usually in a way slightly different to that suggested in Boyd's play. Moreover, just eight months prior to the play's Lyric Theatre production, a controversial 34-hour curfew had been imposed on the predominantly nationalist Falls Road. This caused widespread alienation among Belfast's nationalist population. The moderate Central Citizens' Defence Committee (CCDC) condemned the British Army's violation of English common law (Lee 1989: 434) and, in a fifty-page booklet, *Law(?) and Orders*, it argued that the Falls curfew had destroyed nationalist confidence in its 'peace-keeping' role in Northern Ireland (*Irish Times*, 18 September 1970: 1). The curfew ended on 5 July shortly after a group of 3,000 women from neighbouring nationalist areas in Belfast defied the army by walking through the military cordon with prams full of bread, milk and other provisions. Within this context, Boyd's play is opposed to the nationalist and republican politics of the Belfast community of Unity Flats and to the political agency expressed by the women's march (see Aretxaga 1997: 56–9). Instead, *The Flats* offers a sentimental effacement of that community's political choices. But, to the extent that *The Flats* deals with a locally recognizable situation in this strikingly artificial manner, one might also say that the play demonstrates not so much the ideological *ease* with which Northern Ireland's sectarian and political divisions may be transcended in the name of a universal humanity, but the sheer recalcitrance of these divisions.

This representation of the Northern Ireland crisis in *The Flats*, however, is by no means exceptional. As with Dublin's NTS, plays performed at the Lyric in the 1970s – works as varied as Wilson John Haire's *Between Two Shadows* (1972–3), Patrick Galvin's *Nightfall to Belfast* (1973–4), and Stewart Parker's *Catchpenny Twist* (1977) – share one characteristic assumption: the persistence and unassimilability of sectarian division. As well as absolving the theatre spectator of all political responsibility, this portrayal of the conflict in terms of an irresolvable social pathology tends to foreclose the possibility of its political resolution. To some extent, this coincides with the Irish and British governments' policies such as internment (1971–5) and the removal of political status or 'special category' status from IRA prisoners (O'Dowd *et al.* 1982). But British policy makers, in particular, also recognized that there existed a corresponding need to establish various forms of community development and community cultural expression in Northern Ireland. With the enthusiastic support of the conservative peer Lord Melchett, for example, this was a major emphasis in terms of ACNI initiatives in the late 1970s (see *ACNI, 35th Annual Report 1977–8*: 10). That the abolition of 'special category' status for republican prisoners soon led to the blanket and dirty protests (1976–7) and then to the more notorious hunger strikes of 1980–1 simply under- lined the need for a more sophisticated 'multiculturalist' approach. There was a growing interest in representing the conflict as arising from the integrity of two opposing cultural traditions. In the Republic of Ireland as well, there was a growing emphasis on the role of culture in underpinning the possibility of a new social contract between nationalists and unionists in Northern Ireland (Bell 1998: 238). In 1980, the Fianna Fáil Taoiseach Charles Haughey spoke of the need 'to promote a deeper understanding among the different communities in the island of the richness and diversity of our heritage' (NA: ARCA A171: Newspaper Clipping from *Clonmel Nationalist*, 10 May 1980), and the joint Anglo–Irish summit between Haughey and Prime Minister Margaret Thatcher in Dublin on 8 December 1980 laid particular stress on the need for both governments to encourage mutual understanding through 'the totality of relationships within these islands' (*Irish Times*,

9 December 1980: 1). It is in this context both of the growing inter-governmental co-operation of the early 1980s, and the emphasis by the two governments on developing culture and heritage as vehicles for political reconciliation (Bell 1998: 228), that the first performance of Brian Friel's play *Translations* may now be considered.

Funded by the Arts Council of Ireland and the Arts Council of Northern Ireland, the première of Brian Friel's *Translations* on 23 September 1980 was hailed as a momentous cultural occasion. As the first performance of the Field Day Theatre Company, a group whose stated objective was the search for a solution to the Northern Ireland crisis through a cultural 'fifth province' that would transcend political differences, *Translations* was received by its first night audience in Derry with intermittent applause and a standing ovation.[4] That the standing ovation was led by an Ulster Unionist Party councillor and several members of Derry City Council, that the play was performed in Derry's Guildhall (the same building that is the setting and symbol of unionist domination in Friel's *The Freedom of the City*), and that *Translations* deals with the decline of the Irish language under the impact of British imperialism made this, the first performance of *Translations*, an unprecedented event. Michael Sheridan in the *Irish Press* described it as 'a watershed in Irish theatre' (*Irish Press*, 25 September 1980: 3), and Irving Wardle, reviewing the London production in May 1981, argued that Friel's play was 'a national classic' comparable to O'Casey's *The Plough and the Stars* (*Times*, 13 May 1981: 11). For most commentators, the fact that *Translations* and the Field Day Theatre Company were inaugurated in Derry's Guildhall marked an important shift in Northern Ireland's post-Stormont political order (see Bell 1998: 137).

Widespread initial praise for *Translations* – described by Seamus Deane as Field Day's 'central text' (Gray 1985: 8) – confirmed what for many was the beginning of a period of improved Anglo–Irish relations. This culminated, in November 1985, with the signing of the Anglo–Irish Agreement. An editorial in the *Irish Times* summarized this concisely when it warmly praised the Field Day project and described the Derry première of *Translations* as a welcome reminder of an essential Irish unity 'across time and territory' (*Irish Times*, 22 August 1980: 9). And yet, despite the praise that *Translations* received in its Field Day and London productions, the play was also the subject of critical controversy, mainly because of its treatment of nineteenth-century Irish history and the supposed relevance of this to the conflict in Northern Ireland. Two directly opposing views have been advanced. On the one hand, Seamus Heaney and Seamus Deane (both co-directors with Field Day) argue that the achievement of *Translations* lies in its demythologizing of traditional conceptions of Irish history in a way that offers healing potential for the war in Northern Ireland. In Heaney's words, Friel diagnoses 'the need we have to create enabling myths of ourselves and the danger we run if we too credulously trust to the sufficiency to these myths' (Heaney 1980: 1119). Thus, Heaney concludes, *Translations*, like Friel's fourteen preceding plays, 'constitutes a powerful therapy, a set of imaginative exercises that give her [Cathleen Ni Houlihan or Ireland] the chance to know and say herself properly to herself again'. But for other critics (such as Edna Longley, Sean Connolly and Bruce Kirkland) *Translations* is seriously flawed because it endorses, rather than questions, traditional nationalist conceptions of Irish history and in particular the notion of Ireland as a once Gaelic-speaking utopia. For these critics, the play expresses a nationalist political perspective because it exaggerates the repressiveness of the British military and because it ignores any direct consideration of militant Irish republicanism. Connolly points out, for example, that the Ordnance Survey in *Translations* is portrayed inaccurately as an almost Cromwellian military force and that Friel's play has soldiers with fixed bayonets and powers of eviction, whereas in all published historical accounts, including the account in J. H. Andrew's *A Paper Landscape* upon which *Translations* is partly based, the principal motive for the Ordnance Survey in Ireland is shown as economic (land valuation) (Connolly 1987: 42–4). The reason that Friel avoids the historical fact that the soldiers involved in the Ordnance Survey were strictly forbidden any involvement in evictions or putting down civil disturbances is so that he can offer 'a crude portrayal of cultural and military imperialism visited on passive victims' (Connolly 1987: 44). '*Translations*', Longley concludes, 'refurbishes an old myth . . . the play does not so much examine myths of dispossession and oppression as repeat them' (Longley 1985: 28–9). More recently, Kirkland criticizes *Translations* for its 'absolute condemnation of territorial appropriation' and the way in which this was concealed by the euphoric reception of the Derry première and the 'tide of reconciliatory impulses which sought unity within the remit of culture' (Kirkland 1996: 137). Adding substance to the controversy is the fact that, despite Friel's own hints that the espousal of a nostalgia for a lost Gaelic Ireland was not his intention in *Translations*, Friel's diary entries written from the period when it was being composed record a recurrent uncertainty as to the political connotations of the play (Friel 1983: 58–9). In addition, Friel's writing of *The Communication Cord* (1982), a farce that lampoons nostalgia for a lost Gaelic and Edenic Ireland, and his description of this as a conscious 'antidote' to *Translations*, suggests a recognition that the earlier play may indeed have evoked a nostalgic view of nationalist Irish history, despite this being contrary to the principal elements of the play's design.

The time and place of *Translations* is politically charged: rural Ireland on the eve of the potato famine and the introduction of English as the emerging dominant vernacular. With its evocation of traditional characters such as the red-coated soldier (Lancey and Yolland), the shawled girl or Cathleen Ni Houlihan figure (Sarah – a potentially dumb woman whom Manus is teaching to speak), the hedge schoolmaster (Hugh) and traditional motifs such as eviction, potato blight and poteen, Friel's play evokes a nationally distinctive way of life that was about to disappear. Furthermore, in so far as the first act reveals a confrontation between an economically impoverished but educationally superior indigenous Irish-speaking culture and an imperial, but philistine, English military, the play seems to confirm traditional views on nineteenth-century Irish history much more than it challenges them. Popular nationalist sentiment is appealed to, for example, when, in the middle of Lancey's patronizing lecture on the purposes of the Ordnance Survey, the learned Jimmy Jack inquires politely, '*nonne Latine loquitur*', and Lancey replies promptly that he does not speak Irish (Friel 1981: 30). As the *Sunday Times* reviewer pointed out with some annoyance, Lancey – supposedly a well-educated British Army captain – is here not even capable of recognizing Latin (*Sunday Times*, 28 September 1980: 40). The Baile Beag hedge school may be set in a context of a deteriorating economy (the opening stage directions describe the school as littered with 'broken and forgotten implements' (Friel 1981: 11)) and may face the anglicizing effects of the Ordnance Survey and the new National School, but, at least in Act I, these threats are countered by the wit and subversive ingenuity of the locals. The atmosphere at the beginning of the play is one of optimism and exuberance, of an Irish national culture surviving despite severe economic and political disadvantage.

The principal complication occurs when Yolland falls in love, first with the place and the Irish language, and then with Maire, a local woman betrothed to Manus. After their first and only meeting as lovers, Yolland mysteriously disappears, and while the audience does not find out what has happened to him, there are several hints that he has been abducted and probably killed by the Donnelly twins (who never once appear in the play) as part of their on-going guerrilla war against the British. In the final scene Lancey retaliates by threatening to destroy the entire area if Yolland is not found. The play ends therefore with a situation very similar to the conflict in Northern Ireland in the early 1980s: an escalating war between the British Army and the guerrilla tactics of republican paramilitaries. But to consider, as some commentators do, that the nationalist appeal of the first act is an indication of the nationalist tendencies of *Translations* as a whole, or that the play's conclusion somehow endorses republican paramilitarism, is to ignore Friel's pervasive irony. Hugh's scorn for English is spoken in English, which the audience, through the play's dramatic convention, understands as Irish. Thus, while Hugh's teaching is based on the view that Gaelic culture and classical culture make 'a happier conjugation' (Friel 1981: 25), his actual formulation of this view is an etymological pedagogy that demonstrates exactly the opposite: that it is English, not Irish, that has extensive roots in Greek and Latin. It is not the etymology of Irish words that Hugh is constantly asking his pupils to conjugate and recite, but English words such as 'baptize' (*baptizein*), 'perambu-lations' (*perambulare*), 'verecund' (*verecundas*), 'conjugation' (*conjugo*), and 'acquiesced' (*acquiesce*). Hugh may declare that the English language is particularly suited 'for the purposes of commerce' (Friel 1981: 25) and that it makes poetry sound 'plebian' (Friel 1981: 41), but this is contradicted by his own ostentatious delight in iambic rhythms, alliteration and words that are polysyllabic and latinate. Even in terms of its own English-language theatrical medium, this is a play that celebrates, not the possibility of recovering the Irish language as a widely-spoken vernacular, but Ireland's skilful appropriation of English.

As the play proceeds, the audience's awareness of this irony becomes increasingly apparent. If, in Act II, Hugh pontificates extravagantly on the aristocratic closeness of the Irish and classical cultures ('I'm afraid we're not familiar with your literature, Lieutenant. We feel closer to the warm Mediterranean. We tend to overlook your island' (Friel 1981: 41)) he is also described by the stage directions as conveying an impression of 'deliberately parodying himself' (Friel 1981: 40). And when Yolland shows no signs of recognizing the self-parody in Hugh's remarks and Owen becomes embarrassed by it, Hugh responds to Yolland's enthusiastic apostrophes for Gaelic culture ('I understand it's enormously rich and ornate' (Friel 1981: 42)) not with approval and agreement as some of Hugh's earlier comments might lead us to expect, but with repeated cautions and qualifications. Repeatedly, Hugh warns Yolland that part of the attraction of the Irish language and its literature is that Irish has tendencies towards quixotic fantasy and self-deception (Friel 1981: 42). Hugh's point, formulated in this scene in phrases that echo and in some cases quote directly from various passages in George Steiner's *After Babel* (Kearney 1983: 54–5), is that the attractive richness of Gaelic culture exists in direct correspondence to that of the material impoverishment from which it arises. Irish is 'a rich language' because it has functioned historically as a compensation for poverty: 'full of mythologies of fantasy and hope and self-deception – a syntax opulent with tomorrows. It is our response to mud cabins and a diet of potatoes; our only method of replying to . . . inevitabilities' (Friel 1981: 42). That Hugh's caveats are delivered with much the same self-indulgent panache as his tossing back of Anna na mBreag's poteen is a further irony that the excited and semi-intoxicated Yolland is unable to detect.

This association between quixoticism and an entirely Irish-speaking culture is relentlessly pursued. In the exchange between Yolland and Owen at the beginning of Act III, Owen argues that since the name 'Tobair Vree' bears an entirely arbitrary relation to its referent (a local crossroads), and since he is the only one in the area who remembers its derivation (an erosion of *Tobair Bhriain* or 'the well of Brian'), there is therefore no reason, except romantic nostalgia, why the name should not be 'standardized' as 'the Cross' or 'The Crossroads'. Yolland, however, remains obdurate that the name should remain exactly as it is. The irony (intended or not) is that not only is 'Tobair Vree' itself an anglicization, since traditionally the letter 'v' is not used in the Irish alphabet, but that 'Tobair Vree' is also a phonetic impossibility since the Irish language would never lose its final nasal consonant in the manner that 'Tobair Vree'/Tobair Bhrian' implies. A similar irony is evident at the beginning of Act III when, in the case of 'The Murren', Owen decides on aesthetic grounds ('Very unattractive name, isn't it' (Friel 1981: 54)) to revert to the original: the 'original' that he chooses is the English 'Saint Muranus,' rather than '*Naomh Muirenn*' or '*Cill Muirenn*', which would be its literal Irish equivalents.[5]

Nevertheless, the idea that retaining 'original' names is romantic folly and a form of self-deception is countered by Friel's persistent suggestion that names also have an ontological importance that cannot be replaced. There is, for example, the exuberance of the opening scene in which Sarah slowly articulates her name and the play's association of this process with an atmosphere of optimism and self-confidence. In Act III, when Sarah loses this ability, she is described as 'more waiflike than ever' [sic] (Friel 1981: 54), as if her physical identity is itself beginning to disappear. As with Martin Heidegger's *Poetry, Language, Thought*, a brief passage of which is quoted in the play's 1980 Field Day programme, there is a strong suggestion in *Translations* that naming and belonging are processes that are inextricably related. Names may be accidental, Friel implies, but they also have a private significance that cannot be so easily dismissed.

The play's ambivalence towards the Irish language (Heaney described it as 'a mixture of irony and elegy' (Heaney 1980: 1199)) is returned to in the final scene. Here, Hugh abandons completely his earlier exclusive commitment to Irish by lecturing Owen on the importance of accepting the new Anglicized place-names and by volunteering to teach Maire English. Again, in terms that echo Steiner's *After Babel*, Hugh draws an analogy between Owen's repudiation of the Name Book ('A mistake, my mistake – nothing to do with us' (Friel 1981: 66)) and Jimmy Jack's proposal to marry Pallas Athene:

OWEN: I know where I live.

HUGH: James thinks he knows too. I look at James and three thoughts occur to me: A – that it is not the literal past, the 'facts' of history, that shape us, but images of the past embodied in language. James has ceased to make that discrimination.

OWEN: Don't lecture me, Father.

HUGH: B – We must never cease renewing those images; because once we do we fossilise.

(Friel 1981: 66)

The implication of Hugh's remarks is that Owen's apostatic commitment to the idea of an autonomous Irish-speaking culture and Jimmy Jack's pathetic fantasies about Athene stem from a similarly flawed perception: a failure to recognize a distinction between history as fact and history as narrative. For Hugh, Jimmy Jack shows this myopia in his belief that the gods and goddesses of classical mythology actually exist, and Owen shows it through his assumption that the Gaelic place-names of the area represent a cultural permanence that must not be changed. Both positions, moreover, may be considered as attempts to resolve or to compensate for an impoverished and isolated condition that results, not in an improvement of that condition, but in the sure guarantee that it will continue. So long as Jimmy Jack chooses goddesses rather than real women, then the companionship that he is longing for will never be found. So long as Irish history is thought of in terms of a loss of an original purity that may be recovered, and so long as this purity is regarded as fact, then the present and future will be condemned to a series of violent repetitions. In this way, the conflict between the mysterious Donnelly twins and the British Army in Act III is presented by Doalty as an echo of earlier situations ('When my grandfather was a boy they did the same thing' (Friel 1981: 63)) and is offered by the play as a whole as a pre-figuration of the conflict in Northern Ireland in the early 1980s. The play's concluding emphasis, therefore, is on the dangers of republican militancy and this is achieved by means of Friel's valorization throughout of the absolute priority of the (patriarchal) family unit. Crucial to this perspective is Hugh's description of setting out for the 1798 rebellion and then opting out of the uprising because of what he considers to be the more enduring reality of the family.

HUGH: We were gods that morning, James; and I had recently married *my* goddess, Caitlin Dubh Nic Reactainn, may she rest in peace. And to leave her and my infant son in his cradle – that was heroic, too. By God, sir, we were magnificent. We marched as far as – where was it? – Glenties! All of twenty-three miles in one day. And it was there, in Phelan's pub, that we got homesick for Athens, just like Ulysses. The *desiderium nostrorum* – the need for our own. Our *pietas*, James, was for older, quieter things.

(Friel 1981: 67)

Like Jimmy Jack's commitment to classical mythology, the militant heroics of the 1798 rebellion, an event central to republican mythology, are presented here as a substitution of abstractions and goddesses for the quotidian actuality of the domestic or, as Hugh describes it, 'the *desiderium nostrorum* – the need for our own' (Friel 1981: 67). One way, then, in which the play's development may be considered is in terms of the audience's gradual recognition of this mistaken substitution in the course of the action. Whereas in Act I Hugh brusquely dismisses Maire's request to learn English so that s he might emigrate to America and earn enough money to subsidize her family at home, Hugh now volunteers his services as an English teacher as if in realization of the inevitability and priority of this. And whereas in Act I the three stalwarts of the hedge school – Manus,

Hugh and Jimmy Jack – are shown as blind or indifferent to the exigencies of the domestic, the outcome of these attitudes in Act III is Manus's hurt rage at Maire's relationship with Yolland, Jimmy Jack's pathetic revelation that he is lonely and, in Hugh's case, the recognition that an exclusive commitment to an all Irish-speaking culture is a mistake.

Hugh's speeches in the final scene offer a radically different perspective, therefore, on the version of nineteenth-century Irish history presented in Act I. That earlier, nationalistically attractive contrast between on the one hand a rich indigenous culture and a deteriorating economy and, on the other, a repressive British military now appears as a more complicated relation. Now, the richness of Gaelic culture appears as a delusive quixoticism that contributes to economic decline. In short, the ending of *Translations* suggests that it is precisely because of the exuberant idealism of the hedge school that its setting is characterized by 'broken and forgotten implements' and 'no trace of a woman's hand' (Friel 1981: 11). In the context of this recognition, Hugh's proposal that the English language should be accepted is a compelling alternative.

Yet while an acceptance of the English language is proposed by Hugh as a corrective to the celibate heroics of Irish republicanism, there is also a definite impression that this change – Irish-speaking Ireland's surrender to modernity – will also involve an unquantifiable ontological loss. Hugh tells Maire that he will provide her with 'the available words and the available grammar', but then adds that he has no idea whether this will allow her to interpret 'between privacies' (Friel 1981: 67). It is not enough for the English place-names to be accepted, Hugh lectures Owen, they must also be made 'our own . . . our new home' (Friel 1981: 66). Friel here defines Irish nationalism not in terms of militant anti-imperialism but, like Hugh's unfinished syllogisms, as a modernizing, and apparently open-ended project of cultural recovery. And in Hugh's final speech – his attempt to recall the beginning of Virgil's *Aeneid* – whether or not Carthage/Ireland can be restored to its former plenitude is a problem that is suspended, quite literally, in mid sentence. In short, *Translations* refutes the existence of a single nationalist narrative, requires a rethinking of the 'facts' of history and accepts an equation between imperialism and modernity.

But if in these respects *Translations* may be regarded as Irish historical revisionism *par excellence*, it is also a conclusion that raises a number of problems. If the movement of the play in general, and Hugh's final speeches in particular, are designed to call attention to the extent to which both history and fiction are 'images of the past embodied in language', why then does *Translations* conceal the extent to which its own version of history is itself a construction? The consistent naturalistic setting and dramaturgy of *Translations*, together with the extensive historical references in the programme notes for the Field Day, and subsequent London, and Abbey Theatre productions all convey an impression that the version of nineteenth-century Irish history presented by the play is grounded, unproblematically, in fact. The play's attempt to show history as 'images of the past constructed in language' (Friel 1981: 66) conflicts with the manner in which *Translations* is presented.

Furthermore, this is a play that treats the emotive subject of the decline of the Irish language in a text from which the Irish language is itself almost completely absent. For Friel, this is the fundamental irony of *Translations* (Agnew 1980: 59), but it is more than just an irony. That the Irish language appears in the play *exclusively* in terms of place-names and that spoken English is made to represent an Irish language vernacular conveys a powerful impression that the two languages are semantically equivalent. The difference between languages in *Translations* is thus rendered simply as a matter of signifiers, the sounds or written images of words. It is the sound of Irish that is shown to have the potential both to exercise a delusive intoxication as in the case of Yolland's raptures about 'Tobair Vree,' and to express the privacy of individual identity as in the case of Sarah's hesitant articulation in the opening scene or, in the case of Hugh's caution to Marie, at the play's conclusion. Constituted as a nomenclature, then, language in *Translations* appears as a system of names for a world of identities that exists clearly and unambiguously outside of language. Drawing on Steiner's Heideggerean view that language is inextricably linked to an essential privacy (see Murray 1981: 238–9 and Kearney 1983: 54–5), the portrayal of language in *Translations* strengthens the impression that authenticity resides in an essential privacy that can never be fully represented either in Irish or in English.

That the Irish language in *Translations* appears only as place-names is not fortuitous, therefore, but crucial to the play's conception of identity as existing outside of language and social relations. It is this particular notion of identity that fortifies the play's conclusion that the loss of the Irish language is a regrettable, but also an insuperable, necessity. Just as the play's naturalistic dramaturgy conceals the extent to which the characters and action are fictional and constructed, so also does Friel's view of language as a nomenclature conceal the extent to which meaning and identity are themselves constructed in language and can thus vary from one language to another. Interestingly, Friel's one instruction to the person charged with the translation of *Translations* into Irish was his insistence that the entire text, including the speeches of the British soldiers, should be done into Irish (Professor B. Ó Doibhlin, Letter to the author, 21 May 1988). This instruction, given in spite of the fact that most late twentieth-century Irish-speaking audiences would be universally capable of understanding English, suggests that Friel's major concern was effacing any impression of the two languages as competing and incommensurable vernaculars. By so erasing the conceptual differences between Irish and English, the play's overall linguistic and cultural conclusion follows naturally: the loss of Irish as a vernacular is presented as a matter of ontological rather than political importance. To this extent, the underlying logic of the play is tautological. It is the audience's acceptance of English as a theatrical convention for Irish and the recognition that this convention is itself a matter of theatrical expediency that serves as Friel's most convincing demonstration of the inevitability of the loss of Irish as a contemporary spoken vernacular. How else, after all, might the play be performed and understood in metropolitan centres like London, New York, Toronto?

The suggestion at the end of *Translations* that both the violent resistance of Doalty and the Donnelly twins and Owen's newfound determination to recover the Irish language are dangerous, mutually reinforcing illusions may also be read as an attack on the politics of contemporary Irish republicanism in the late 1970s. In particular, *Translations* serves as a response to a Provisional Sinn Féin campaign that stressed the separatist potential of the Irish language and emphasized the colonial origins of the conflict. As a perusal of the Sinn Féin weekly *An Phoblacht/Republican News* from 1978 to 1980 demonstrates, the colonial context of the conflict and the fundamental untranslatability of the Irish language were increasingly important lines of argument. Disparagement of the Irish language by the British and Irish political establishments is one of 'the more obvious signs that this country is a colony' argues one article (*An Phoblacht/Republican News*, 14 October 1978: 7), while a later editorial describes the separatist political potential of the Irish language as a 'separatism that is built into it, as it is in every language' (*An Phoblacht/Republican News*, 6 January 1979: 2). Within this context, Friel's suggestion that the differences between languages are a matter of ontological rather than semantic importance bears a distinct political colour. At a time when the campaign for political status for republican prisoners was turning out parades similar in size to the civil rights marches of the early 1970s (Bew *et al.* 1995: 209), *Translations* underlines the need for a *via media* of political accommodation based on an acceptance of inherited political and cultural realities, and, to this extent, constitutes a rebuttal of republican militancy.

It is not at all surprising, however, that the anti-republicanism of Friel's play has been unremarked whereas *Translations* has been criticized, and criticized extensively, for nursing nationalist grievance. If the play's concluding emphasis on the need for political accommodation is based on an audience's recognition of the universality and permanence of the English language in Ireland and on the play's association of English imperialism with post-Enlightenment modernity, then the corollary of this assertion is the plangency of cultural loss. Moreover, the play's construction of language difference in terms of ontology rather than semantics necessarily privileges the idea of a lost Irish-speaking essence or 'privacy.' In so far as nationalist Ireland has an identity to be recovered it is an ontological entity, a state of being rather than a state of politics. As with the British and Irish government initiatives of the early 1980s, the basis of conflict resolution in Northern Ireland is adumbrated in terms of nationalist Ireland's acceptance of the political status quo, in return for a recognition of its historical cultural trauma (Bell 1998: 238). A notable feature of the 1980 Anglo–Irish summit, the New Ireland Forum (1983–4) and the Anglo–Irish Agreement (1985), for example, was their emphases on the primacy of constitutional politics: an acceptance of the political entity known as Northern Ireland *and* the need to establish new structures capable of accommodating together 'two sets of legitimate rights.'

> 4.15 The solution to both the historic problem and the current crisis of Northern Ireland and the continuing problem of relations between Ireland and Britain necessarily requires new structures that will accommodate together two sets of legitimate rights:
> – the right of nationalists to effective political, symbolic and administrative expression of their identity; and
> – the right of unionists to effective political, symbolic and administrative expression of their identity, their ethos and their way of life.
>
> (New Ireland Forum 1984: 23)

That these two assertions are presented as equal and balancing (and yet are expressed as an awkward, unexplained asymmetry) indicates the extent to which the 'multiculturalist' approach to Northern Ireland was, from its beginning, plagued by a contradiction. If Northern Ireland's political integrity was accepted, how could the rights of its nationalist population be cherished equally to those of Northern Ireland's unionist majority? Given the British government's 1984 rejection of one of the New Ireland Forum's proposed solutions – joint British and Irish sovereignty in Northern Ireland – the vexed issue of political equality was rendered increasingly as an issue of cultural traditions. But from a unionist perspective the difficulty remained: to concede any equivalence between nationalist and unionist rights was to reinscribe the basic terms of the conflict. Thus, for one commentator, the difference between revisionist nationalism's acceptance that Irish unification may only take place with unionist consent and an anti-unionist nationalism that seeks unity by armed insurrection was simply a matter of tactics (English 1996: 228–9). In both cases, the assertion of a nationalist cultural identity (in *Translations*, the very idea that there is an identity to be recovered) was seen as lending credibility to a dangerous impression of minority grievance. Bluntly put, to recognize nationalist minority culture in Northern Ireland as equal was to undermine the legitimacy of the state (English 1994: 99 and see Gibbons 1994: 17). To this extent the asymmetry evident in paragraph 4.15 of the New Ireland Forum's *Report* is unusually revealing of a cultural realpolitik.

Recognizing and giving expression to the differential relationship between Protestant/unionist culture and Catholic/nationalist culture in relation to the state becomes an increasingly important issue for Irish theatre in the 1980s and 1990s. How, in this context, should Ireland's state-funded national theatre react? In particular, how might the cultural issues involved in the Northern Ireland conflict be addressed in a manner that would avoid the apparent partisanship of Field Day's *Translations* and yet express the NTS's commitment to inclusiveness?

One major response to these questions was the Peacock Theatre's celebrated 1985 production of Frank McGuinness's *Observe the Sons of Ulster Marching Towards the Somme*. Written in the wake of a hostile unionist reaction to the New Ireland Forum, McGuinness's play was an attempt to engage positively with the loyalist ideology of Ulster Protestantism. It was performed in February 1985 and may be read as a counterweight to Friel's earlier *Translations*, from which Protestant/unionist culture is entirely absent. Beneath the jingoistic rhetoric of the First World War and the bombast of Orangeism, McGuinness's play suggests, there lie personal bonds of sympathy and communal solidarity which outsiders, and especially southern Irish outsiders, must respect and take note of. The exhortation of the play's title, 'observe', encapsulates this deferential and non-judgemental attitude towards unionism that the play tries to encourage. Framed by the recollections of the two versions of the character Pyper, the play's narrative explores the contradictions and emotional attachments of unionist ideology as manifest in Pyper's fellow soldier volunteers in the period prior to the Battle of the Somme. The older Pyper, the only survivor of the Somme, introduces himself as a stalwart of the Stormont years. As one who 'helped organize the workings of this province' (McGuinness 1986: 10), Pyper emphasizes the unspoken heroism of Ulster Protestantism by alluding ironically to the English meaning of Sinn Féin ('ourselves'): 'It is we, the Protestant people, who have always stood alone' (McGuinness 1986: 10). Indeed, a major emphasis of *Observe the Sons of Ulster Marching Towards the Somme* is its articulation of a deliberate counter to nationalist ideology: in place of the 1916 Rising, McGuinness offers a seminal moment in Northern Irish Protestant identity, the Battle of the Somme, and in place of the painful history of Northern Ireland's Catholic minority, McGuinness places the cultural isolation of Ulster Protestants. The play's tone is both elegiac and celebratory: as the soldiers move towards the moment of slaughter they also move from 'remembrance' to 'initiation' to 'pairing' to 'bonding'. By such means the audience's impression is that at the core of unionist mentality lies a deeply felt personal bonding.

In addressing the topic of Northern Ireland's loyalist identity, the play does acknowledge anti-Catholicism but it suggests that within the context of the appalling sacrifices that took place at the Battle of the Somme, this is relatively unimportant. Beneath the façade of sectarian bigotry, the audience is made to recognize a passionate devotion to place. In Part III, when Anderson and McIlwaine address the audience as an Orange Lodge (McGuinness 1986: 58–60), the spectator allows that the rhetoric of Orangeism may be composed of lies, and that the two soldiers are partly aware of this, but also recognizes that this rhetoric has a potent emotionalism and sincerity (Murray 1997: 205). For Ulster Protestantism, the play suggests, the Battle of the Somme was not for nothing, but for Ulster.

YOUNGER PYPER: The house has grown cold, the province has grown lonely.

ELDER PYPER: Ulster.
YOUNGER PYPER: You'll always guard Ulster.
ELDER PYPER: Ulster.
YOUNGER PYPER: Save it.
ELDER PYPER: Ulster.
YOUNGER PYPER: The temple of the Lord is ransacked.
ELDER PYPER: Ulster.
   (*Pyper reaches towards himself*)
YOUNGER PYPER: Dance in this deserted temple of the Lord.
ELDER PYPER: Dance.
   (*Darkness*)   (McGuinness 1986: 80)

This final elegiac movement of the play reinforces McGuinness's central point. At the core of Northern Irish Protestantism is a loneliness that beseeches the audience's sympathy. Ulster may well have grown 'cold' for its Catholic minority population, but the existential experience of Protestants is just as intensely felt. For Ulster Protestants, moreover, the province of 'Ulster' is, unequivocally, Northern Ireland, and it is this – the political reality of partition – that *Observe the Sons of Ulster Marching Towards the Somme* exhorts its audience to accept and to celebrate (Murray 1997: 206). That McGuinness's play was elevated to the main Abbey Theatre stage just one month after the signing of the Anglo–Irish Agreement in November 1985 – an agreement that conceded that Ireland would have a consultative role in the government of Northern Ireland in return for its acceptance of Northern Ireland as a valid political entity (Bew *et al.* 1995: 214) – indicates the extent to which the political vision of the play coincided with the state's own official response to the conflict.

   Observe the Sons of Ulster Marching Towards the Somme thus demonstrates an important trend in the still-dominant national theatre tradition of twentieth-century Ireland: ideological conformity to the political interests of the state. And yet, as in so many of the plays written for the NTS, this is a conformity that seldom fully neutralizes or exhausts the theatre's subversive potential. That McGuinness's play uses homosexual friendship as part of its celebration of the loyalties of Ulster unionism – at a time when the public expression of gay identities in Ireland remained anathema to both main religious and political traditions – illustrates the extent to which theatrical performance is often in excess of the meanings proffered by the state. The political dynamism of Irish theatre lies more in its development and exploration of this excess than in any self-conscious articulation of state policy.

NOTES

1 HOME RULE AND THE IRISH LITERARY THEATRE, 1893–1902

1 The prompt copy of *The Countess Cathleen* at the University of Texas indicates that Yeats did alter the previously published text of his play, perhaps on clerical advice, before the 1899 performance. Instead of the starving peasant Shemus 'kicking' the shrine of Our Lady 'to pieces' (as indicated in the 1899 printed version of the play), Yeats cancelled the direction and gave a new line to Maire: 'Look, look. The shrine has fallen from its nail / And shrine and image have broken in two.' (Yeats 1997: 379n.) As it was too late to change the 1899 *Poems*, Yeats changed the 1901 edition so that Shemus crushed the shrine 'underfoot' (Yeats 1997: 380).

2 See 'Tableaux Vivants at the Chief Secretary's Lodge', *The Daily Express*, 26 January 1899: 6 (cited in Hogan and Kilroy 1975: 150–1).

3 Following the Phoenix Park performance of *The Countess Cathleen*, Yeats was especially anxious that no special reception be given to a visit to the National Literary Society by Lady Cadogan, wife of the British Lord-Lieutenant (see Yeats 1997: 342).

4 Plunkett comments that 'excepting Ulster, whose staple industry was not interfered with, and where English individualism succeeds, we have a country without town life, and therefore without industrial spirit, mainly dependent upon agriculture. . . . In some way or another the economic thought of the country must be transformed until the people come to see that they must work out their own economic salvation' (*Daily Express*, 1 November 1898: 6). Boylan and Foley comment that 'By and large, Catholicism was regarded as a force inimical to political economy' and cite in particular Charles Gide's contribution to R. H. I. Palgrave's *Dictionary of Political Economy* (1894) (Boylan and Foley 1992: 145–7).

5 See Horace Plunkett, Diary entry for 7 May 1896, Plunkett Foundation. Unionist calls for the abolition of the vice-royalty were not unprecedented. Earlier in the century the Protestant political economist,

Archbishop Whately, made a similar call in order to better assimilate Ireland and England (see Boylan and Foley 1992: 125).

6 For a useful discussion of the relationship between moderate nationalism and the Anglo-Irish Ascendancy, see Foster 1993: 62–7.

7 George Russell to T. P. Gill; Art Loan Exhibition, Dublin; Leinster House; bs; ALS. (NLI: 13,481 (1)) My thanks to Adrian Frazier for drawing my attention to this reference.

8 John Redmond described as a 'social revolution' the 1898 Local Government Act's replacing of the landlord-appointed grand juries with local county councils (quoted in Bew 1987: 32).

9 See Howes 1996: Chapter 3.

10 In her unpublished memoirs Lady Desart writes nostalgically about the Private Theatre of Kilkenny in the early nineteenth century 'when all that was fairest and wealthiest in Ireland had flocked every winter to the Season of the Kilkenny theatre where the Gentlemen of the County as the actors and the most brilliant stars of the Dublin Stage as actresses provided entertainment for the well to do and money for the poor, and the list of box and stallholders reads like pages out of the Peerage'. Ellen, Countess of Desart, Unpublished Memoirs, no pagination; see also Farrelly 1996: 52–72; 82–107. I am most grateful to Mr Farrelly for providing me with a photocopy of Lady Desart's memoirs.

11 The extent to which theatre as an institution is bound up with nationalism can be illustrated by the complete effacement of other forms of theatrical practice from Irish theatre history. Even Séamus Wilmot, writing of Irish drama in the Irish language, shares this tendency:

> . . . for years, the seldom time a play was produced, it was usually featured as just another item of entertainment between songs, dances and recitations at concerts, before theatrically unsophisticated audiences, at *feiseanna, aeríochtanna* or in parish halls. (It is interesting to note that the Irish word for 'play' in those early days was *cluiche*, which literally means game, sport or pastime: when things were taken more seriously, that word was dropped for *dráma*.)
>
> (Wilmot 1968: 64)

12 For the story of the genesis of *The Bending of the Bough* in George Moore and Yeats's rewriting of Edward Martyn's play *A Tale of a Town*, see Frazier 2000: 281–8.

13 For Gill, see (Moore 1911/1985: 122–3); Curran regards Yeats's decision 'to represent the issue as solely touching the liberty of the artist and . . . a proper critical approach' was a disingenuous attempt to ignore the validity of the students' objections (Curran 1970: 103–4).

14 See 'The Battle of Two Civilizations' reprinted in Moran (n.d.: 106): 'The Irish language is now the ultimate goal of the Irish Literary Theatre.'

15 That Synge's account conflicts with another contemporary description
    of the first October 1901 production of *Casadh an tSúgáin* which
    registers a contrary impression merely underlines the political nuance
    of the performance. For the critic Stephen Gwynn the production of
    Hyde's play was a momentous cultural event that galvanized nationalist
    audiences and that was greeted with popular acclaim.

> [B]eing on the floor of the house, I was nearer the uneducated
> people in the pit who understood what was being said. . . .
> Here the words were caught up almost before they were out of
> the speaker's mouth; and I heard from behind me shouts in
> Irish of encouragement to the performers in the dance. I was
> never in an audience so amusing to be among; there was
> magnetism in the air. In the entr' actes' a man up in the gallery
> with a fine voice, sang song after song in Irish, the gallery
> joining in the chorus. One began to realise what the Gaelic
> League was doing – and one felt a good deal out in the cold
> because one had to rely on the translation.
>
> (Gwynn 1901: 1058)

16 See, for example, Constance Markiewicz's comment, 'That play of Yeats
    was a sort of gospel to me,' in Markiewicz 1934: 241 and Dudley
    Edwards 1990: 101. Stephen Gwynn later questions whether 'such plays
    should be produced unless one was prepared for people to go out to
    shoot and be shot, and for Yeats, Gonne's acting had a 'wierd power''
    (Yeats 1999: 167).

2 J. M. SYNGE AND THE COLLAPSE OF
CONSTRUCTIVE UNIONISM, 1902–9

1 I am extremely grateful to Helen Laird's daughter, Mrs Elizabeth
   Solterer, for clarifying the unlikelihood of this story, and for pointing
   out that Helen Laird left the INTS solely because she did not wish to
   become a professional actress (letter to the author; 24 June 1998).
2 Although such opinions were predominantly a phenomenon of Irish
   Protestant and unionist culture, they were not exclusively so. Dissenting
   nationalist journals such as *Dána*, and *The Shanachie* and *The Peasant*
   were highly critical of the majoritarian tendencies of the Irish Parliamentary Party and Sinn Féin and were emphatic in insisting on the need
   to preserve intellectual independence
3 'With brutal indifference to his feelings Cardinal Logue and Archbishop
   Walsh have shown the country that they are, and intend to
   remain, masters of the situation. Secure in their authority and
   contemptuous of the weakness of the present Liberal Government, they
   have not hesitated to announce definitely to the world that Home

Rule is still Rome Rule.' (*Church of Ireland Gazette*, 12 January 1906: 33).

4 Quinn then went on to suggest that Synge should write a play that would engage even more directly with contemporary nationalist self-inflation: 'take all the absurdities of Sinn Feinism and of the "nation builders" with their foreign consuls and their delegates to the Hague convention, with their invitations to the colonial premiers to attend the so-called "National Council" in Dublin, and so on, and laugh at them' (TCD: MS 4425/364, John Quinn to J. M. Synge, 23 August 1907: 5–6).

3 NTS, LTD AND THE RISE OF SINN FÉIN, 1910–22

1 Hogan and Kilroy remark 'the main reason for [*Falsely True's*] production was undoubtedly that its author was the daughter of John Redmond, the leader of the Irish Parliamentary Party' (Hogan *et al.* 1979: 149).

2 The explanation of the whole uproar is that there is now an educated patriotic Ireland. Up to about 20 years ago the only patriotic Ireland we had was practically ignorant. The educated people were hostile or indifferent. The new patriotic educated Ireland is insisting on its standards being recognised, and upon having life put as freely at the service of the artist as it is in all other countries. The old Ireland is making its protests heard more and more fully. Ireland is ceasing to object, but the Irish-American is in the state of mind that Ireland was 20 years ago.

(W. B. Yeats, *Irish Times*, 20 January 1912: 8)

3 A letter from Lady Gregory to Constant Huntington (Berg: 10 October 1912) indicates that Gregory quickly finished the MS of *Our Irish Theatre*, so that its publication would be ready in time for the second Abbey tour. I am very grateful to James Pethica for information on this point.

4 According to Foster, Yeats wrote to the *Irish Times* claiming that American opposition was composed of 'half-educated men' and mendacious priests (Foster 1997: 450).

5 As well as *The Irish Revolution*, McCarthy's famous *Priests and People in Ireland* (1902) was reissued in a 1912 edition sponsored by a consortium of Belfast unionists. My thanks to Barra Ó Seaghdha for information on this point.

6 As Foster points out, discussions about the establishment of a government appointed senate as part of Irish home rule were taking place in 1912 (Foster 1997: 459).

7 See Gregory 1974: 459–61. A few weeks after his appearance at the production of *The Playboy of the Western World*, Roosevelt published an appreciative essay on the Abbey, 'In the Eyes of our Friends: The Irish Theatre', *Outlook*, 16 December 1911.

8 The 'Cork Realists' also included Suzanne R. Day, G. D. Cummins and J. Bernard McCarthy. See *New Ireland*, 10 February 1917: 227.

9 For a detailed account of the integrationist tendencies of Southern Irish 'city Protestants', see Buckland 1966–67: 228–55 and d'Alton, 1973: 71–88.

10 John Cronin describes Ervine's appointment as 'a bizarre choice of manager of a national theatre' (Ervine 1988: 8).

11 The Lane picture controversy arose following the disputed will of Lady Gregory's nephew, the art collector Sir Hugh Lane. Lane possessed an extensive collection of modern art including some notable impressionists which, in 1913, he bequeathed to the City of Dublin on condition that it erect an art gallery to house the collection. Lane's favoured idea was a gallery to be built on a specially constructed bridge spanning the Liffey. Not unexpectedly many nationalist members of Dublin corporation objected to what they regarded as yet another public monument to Ascendancy prestige in Ireland's capital city. There were also murmurings about the artistic worth of the collection. Lane withdrew his offer, and left the collection instead to the National Gallery in London. In February 1915 Lane returned to his original decision and, in an unwitnessed codicil to his will, he bequeathed the paintings once more to Dublin. After Lane's death in May 1915 the pictures were sent to London. This was disputed by Dublin Municipal Gallery and there followed an on-going campaign to have the pictures restored to Ireland. For Lady Gregory, returning the Lane pictures to Ireland became a major preoccupation.

12 For this point I am indebted to Professor R. F. Foster (letter to author, 17 December 1999).

4 CUMANN na nGAEDHEAL AND THE ABBEY THEATRE, 1922–32

1 Plunkett was also a prominent member of the Irish Dominion League (June 1919–November 1921) and regarded the treaty as the League's 'conspicuous vindication' (see NLI Ir 94,109: 24).

2 'I believe we shall have a very poor chance of receiving such help unless we offer in return to do all we can to create and foster a Gaelic Theatre. . . . We should also promise to give special performances on occasion when asked to do so by the Government and should accept suggestion from them as to the plays given on such occasions' (quoted in Hogan and Burnham 1992: 94).

3 Oliver St John Gogarty's *Blight*, an earlier play about slum conditions in Dublin, was performed at the Abbey Theatre in December 1917 (Hogan and Burnham 1984: 108–13).

4 P. S. O'Hegarty was Secretary of the Department of Posts and Telegraphs from 1922 to his retirement in 1944.

5 The earliest and still by far the most comprehensive critique of O'Casey's representation of Irish politics can be found in Deane 1985: 108–22. For a discussion of O'Casey's own political background and that of his plays, see Greaves 1979.

6 George O'Brien (Professor of Economics at University College, Dublin) belonged to the O'Higgins wing of Cumann na nGaedheal (Regan 1999: 244) and served as the government's appointee on the Abbey Theatre's board of directors from 1925 until 1927. His specific objection was that Rosie Redmond's role as a prostitute had been given unnecessary emphasis in the play (see Hogan and Burnham 1992: 282).

5 FIANNA FÁIL AND 'THE NATION'S PRESTIGE', 1932–48

1 The text of a motion proposed by Fianna Fáil Inc. reads as follows:

> the money of Irish taxpayers [should] be not spent to subsidize the Abbey Theatre in Dublin, which is responsible for presenting these plays with their filthy language, their drunkenness, murder, and prostitution, and holding up the Irish character generally to be scoffed at and ridiculed by people of other races.
>
> (NA: S 6284 A)

2 As Dunphy's history of Fianna Fáil points out, de Valera had conducted successful fund-raising tours of the United States in the late 1920s and had helped establish a network of Fianna Fáil support committees. This, and the outcome of the Sinn Féin Funds case of 1927 when money donated to Dáil Éireann in the early phase of national independence was diverted to de Valera who used the money to launch the *Irish Press* in 1931, had a major role in contributing to Fianna Fáil electoral successes (Dunphy 1995: 80–1).

3 Kevin Rockett makes a similar observation in relation to the government's attitude to the cinema in the early 1930s. Eight months before becoming Minister for Finance, Seán MacEntee called for a redirection in film policy away from a dependence on Anglo-American corporations (Rockett 1988: 51).

4 Patrick J. Little (1884–1963) was the Fianna Fáil TD for Waterford and had a longstanding interest in theatre and the arts. He served as the theatre critic for *New Ireland* during the war of independence and was

editor of *An Phoblacht*. Little went on to become Minister for Posts and Telegraphs (1933–9) and the first chairperson of the Arts Council of Ireland, An Chomhairle Ealaion (Kennedy n.d.: 41).

5 My thanks to Dr John Devitt of the Mater Dei Institute, Dublin for helpful advice and information on the relationship between modernism and the Catholic Church.

6 I am grateful to my colleague, Professor Hubert McDermott, for information on Dr Murphy's academic career in Galway.

6 IRISH THEATRE AND MODERNIZATION, 1948–68

1 For information on the McCaughey hunger strike, I am indebted to Caoilfhionn Ní Bheacháin's unpublished MA dissertation, and to Ms Ní Bheacháin's on-going doctorate research into the narratives of Irish republican prisoners in the 1940s.

2 Morash comments as follows: 'Post-utopian "realism," and not visionary illusion, was to be the aesthetic of a National Theatre which Blythe enlisted in a double-edged campaign in the cultural sphere both to defeat the IRA and to end Partition' (Morash 2000: 75).

7 NATIONAL THEATRES IN NORTHERN IRELAND, 1922–72

1 Part of this chapter was previously published as 'Theatre and Cultural Politics in Northern Ireland: The *Over the Bridge* Controversy, 1959' in *Éire-Ireland* 30, April 1996: 76–93. I am grateful to Philip O'Leary, Senior Consulting Editor of *Éire-Ireland* for permission to republish.

2 For a general history of theatre in Northern Ireland see Bell 1972, and Byrne 1997. Archives relating to the Northern Drama League are held in the Public Records Office of Northern Ireland.

3 I am grateful to Kathryn Mullan for drawing my attention to Lynch's play.

4 The *Derry Journal* was banned for six months in 1940 (Farrell 1976: 94).

5 Northern Ireland's parliament had been in operation since 1921 and, from November 1932, was housed in a new chamber at Stormont Castle in Belfast.

6 The representative in question was Patrick J. Little.

7 See also 'Belfast Cinema may Become a State Theatre', *Belfast Telegraph* 18 September 1956: 1; 'The Living Theatre,' *Belfast Telegraph*, 20 September 1956: 4 and 'Group Puts Case Against New Theatre', *Belfast Newsletter*, 24 September 1956: 5.

8 O'Leary and McGarry note that after the introduction of universal suffrage by the British Labour government in 1945, the Stormont Parliament responded by passing 'its own representation of the People Act (1946) which retained most of the old system, but restricted it

further by removing the franchise from lodgers who were not rate-payers' (O'Leary and McGarry 1993: 129).

9 A prompt script of *The Bonefire* is contained in the Linen Hall Library, Belfast. I am most grateful to the Librarian, John Gray, and to the Linen Hall Library theatre archivist, Ms Ophelia Byrne, for granting me access to this play.

10 The rehearsal copy of *Over the Bridge* is available in the Sam Thompson Archive in Belfast City Library. I am very grateful to Mrs May Thompson for permission to cite from this archive and from the rehearsal copy of *Over the Bridge*. I would also like to acknowledge the kind assistance of Mr Roger Dixon, former Irish and Local Studies Librarian with Belfast Public Libraries.

11 Sir James Craig (Viscount Craigavon) was Prime Minister of Northern Ireland from 1921 to 1940.

12 Such interaction was almost exclusively a middle-class phenomenon. Lee points out that whereas the proportion of Catholics at Queen's University Belfast increased dramatically between 1955 and 1959, there was a worsening of the differential in employment between Catholics and Protestants (Lee 1989: 413–14).

13 For a detailed history of the Lyric Players Theatre, see O'Malley 1988 and O'Malley 1988b, and Boyd and O'Malley 1979. For access to the original records of the early years of the Lyric and related documents, I am indebted to Dr and Mrs O'Malley. These documents are now part of the Lyric Theatre O'Malley Archive at NUI, Galway.

14 Entitled 'Appeal to Leaders of Nationalist Opinion in the North', Blythe's 1957 memorandum urges nationalists to accept partition by transferring their 'nationalist zeal and energy from the political to the cultural field and labour there with increasing diligence for basic Irish Nationality (Blythe 1997: 4–5): 'They should support Irish language classes, literary, historical and antiquarian societies with an Irish outlook; Anglo-Irish and Gaelic dramatic companies; Gaelic choirs: Irish dancing competitions . . .' (Blythe 1997: 5). A copy of this memorandum exists in the Lyric Theatre O'Malley archive at NUI, Galway, and was published, with Dr O'Malley's response, in 1997.

8 NATIONAL THEATRE AND THE POLITICAL CRISIS IN NORTHERN IRELAND, 1968–92

1 I am most grateful to the Abbey Theatre's archivist, Mairead Delaney and to Kathleen Barrington (actor, Abbey Theatre) for information on this point.

2 Several of the Judge's speeches in the play echo or quote directly from Lord Widgery's published report. For example, the third of the Judge's conclusions in Friel's play – 'There is no reason to suppose that the soldiers would have opened fire if they had not been fired on first' (Friel

1974: 95) – is a direct quotation from Widgery's *Report of the Tribunal*. The same is true for several phrases used by Friel's Judge when outlining the parameters of the inquiry at the beginning of Act I: 'this tribunal of inquiry . . . *is essentially a fact-finding exercise*' (Friel 1974: 18), 'our only function is *to form an objective view of the events which occurred*', and 'it is none of our function to *make moral judgements*' (Friel 1974: 18–19; italics indicate direct quotations from Widgery 1972). (See also Winkler 1982: 413–15.)

3 Boyd's *The Assassin* has an earlier date (29 September 1969), but was first performed in Dublin.

4 For a detailed analysis of the early years of the Field Day Theatre Company, see Richtarik 1994.

5 I am most grateful to Professor Ann Dooley (University of Toronto) for information on this point.

GLOSSARY AND ABBREVIATIONS

ACNI = Arts Council of Northern Ireland
CEMA = Council for the Encouragement of Music and the Arts
Dáil Éireann = the lower house of the Parliament of Ireland
ILT = Irish Literary Theatre
IRA = Irish Republican Army
NTS = National Theatre Society
Oireachtas = the legislature of Ireland
RIC = Royal Irish Constabulary
RUC = Royal Ulster Constabulary
Seanad Éireann = the Senate (or upper house) of the Parliament of Ireland
Saorstát Éireann = Irish Free State
Taoiseach = Prime Minister (literally, leader)
TD = Teachta Dála (Member of the Dáil)
UIL = United Irish League

WORKS CITED

Archive and manuscript sources

Abbey Theatre Archive
ACNI   Arts Council of Northern Ireland (Council Archives)
Desart papers   Memoirs of Ellen, Countess of Desart, Desart Court, Co. Kilkenny
DAA   Dublin Archdiocesan Archives (McQuaid papers)
CLB   Central Library, Belfast (Sam Thompson Archive)
LHB   Linenhall Library, Belfast Theatre Archive
Northern Ireland Political Collection (NIPC)
NA   National Archives, Dublin
   S files   President of the Executive Council/Department of Taoiseach
   F files   Department of Finance
   AG files   Office of the Attorney General
   ARCA   Arts Council files
NLI   National Library of Ireland, Dublin
NUIG   National University of Ireland, Galway, Special Collections Department, James Hardiman Library (Lyric Theatre O'Malley Archive)
NYPL   New York Public Library, Henry W. and Albert A. Berg Collection, (Lady Gregory Archive)
Plunkett   Plunkett Foundation, Oxford (Sir Horace Plunkett Archive)
PRONI   Public Record Office of Northern Ireland, Belfast
   AC files   Arts Council of Northern Ireland
   CAB files   Files of the Northern Ireland cabinet
   ED files   Department of Education, Northern Ireland
SIUC   Southern Illinois University, Carbondale, Special Collections Department, Morris Library (Lennox Robinson Archive)
TCD   Trinity College Dublin, Manuscripts Room (Pike Theatre Archive)
UCC   University College Cork, Special Collections Department (Daniel Corkery Archive)
UCD   Archives Department, University College Dublin (Ernest Blythe Collection)

Newspaper and periodical sources

An Phoblacht/Republican News
Belfast Telegraph
Catholic Bulletin
Church of Ireland Gazette
Derry Journal
L'Européen
Freeman's Journal
Hibernia
Ireland Today
Irish Homestead
Irish Independent
Irish Monthly
Irish Nation
Irish Press
Irish Statesman
Irish Times
Kilkenny Journal
Leader
Nation
New Ireland
Observer
Sinn Féin
Spark
Standard
Star
Sunday Times
United Irishman

Printed reports

Reports of the Arts Council/An Chomhairle Ealaíon
Reports of the Arts Council of Northern Ireland
CEMA Annual Reports
Dáil Reports
Northern Ireland Hansard

References and bibliography of published sources

Agnew, P. (1980) '"Talking to Ourselves": Brian Friel Talks to Paddy Agnew', *Magill* 4 (3): 59–61.
Althusser, L. (1982) *For Marx*, translated by E. Brewster, London: Venso editions/NLB.

Arensberg, C. and Kimball, S. (1940) *Family and Community in Ireland*, Cambridge, Mass.: Harvard University Press.

Aretxaga, B. (1997) *Shattering Silence: Women, Nationalism, and Political Subjectivity in Northern Ireland*, Princeton, NJ: Princeton University Press.

Arnold, B. (1982) 'Politics and the Arts in Ireland – the Dáil Debates', in F. Litton (ed.) *Unequal Achievement: The Irish Experience 1957–1982*, Dublin: Institute of Public Administration.

Ashtown, Lord (1907) *The Unknown Power Behind the Irish Nationalist Party: Its Present Work and Criminal History*, London: Swann Sonnenschein.

Barrett, W. (1895) 'Irish Drama', *New Ireland Review*, March–August: 38–41.

Behan, B. (1956) *The Quare Fellow*, London: Methuen.

—— (1992) *The Letters of Brendan Behan*, E. H. Mikhail (ed.), Montreal and Kingston: McGill-Queen's University Press.

Bell, D. (1998) 'Modernising History: The Realpolitik of Heritage and Cultural Tradition in Northern Ireland', in D. Miller (ed.) *Rethinking Northern Ireland: Culture, Ideology and Colonialism*, London & New York: Longman.

Bell, S. H. (1972) *The Theatre in Ulster: A Survey of the Dramatic Movement in Ulster from 1902 to the Present Day*, Dublin: Gill & Macmillan.

Bew, P. (1987) *Conflict and Conciliation in Ireland 1890–1910: Parnellites and Radical Agrarians*, Oxford: Clarendon Press.

—— (1994) *Ideology and the Irish Question: Ulster Unionism and Irish Nationalism, 1912–1916*, Oxford: Clarendon Press.

Bew, P., Gibbon, P. and Patterson, H. (1995) *Northern Ireland 1921–1994: Political Forces and Social Classes*, London: Serif.

Bew, P., Hazelkorn, E. and Patterson, H. (1989) *The Dynamics of Irish Politics*, London: Lawrence & Wishart.

Birmingham, G. A. (1912) *The Lighter Side of Irish Life*, London and Edinburgh: Foulis.

Blythe, E. (1997) *An Appeal to Leaders of Nationalist Opinion in Northern Ireland: A Memorandum Written in 1957 by Ernest Blythe (Earnan de Blagdh) With a Response by Dr Pearse O'Malley*, Dublin: Elo Publications.

—— (1965) *The Abbey Theatre*, Dublin: The National Theatre Society Ltd.

Bowen, K. (1983) *Protestants in a Catholic State: Ireland's Privileged Minority*, Kingston and Montreal: McGill-Queen's University Press.

Boyd, J. (1981) *Collected Plays, Volume 1: The Flats, The Farm, Guests*, Dundonald: Blackstaff Press.

Boyd, J. and O'Malley, M. (eds) (1979) *A Needle's Eye*, Belfast: Lyric Player's Theatre.

Boylan, T. A. and Foley, T. P. (1992) *Political Economy and Colonial Ireland: The Propagation and Ideological Function of Economic Discourse in the Nineteenth Century*, London: Routledge.

Breen, R., Hannan, D. F., Rottman, D. B. and Whelan, C. T. (1990) *Understanding Contemporary Ireland: State, Class and Development in the Republic of Ireland*, London: Macmillan.

Brewer, J. D. with Higgins, G. I. (1998) *Anti-Catholicism in Northern Ireland, 1600–1998*, London: Macmillan Press Ltd.

Brown, T. (1985) *Ireland: A Social and Cultural History 1922–1985*, London: Fontana.

—— (1991) 'The Counter-Revival, 1930–60: Drama', *The Field Day Anthology of Irish Writing*, Volume 3, S. Deane (ed.), Derry: Field Day Publications.

—— (1995) 'Ireland, Modernism and the 1930s', in P. Coughlan and A. Davis (eds) *Modernism and Ireland: The Poetry of the 1930s*, Cork: Cork University Press.

Bryson, L. and McCartney, C. (1994) 'Clashing Symbols? A Report on the Use of Flags, Anthems and Other National Symbols in Northern Ireland', Belfast: the Institute of Irish Studies.

Buckland, P. (1966–7) 'The Southern Irish Unionists, the Irish Question and British Politics 1906–14', *Irish Historical Studies* 15: 228–55.

—— (ed.) (1973) *Irish Unionism 1885–1923: A Documentary History*, Belfast: Her Majesty's Stationery Office.

Butler, H. (1986) *Escape from the Anthill*, Mullingar: Lilliput Press.

Byrne, O. (1997) *The Stage in Ulster from the Eighteenth Century*, Belfast: The Linen Hall Library.

Byrne, S. (1956) *Design for a Headstone*, Dublin: Progress House.

Carney, J. (1986) *The Playboy and the Yellow Lady*, Dublin: Poolbeg.

Carroll, P. (1948) *Two Plays:* The Wise Have Not Spoken *and* Shadow and Substance, London: Macmillan.

Cathcart, R. (1984) *The Most Contrary Region: the BBC in Northern Ireland, 1924–84*, Belfast: Blackstaff Press.

Clark, B. K. and Ferrar, H. (1979) *The Dublin Drama League 1918–1941*, Dublin: Dolmen Press.

Colum, P. (1926) *The Road Round Ireland*, New York: Robert M. McBride & Company.

—— (1957) 'The Nation and the State', *Threshold* 1(3): 33–9.

Connolly, S. (1987) 'Dreaming History: Brian Friel's Translations', *Theatre Ireland*, 13: 42–4.

Coogan, T. P. (1970) *The IRA*, London: Fontana/Collins.

Corkery, D. (1931) *Synge and Anglo-Irish Literature*, Cork: Cork University Press.

—— (1924) 'The Literature of Collapse', unpublished manuscript (UCC: UC/DC/422).

Cronin, M. and Regan, J. M. (2000) 'Introduction: Ireland and the Politics of Independence 1922–49, New Perspectives and Re-considerations', in M. Cronin and J. M. Regan (eds) *Ireland: The Politics of Independence, 1922–49*, London: Macmillan Press.

Crotty, R. (1966) *Irish Agricultural Production: Its Volume and Structure*, Cork: Cork University Press.

Curran, C. P. (1970) *Under the Receding Wave*, Dublin: Gill & Macmillan.

D.83222 (1945) *I Did Penal Servitude* (with a Preface by Séan O'Faolain), Dublin: Metropolitan Publishing.

D'Alton, I. (1973) 'Southern Irish Unionism: A Study of Cork Unionists, 1884–1914', *Transactions of the Royal Historical Society* 23 (January): 71–88.

D'Alton, L. (1970) *This Other Eden: A Play in Three Acts*, Dublin: P. J. Bourke.

Dash, S. (1972) *Justice Denied: A Challenge to Lord Widgery's Report on 'Bloody Sunday'*, New York: The Defense and Education Fund of the International League for the Rights of Man.

Davis, T. C. (1992) 'Indecency and Vigilance in the Music Halls', in T. C. Davis and R. Foulkes (eds) *British Theatre in the 1890s: Essays on Drama and the Stage*, Cambridge: Cambridge University Press.

Deane, S. (1985) *Celtic Revivals: Essays in Modern Irish Literature 1880–1890*, London: Faber and Faber.

——(1992) 'Foreword', in E. McCann with M. Shiels and B. Hannigan, *Bloody Sunday in Derry: What Really Happened*, Dingle: Brandon.

De Blacam, A. (1935) 'What do we owe the Abbey', *Irish Monthly* 63: 191–200.

Deevy, T. (1939) *Three Plays: Katie Roche, King of Spain's Daughter, The Wild Goose*, London: Macmillan.

Deutsch, R. and Magowan, V. (1974) *Northern Ireland 1968–73: A Chronology of Events*, Volume 1, 1968–71, Belfast: Blackstaff Press.

Dowling, J. (1937) 'The Abbey Theatre Attacked I', *Ireland To-Day* 2 (1) (January) 35–43.

Doyle, B. (1986) 'The Invention of English', in R. Colls and P. Dodd (eds) *Englishness: Politics and Culture 1880–1920*, London: Croom Helm.

Dudley Edwards, R. (1990) *Patrick Pearse: The Triumph of Failure*, London: Gollancz.

Dunleavy, G. W. (1987) 'The Pattern of the Threads: The Hyde Gregory Friendship', in A. Saddlemyer and C. Smythe (eds) *Lady Gregory Fifty Years After*, Gerrards Cross, Bucks: Colin Smythe.

Dunphy, R. (1995) *The Making of Fianna Fáil Power in Ireland 1923–1948*, Oxford: Clarendon Press.

Dwyer, T. R. (1991) *De Valera: The Man and the Myths*, Dublin: Poolbeg.

Editorial (1894) *New Ireland Review* 1 (March–August) 1–3.

English, R. (1994) ' "Cultural Traditions" and Political Ambiguity', *Irish Review* 15 (Spring): 97–106.

—— (1996) 'The Same People with Different Relatives? Modern Scholarship, Unionists and the Irish Nation', in R. English and G. Walker (eds) *Unionism in Modern Ireland: New Perspectives on Politics and Culture*, Dublin: Gill & Macmillan.

Ervine, St J. G. (1988) *Selected Plays of St. John Ervine*, chosen and with an introduction by J. Cronin, Gerrards Cross: Colin Smythe.

Everson, I. G. (1966) 'Young Lennox Robinson and the Abbey Theatre's First American Tour (1911–1912)', *Modern Drama* 1: 74–89.

Fallon, B. (1998) *An Age of Innocence: Irish Culture 1930–1960*, Dublin: Macmillan.

Fallon, G. (1936) 'Those Dramatists of Inish', *Irish Monthly* 64: 615–23.

—— (1937) 'Drama of Lost Leaders', *Irish Monthly* 65: 769–76.

—— (1938) 'Words on a National Theatre', *Irish Monthly* 66: 631–38.

—— (1948) 'The Abbey Theatre Speaks', *The Irish Monthly* 76: 88–92.

Farquharson, D. (1997) 'Brian Friel', in B. Shrank and W. Demastes (eds) *Irish Playwrights, 1880–1995: A Research and Production Sourcebook*, Westport, CT: Greenwood Press.

Farrell, M. (1941) 'Drama in Ulster Now', *The Bell* 2 (4): 82–8.

—— (1976) *Northern Ireland: The Orange State*, London: Pluto Press.

—— (1986) *The Apparatus of Repression*, Derry: Field Day Theatre Company.

Farrelly, P. V. (1996) *600 Years of Theatre in Kilkenny, 1366–1996*, Kilkenny: P. V. Publications.

Fay, F. J. (1970) *Towards a National Theatre: The Dramatic Criticism of Frank J. Fay*, edited and with an introduction by R. Hogan, Dublin: The Dolmen Press.

Fay, G. (1958) *The Abbey Theatre: Cradle of Genius*, London: Hollis and Carter.

Ferrar, H. (1973) *Denis Johnston's Irish Theatre*, Dublin: The Dolmen Press.

FitzPatrick, D. (1977) *Politics and Irish Life, 1913–21*, Dublin: Gill & Macmillan.

—— (1975) 'W. B. Yeats in Seanad Éireann', in R. O'Driscoll and L. Reynolds (eds) *Yeats and the Theatre*, Toronto: Maclean Hunter Press.

Foley, C. (1992) *Legion of the Rearguard: The IRA and the Modern Irish State*, London: Pluto Press.

Foster, R. F. (1988) *Modern Ireland 1600–1972*, London: Penguin.

—— (1993) *Paddy and Mr Punch: Connections in Irish and English History*, London: Allen Lane.

—— (1997) *W. B. Yeats: A Life: I The Apprentice Mage 1865–1914*, Oxford: Oxford University Press.

Frazier, A. (1990) *Behind the Scenes: Yeats, Horniman, and the Struggle for the Abbey Theatre*, Berkeley, CA: University of California Press.

—— (2000) *George Moore: 1852–1933*, London and New Haven: Yale University Press.

Friel, B. (1974) *The Freedom of the City*, London: Faber and Faber.
—— (1965) *Philadelphia, Here I Come!*, London: Faber and Faber.
—— (1972) 'Plays Peasant and Unpeasant', *Times Literary Supplement*, 17 March 1972: 305–6.
—— (1979) *The Enemy Within*, with introductory notes by the author and T. Kilroy, Dublin: Gallery Books.
—— (1981) *Translations*, London: Faber and Faber.
—— (1983) 'Extracts from a Sporadic Diary', in Coogan, T. P. (ed.) *Ireland and the Arts: A Special Issue of the Literary Review*, London: Namara, 56–51.
Gailey, A. (1987) *Ireland and the Death of Kindness: The Experience of Constructive Unionism 1890–1905*, Cork: Cork University Press.
Gibbons, L. (1996) *Transformations in Irish Culture*, Cork: Cork University Press.
—— (1994) 'Do you have to be Irish to be Irish?', *The Tribune Magazine* (23 October 1994): 17.
Girvan, B. (1989) *Between Two Worlds: Politics and Economy in Independent Ireland*, Dublin: Gill & Macmillan.
Gray, J. (1985) 'Field Day Five Years On', *The Linenhall Review* 2(2): 8.
Greaves, C. D. (1979) *Sean O'Casey: Politics and Art*, London: Lawrence and Wishart.
Greene, D. H. and Stephens, E. M. (1961) *J. M. Synge 1871–1909*, New York: Collier Books.
Gregory, A. (ed.) (1901) *Ideals in Ireland*, London: Unicorn.
Gregory, A. (1893) *A Phantom's Pilgrimage; or Home Ruin*, London: W. Ridgeway.
—— (1912) 'The Irish Theatre and the People', *The Yale Review* January: 181–91.
—— (1913a) *Our Irish Theatre*, New York and London: G. P. Putnam's Sons, The Knickerbocker Press.
—— (1913b) 'Synge', *The English Review* March: 556–66.
—— (1974) *Seventy Years: Being the Autobiography of Lady Gregory*, C. Smythe (ed.) Gerrards Cross: Colin Smythe.
—— (1978) *Lady Gregory's Journals, Volume I, Book 1–29, 10th October 1916 to 24 February 1925*, Gerrards Cross: Colin Smythe.
—— (1995) *Selected Writings*, edited with an introduction by L. McDiarmid and M. Waters, London: Penguin.
Grene, N. (1999) *The Politics of Irish Drama: Plays in Context from Boucicault to Friel*, Cambridge: Cambridge University Press.
Gwynn, S. (1901) 'The Irish Literary Theatre and its Affinities', *Fortnightly Review*, 1055–8.
Hanley, B. (1999) 'Poppy Day in Dublin in the '20s and '30s', *History Ireland* 7(1), (Spring): 5–6.
Heaney, S. (1980) '. . . English and Irish', Review of *Translations*, by Brian Friel, *The Times Educational Supplement*, 24 October 1980, 1199.

Hickey, D and Smith, G. (eds) (1972) *A Paler Shade of Green*, London: Leslie Frewin.

Hickey, M. P. (1898) 'Nationality according to Thomas Davis – I', *New Ireland Review* 9 (May): 129–38.

Hill, J. (1998) *Irish Public Sculpture: A History*, Dublin: Four Courts Press.

Hogan, R. (1967) *Seven Irish Plays: 1946–1964*, Minneapolis, MN: University of Minnesota Press.

Hogan, R. and Burnham, R. (1984) *The Modern Irish Drama Volume 5: The Art of the Amateur 1916–1920*, Portlaoise: Dolmen Press.

—— (1992) *The Years of O'Casey, 1921–1926: A Documentary History*, Gerrards Cross: Colin Smythe.

Hogan, R. and Kilroy, J. (1975) *The Irish Literary Theatre 1899–1901*, Dublin: Dolmen Press.

—— (1976) *The Modern Irish Drama II: Laying the Foundations 1902–1904*, Dublin: Dolmen Press.

Hogan, R. and O'Neill, M. J. (1967) *Joseph Holloway's Abbey Theatre: A Selection from his Unpublished Journal 'Impressions of a Dublin Playgoer'*, Carbondale, IL: Southern Illinois Press.

Hogan, R., Burnham, R. and Poteet, D. P. (1979) *The Rise of the Realists, 1910–1915*, Volume 4, *The Modern Irish Drama: A Documentary History*, Dublin: Dolmen Press.

Howes, M. (1996), *Yeats's Nations: Gender, Class and Irishness*, Cambridge: Cambridge University Press.

Hunt, H. (1979) *The Abbey: Ireland's National Theatre 1904–1979*, Dublin: Gill & Macmillan.

Inglis, B. (1962) *West Briton*, London: Faber and Faber.

Johnston, D. (1960) *The Collected Plays of Denis Johnston*, Volume 2, London: Jonathan Cape.

—— (1977) *The Dramatic Works of Denis Johnston: Volume 1*, Toronto: Macmillan of Canada.

Kavanagh, P. (1950/1984) *The Story of the Abbey Theatre* (1984 facsimile reprint), Orono, ME: University of Maine.

Keane, J. B. (1961) *Many Young Men of Twenty: A Play with Music*, Dublin: Progress House.

Kearney, R. (1983) 'Language Play: Brian Friel and Ireland's Verbal Theatre', *Studies* 62: 20–56.

Kennedy, B. P. (n.d.) *Dreams and Responsibilities: The State and the Arts in Independent Ireland*, Dublin: Arts Council of Ireland.

—— (1992) 'The Failure of the Cultural Republic: Ireland 1922–39', *Studies* (Spring): 14–22.

Kennedy, D. (1946) 'The Ulster Region and the Theatre', *Lagan* 4: 51–5.

—— (1953) 'The Theatre in Ulster: 1944–1953', *Rann* 20 (June): 39–42.

Kennedy, K. A. (1986) *Ireland in Transition: Economic and Social Change since 1960*, Cork: Mercier Press.

Kenny, P. D. (1907) *The Sorrows of Ireland*, Dublin: Maunsel.

Keogh, D. (1986) *The Vatican, The Bishops and Irish Politics 1919–39*, Cambridge: Cambridge University Press.

——(1995) *Ireland and the Vatican: The Politics and Diplomacy of Church–State Relations, 1922–1960*, Cork: Cork University Press.

Kettle, T. (1937) *The Day's Burden: Studies, Literary & Political and Miscellaneous Essays*, Dublin: Browne and Nolan.

Kiberd, D. (1995) *Inventing Ireland*, London: Jonathan Cape.

Kilroy, J. (1971) *The 'Playboy' Riots*, Dublin: Dolmen Press.

Kirkland, B. (1996) *Literature and Culture in Northern Ireland Since 1965: Moments of Danger*, London: Adison-Wesley Longman.

Kotsonouris, M. (1994) *Retreat from Revolution: The Dáil Courts 1920–24*, Dublin: Irish Academic Press.

Kostick, C. (1996) *Revolution in Ireland: Popular Militancy 1917 to 1923*, London: Pluto Press.

Kruger, L. (1992) *The National Stage: Theatre and Cultural Legitimation in England, France and America*, Chicago, IL: University of Chicago Press.

Lacy, S. (1995) *British Realist Theatre: The New Wave and its Context 1956–1965*, London: Routledge.

Lee, J. J. (1989) *Ireland 1912–1985: Politics and Society*, Cambridge: Cambridge University Press.

Lewis-Crosby, J. E. C. (1959) 'CEMA and the Professional Theatre', *Threshold* 3(2): 21–3.

Litton, F. (1982) *Unequal Achievement: The Irish Experience 1957–1982*, Dublin: Institute of Public Administration.

Longley, E. (1985) 'Poetry and Politics in Northern Ireland', *The Crane Bag* 9(1): 28–9.

Loudan, J. (1946) 'Ulster and a Subsidized Theatre', *Lagan* 4: 57–62.

Louvre, A. (1992) 'The New Radicalism: the Politics of Culture in Britain, America and France, 1956–73', in B. Moore-Gilbert and J. Seed (eds) *Cultural Revolution? The Challenge of the Arts in the 1960s*, London: Routledge.

Lynch, L. D. (1936) *Heritage: A Drama in Three Acts* (with a foreword by Very Rev. J. McShane), Omagh: the North-West of Ireland Printing and Publishing.

Lyons, F. S. L. (1948) 'The Irish Unionist Party and the Devolution Crisis of 1904–5', *Irish Historical Studies* 6 (21) (March): 1–22.

MacBride, M. G. (1992) *The Gonne–Yeats Letters 1893–1938*, A. MacBride White and A. N. Jeffares (eds), New York: Norton.

McCartney, D. (1994) *W. E. H. Lecky: Historian and Politician 1838–1903*, Dublin: Lilliput Press.

McCarthy, M. J. F. (1902) *Priests and People in Ireland*, London: Hodder and Stoughton.

—— (1912) *The Irish Revolution: Vol. 1. The Murdering Time, from the Land League to the First Home Rule Bill,* Edinburgh and London: William Blackwood.

McCormack, W. J. (2000) *Fool of the Family: A Life of J. M. Synge,* London: Weidenfeld & Nicolson.

MacDermott, E. (1998) *Clann na Poblachta,* Cork: Cork University Press.

McDiarmid, L. (1994) 'Augusta Gregory, Bernard Shaw, and the Shewing-Up of Dublin Castle,' *PMLA* 109(1) (January): 26–44.

McDowell, R. B. (1970) *The Irish Convention 1917–18,* London: Routledge.

—— (1997) *Crisis and Decline: The Fate of Southern Unionists,* Dublin: Lilliput Press.

MacEoin, U. (1997) *The I.R.A. in the Twilight Years,* Dublin: Argenta Publications.

McGuinness, F. (1986) *Observe the Sons of Ulster Marching Towards the Somme,* London: Faber and Faber.

—— (1988) *Carthaginians and Baglady,* London: Faber and Faber.

McHugh R. (1951) 'Tradition and the Future of Irish Drama,' *Studies* 40: 469–74.

—— (1972) 'Foreword' to 1972 edition of A. Gregory, *Our Irish Theatre: A Chapter of Autobiography by Lady Gregroy,* Gerrards Cross: Colin Smythe.

McIntosh, G. (1999) *The Force of Culture: Unionist Identities in Twentieth-Century Ireland,* Cork: Cork University Press.

Macken, W. (1956) *Twilight of a Warrior: A Play,* London: Macmillan.

MacMahon, B. (1949) 'The Bugle in the Blood: A Tragedy in 3 Acts', unpublished manuscript NLI, Ms 29,339.

MacNamara, B. (1928) 'The Master', unpublished manuscript, NLI: MS 2,107.

Malone, E. (1929) *The Irish Drama,* London: Constable.

Markiewicz, C. (1934) *Letters of Constance Markiewicz,* London: Longman.

Maume, P. (1993) *'Life that is Exile': Daniel Corkery and the Search for Irish Ireland,* Belfast: The Institute of Irish Studies.

Maxwell, D. E. S. (1973) *Brian Friel,* Lewisburg, Penn.: Bucknell University Press.

—— (1973) 'Imagining the North: Violence and the Writers', *Éire-Ireland* 8(2): 91–107.

—— (1991) 'Irish Drama 1899–1929: The Abbey Theatre', in S. Deane (ed.) *The Field Day Anthology of Irish Writing,* Volume II, Derry: Field Day Publications.

Mengel, H. (1986) *Sam Thompson and Modern Drama in Ulster,* Frankfurt am Main: Verlag Peter Lang.

Miller, J. H. D. (1907) *Clericalised Education in England: A Plea for Popular Control (Part 1),* Dublin: Maunsel & Co.

Minihan, J. (1977) *The Nationalization of Culture: The Development of State Subsidies to the Arts in Great Britain,* London: Hamish Hamilton.

Mitchell, A. (1995) *Revolutionary Government in Ireland: Dáil Éireann 1919–22*, Dublin: Gill & Macmillan.

Molloy, M. J. (1998) *Selected Plays of M. J. Molloy*, chosen and introduced by R. O'Driscoll, Gerrards Cross: Colin Smythe.

Moore, G. (1911/1985) *Hail and Farewell: Ave, Salve, Vale*, Gerrards Cross: Colin Smythe.

Moore, G. and Martyn, E. (1995) *Selected Plays of George Moore and Edward Martyn*, chosen, with an introduction by D. B. Eakin and M. Case, Gerrards Cross: Colin Smythe.

Morash, C. (2000) ' "Something's Missing": Theatre and the Republic of Ireland Act, 1949', in R. Ryan (ed.) *Writing in the Republic: Literature, Culture, Politics in the Republic of Ireland, 1949–1999*, London: Macmillan.

Moran, D. P. (n.d.) *The Philosophy of Irish Ireland*, Dublin: James Duffy.

Morison, E. E., Blum, J., Chandler, A. D. Jr and Rice, S. (eds) (1954) *The Letters of Theodore Roosevelt*, Volume VII, 'The Days of Armageddon 1909–1914', Cambridge, MA, Harvard University Press.

Morrisey, T. J. (1983) *Towards a National University: William Delany SJ (1835–1924)*, New Jersey: Humanities Press.

Mulhare, E. *et al.* (1958) Letter to the Editor, *Evergreen Review* 6: 184–5.

Munck, R. (1985) *Ireland: Nation, State, and Class Struggle*, Boulder, CO: Westview.

Murphy, T. (1989) *A Whistle in the Dark and Other Plays*, London: Methuen.

Murray, C. (1981) 'Review of *Translations*, by Brian Friel', *Irish University Review* 11(2) (Autumn): 238–9.

——(1997) *Twentieth-Century Irish Drama: Mirror up to Nation*, Manchester: Manchester University Press.

Murray, P. (2000) *Oracles of God: The Roman Catholic Church and Irish Politics 1922–37*, Dublin: University College Dublin Press.

Murray, T. C. (1956) *Spring: A Play in One Act*, Dublin: James Duffy.

——(1998) *Selected Plays of T. C. Murray*, chosen and introduced by R. A. Cave, Gerrards Cross: Colin Smythe.

New Ireland Forum (1984) 'Report', Dublin: The Stationery Office.

Ní Bheacháin, C. (1997) 'The Lost Republicans: Seán McCaughey and the Disruption of Free State Narrative', unpublished MA dissertation; MA in Culture and Colonialism, National University of Ireland, Galway.

Nic Shiubhlaigh, M. (1955) *The Splendid Years*, Dublin: James Duffy.

O'Brien, J. V. (1982) *'Dear, Dirty Dublin': A City in Distress*, Berkeley, CA: University of California Press.

——(1976) *William O'Brien and the Course of Irish Politics, 1881–1918*, London: University of California Press.

O'Callaghan, M. (1984) 'Language, nationality and cultural identity in the Irish Free State, 1922–7: the *Irish Statesman* and the *Catholic Bulletin* reappraised', *Irish Historical Studies* 24(94) (November): 226–45.

—— (1994) *British High Politics and a Nationalist Ireland: Criminality, Land, and the Law under Forster and Balfour*, Cork: Cork University Press.

—— (1997) 'Franchise Reform, First-Past-the-Post, and the Strange Case of Unionist Ireland', *Parliamentary History* 16(1): 85–106.

O'Casey, S. (1960) *Three Plays: Juno and the Paycock, The Shadow of a Gunman* and *The Plough and the Stars*, London: Macmillan.

—— (1975) *The Letters of Sean O'Casey 1910–41, Volume 1* (edited by D. Krause), London: Cassell.

O'Donnell, F. H. (1899) *Souls for Gold!: Pseudo-Celtic Drama in Dublin*, London: Nassau Press.

O'Donovan, J. (n.d.) 'The Less We Are Together', unpublished manuscript, NLI: MS 29,423–29,424.

O'Dowd, L., Rolston, B. and Tomlinson, M. (1982) 'From Labour to the Tories: The Ideology of Containment in Northern Ireland', *Capital and Class* 18: 72–90.

O'Faolain, S. (1941) [The Bellman] 'Meet Mr Blythe', *The Bell* 3(1) (October): 49–56.

—— (1943) 'Gaelic: the Truth', *The Bell* 5(5) (February): 335–40.

O'Hegarty, P. S. (1998) *The Victory of Sinn Féin: How It Won It and How It Used It*, Dublin: University College Dublin Press.

O'Leary, B. and McGarry, J. (1993) *The Politics of Antagonism: Understanding Northern Ireland*, London: Athlone Press.

O'Malley, C. (1988) *A Poet's Theatre*, Dublin: Elo Press.

O'Malley, M. (1988b) *Never Shake Hands with the Devil*, Dublin: Elo Press.

O'Neill, M. (1999) *The Abbey at the Queen's: The History of the Irish National Theatre in Exile*, Nepean, Ontario: Borealis Publications.

—— (1964) *Lennox Robinson*, New York: Grosset Dunlap.

O'Riordan, M. (1906) *Catholicity and Progress in Ireland*, London: Kegan Paul, Trench, Trubner.

Ó Siadhail, P. (1993) *Stair Dhrámaíocht na Gaeilge 1990–1970*, Indreabhán, Galway: Cló Iar-Chonnachta.

O'Sullivan, S. (1988) 'How our Theatre Began', in E. H. Mikhail (ed.) *The Abbey Theatre: Interviews and Recollections*, Totawa, NJ: Barnes and Noble.

O'Tuathaigh, M. A. G. (1996) 'Decolonization, Identity and State-Formation: The Irish Experience', in González, R. (ed) *Culture and Power: Institutions*, Barcelona: PPU.

O'Toole, F. (1985) 'Brian Friel: The Healing Art', *Magill*, January: 31.

—— (1987) *The Politics of Magic: The Work and Times of Tom Murphy*, Dublin: Raven Arts Press.

Paseta, S. (1999) *Before the Revolution: Nationalism, Social Change and Ireland's Catholic Élite 1879–1922*, Cork: Cork University Press.

Pethica, J. (1996) (ed.) *Lady Gregory's Diaries 1892–1902*, Gerrards Cross: Colin Smythe.

Phoenix, E. (1994) *Northern Nationalism: Nationalist Politics, Partition, and the Catholic Minority in Northern Ireland 1890–1940*, Belfast: Ulster Historical Foundation.

Plunkett, H. (1905) *Ireland in the New Century, with an Epilogue in Answer to Some Critics*, London: John Murray.

—— (1908) *Noblesse Oblige: An Irish Rendering*, Dublin: Maunsel.

—— (1907) 'Editorial', *The Irish Homestead*, 19 January 1907: 45–6

Raymond, R. J. (1983) 'De Valera, Lemass and Irish Economic Development: 1933–1948', in J. P. O'Carroll and J. A. Murphy (eds) *De Valera and His Times*, Cork: Cork University Press.

Regan, J. M. (1999) *The Irish Counter-Revolution 1921–1936: Treatyite Politics and Settlement in Independent Ireland*, Dublin: Gill & Macmillan.

Richtarik, M. (1994) *Acting Between the Lines: The Field Day Theatre Company and Irish Cultural Politics 1980–1984*, Oxford: Clarendon Press.

Rockett, K., Gibbons, L. and Hill, J. (1988) *Cinema and Ireland*, Syracuse, NY: Syracuse University Press.

Robinson, L. (1911) *Two Plays: Harvest, The Clancy Name*, Dublin: Maunsel.

—— (1951) *Ireland's Abbey Theatre: A History 1899–1951*, London: Sidgwick and Jackson.

—— (ed.) (1939a) *The Irish Theatre: Lectures Delivered during the Abbey Theatre Festival held in Dublin in August 1938*, New York: Haskell House [reprint].

—— (1939b) *Killycreggs at Twilight*, London: Macmillan.

—— (1982) *Selected Plays of Lennox Robinson*, chosen with an introduction by C. Murray, Gerrards Cross: Colin Smythe.

Rottman, D. and P. O'Connell (1982) 'The Changing Social Structure of Ireland', in F. Litton (ed.) *Unequal Achievement: the Irish Experience 1957–1982*, Dublin: Institute of Public Administration.

Saddlemyer, A. (ed.) (1982) *Theatre Business: the Correspondence of the First Abbey Theatre Directors: William Butler Yeats, Lady Gregory and J. M. Synge*, Gerrards Cross: Colin Smythe.

Schrank, B. and W. Demastes (eds) (1997) *Irish Playwrights 1880–1995: A Research and Production Sourcebook*, London: Greenwood Press.

Shiels, G. (1942) *The Rugged Path and The Summit: Plays in Three Acts*, London: Macmillan.

Showalter, E. (1990) *Sexual Anarchy: Gender and Culture at the Fin de Siècle*, Harmondsworth: Penguin.

Simpson, A. (1962) *Beckett and Behan and a Theatre in Dublin*, London: Routledge & Kegan Paul.

Sitzmann, Fr. Marion (1975) *Indomitable Irishery Paul Vincent Carroll: Study and Interview*, Salzburg: Universitat Salzburg, Institut für Englische Sprache und Literatur.

Swift, C. (1985) *Stage by Stage*, Dublin: Poolbeg.

WORKS CITED

Synge, J. M. (1968) *Collected Works, Volume III: Plays Book 1*, A. Saddlemyer (ed.), London: Oxford University Press.

—— (1982a) *Collected Works, Volume II: Prose*, A. Price (ed.), Gerrards Cross: Colin Smythe.

—— (1982b) *Collected Works, Volume IV: Plays Book II*, A. Saddlemyer (ed.), Gerrards Cross: Colin Smythe.

—— (1983) *The Collected Letters of John Millington Synge Volume One: 1871–1907* A. Saddlemyer (ed.), Oxford: Clarendon Press.

—— (1984) *The Collected Letters of John Millington Synge* Volume Two 1907–1909, A. Saddlemyer (ed.), Oxford: Clarendon Press.

Talbot-Crosbie, F. (1906) *After the Battle, or Imperial Home Rule: What Is It?* Dublin: Hodges Figgis.

Thompson, S. (1970) *Over the Bridge*, S. Parker (ed.), Dublin: Gill & Macmillan.

Tobin, F. (1984) *The Best of Decades: Ireland in the Nineteen Sixties*, Dublin: Gill & Macmillan.

Townshend, C. (1983) *Political Violence in Ireland: Government and Resistance since 1848*, Oxford: Oxford University Press.

Varley, A. (1994) *The Politics of Agrarian Reform: the State, Nationalists, and the Agrarian Question in the West of Ireland*, Michigan, IN: UMI.

Viswanathan, G. (1987) 'The Beginnings of English Literary Study in British India', *Oxford Literary Review* 9(1–2): 2–26.

Waldron, J. (1992) *Maamtrasna: The Murders and the Mystery*, Dublin: Edmund Burke.

Ward, A. J. (1969) *Ireland and Anglo-American Relations 1899–1921*, London: Weidenfeld and Nicolson.

Ward, M. (1989) *Unmanageable Revolutionaries: Women and Irish Nationalism*, London: Pluto Press.

—— (1990) *Maud Gonne: A Life*, London: Pandora Press.

Welch, R. (1999) *The Abbey Theatre 1899–1999: Form and Pressure*, Oxford: Oxford University Press.

West, T. (1986) *Horace Plunkett: Co-operation and Politics, An Irish Biography*, Gerrards Cross: Colin Smythe.

Whitaker, T. K. (1958) *Economic Development*, Dublin: The Stationery Office.

White, J. (1967) 'Social Life in Ireland', in F. MacManus (ed.) *The Years of the Great Test*, Cork: The Mercier Press.

—— (1975) *Minority Report: The Anatomy of a Southern Irish Protestant*, Dublin: Gill & Macmillan.

Whyte, J. H. (1971) *Church and State in Modern Ireland 1923–1970*, Dublin: Gill & Macmillan.

Widgery, Lord (1972) *Inquiry into the Events on 30 January which led to the Loss of Life in Connection with the Procession in Londonderry on that Day: Report of the Tribunal appointed under the Tribunal of Inquiry (Evidence) Act 1921*, London: Her Majesty's Stationery Office.

Williams, R. (1979) 'The Arts Council', *Political Quarterly* 50(2): 157–71.
—— (1993) 'Culture is Ordinary', in A. Gray and J. McGuigan (eds) *Studying Culture: an Introductory Reader*, London: Edward Arnold.

Wilmot, S. (1968) 'The Gaelic Theatre', *Éire-Ireland: A Journal of Irish Studies* 3(2): 63–71.

Winkler, E. H. (1982) 'Reflections on Derry's Bloody Sunday in Literature', in H. Kosok (ed.) *Studies in Anglo-Irish Literature*, Bonn: Bouvier.

Woodman, K. (1985) *Media Control in Ireland 1923–1983*, Galway: Officina Typographica, Galway University Press.

Wyndham, G. (1915) *Letters of George Wyndham 1877–1913*, compiled by Guy Wyndham, 2 volumes, Edinburgh: T. and A. Constable.

Yeats, W. B. (1901) 'Windlestraws', *Samhain: Edited for the Irish Literary Review by W. B. Yeats*, Sealy, Bryers & Walker.

—— (1903) *Samhain: An Occasional Review edited by W. B. Yeats*, London: Sealy Bryers & Walker.

—— (1911) *Synge and the Ireland of his Time*, Dundrum, Ireland: Cuala Press.

—— (1953) *The Collected Plays of W. B. Yeats*, London: Macmillan.

—— (1954) *The Letters of W. B. Yeats*, Allan Wade (ed.), London: Hart Davis.

—— (1955) *Autobiographies: Memories and Reflections*, London: Macmillan.

—— (1962) *Explorations*, New York: Collier Books.

—— (1972) *Memoirs: Autobiography – First Draft, Journal*, Donoghue (ed.), London.

—— (1975) Frayne, J. P. and Johnson, C. (eds) *Uncollected Prose of W. B. Yeats: Volume 2, Reviews, Articles and Other Miscellaneous Prose*, London: Macmillan.

—— (1977) *The Collected Poems of W. B. Yeats*, London: Macmillan.

—— (1986) *The Collected Letters of W. B. Yeats: Volume One 1865–1895*, J. Kelly and E. Domville (eds), Oxford: Clarendon Press.

—— (1994) *The Collected Letters of W. B. Yeats: Volume Three 1901–1904*, J. Kelly and R. Schuchard (eds), Oxford: Clarendon Press.

—— (1997) *The Collected Letters of W. B. Yeats: Volume Two 1896–1900*, W. Gould, J. Kelly, and D. Toomey (eds), Oxford: Clarendon Press.

INDEX

Abbey Theatre 54, 59, 186; ambivalent attitude towards Synge 67; anti-imperialist themes at 73–5; as artistic/literary institution 39; broadening of repertoire 126–35; claim to national status 136–8; condemned as 'Cromwellian' 98; controversial tours of USA 70–1, 118–20, 121; and death of hunger striker 84; and the Easter Rising (1916) 78–9; end of first of phase 64–5; Endowment Fund set up 65–6; establishment of 1–2; foreign tours by 67, 68, 70–1, 114–16, 118–20, 121; funding withdrawn from 64–5; and generation of tourist revenue 149; Golden Jubilee 149–50; government subsidy for 88–90, 95–9; importance to Sinn Féin 81–2; Irish language policy 89, 137–8, 139–40, 152; and irrelevance of nationalistic concerns 159–65; lack of political hostility/satire in plays at 121; and maintaining balance between unionist/republican politics 81–5; national accountability of 121–30, 144; as national institution 71, 80–5, 88, 96, 97–8, 120; and nationalist ideology 61, 62, 104–11, 131–6; new sense of purpose 90–1; and plays of rural backwardness/national introspection 71–3, 75, 79–80; political aspects 4–5; political function/role 4; praise for 60;

pro-British position of 77–8; protest concerning 139, 140, 141, 142–3; public lectures (1918) 80–1; rebuilt 191–2; relationship with Fianna Fáil 114–21, 134–5; relationship with Irish intellectual life 126; self-conscious renewal of 145; support for 125–6; support for the government 102; and tradionalist/individualist theme 102–4; unadventurous character of plays at 113–14; and use of sexuality as determinant of identity 98–102

Abbey Theatre Advisory Committee 126

Abbey Theatre Playwright's Workshop 191

Aberdeen, Lord 62, 66

Act of Union (1800) 9, 12

Acting 32, 98, 105, 119

AE, *see* Russell, George 21, 87

agricultural co-operative movement 2

Agriculture and Technical Instruction, Department of 12, 70

All the King's Horses (McDonnell) 161

Althusser, Louis 183

An Comhar Drámuíochta 89–90, 135

An Phoblacht/Republican News 219

An Tóstal 149, 157

Andrew, J. H. 211

Anglo–Irish Agreement (1985) 220, 223

Anglo–Irish Free Trade Agreement (1965) 158

Anglo–Irish Treaty (1921) 83, 87, 138

INDEX

Cadogan, Lady 7
Carney, Frank 149
Carney, J. 57
Carroll, Paul Vincent 115, 131, 136, 137
Carson, Edward 69, 75
Casadh an tSúgáin (Hyde) 31–2, 41, 56
Castletown, Lord 14
Catchpenny Twist (Parker) 202, 209
Cathcart, R. 178
Cathleen Listens In (O'Casey) 90
Cathleen ni Houlihan (Yeats and Gregory) 18, 41, 136; gender roles in 32–4; nationalist sentiments 32–4
Catholic Action movement 131
Catholic Bulletin 98, 120, 125
'The Catholic Theory of the State' (Abbey Theatre lecture, 1918) 80
Catholic University 22, 47–8
Catholic Young Men's Societies (CYMS) 127, 131
Catholics *see* Roman Catholics
Celticism 8–9, 14, 15, 16–17, 52
censorship 119–20, 156–8, 192
Censorship Board 116, 155, 157
Censorship of Publications (1929) 113
Childers, Erskine 143, 144
Church of Ireland 108, 124, 157–8
Church of Ireland Gazette 59
Church Street (Robinson) 121, 124
Churchill, Lord Randolph 62
Citizen's Defence Committee 205–7
Civil Authorities (Special Powers) Act (1922) 174
civil rights movement 185, 192, 203–9
Clann na Gael 57, 70, 71
Clann na Poblachta 142, 143, 145
Clark, K. and Ferrar, H. 83
Clarke, Austin 185
clericalism 47–50, 128–9, 157–8
Clongownians 97
Clonmel Nationalist 209
The Closed Door (Reid) 202
Colley, George 192
Collins, Michael 3, 85, 86
colonialism 13–14, 24–5
Colum, Padraic 37, 123, 125, 130, 187, *see also* named plays
Committee of Inquiry on Evil Literature (1926) 116

Congested Districts Board (1890) 3, 76
Connolly, James 27, 43, 78
Connolly, Seán 211
Conservative Party 2, 11
Corkery, Daniel 93, 96, 122–4, 136
Costello, John A. 144
Council for the Encouragement of Music and the Arts (CEMA) 166, 188; and *Bonefire* controversy 177–8; and control of the theatre 172–4; establishment of 168; and playing of British National Anthem 170–2; and promotion of national/regional culture 169
The Countess Cathleen (Yeats) 82, 191; muted controversy surrounding 6, 9–10, 21–9, 35–6; première of 6–9
Craig, Sir James, Viscount Craigavon 184, 231
Crimes Act 47
Cronin, John 228
Cronin, M. and Regan, J. M. 87
Crossland, Anthony 153
Crotty, R. 74
Cuffe, The Hon. Otway 17
Cultural Relations Committee 144
culture 11, 209; Abbey Theatre's role in refining of Irish 82; Catholic debate on 35–6; folk practices 18; national aspects 143–4; nationalist views on 122–6; Northern Ireland controversies 169–90; two meanings of 113
Cumann na nGaedheal (political party) 4, 105, 107, 109, 114, 116, 118, 127, 130, 138, 229; benevolence towards southern unionist minority 96–7; period of reconciliation for 87; support for Abbey Theatre 89–90, 95–9
Cumann na nGaedheal (Theatre Company) 38, 39, 40, 44
Curran, C. P. 24, 225
Cusack, Cyril 6, 151

Dáil Éireann 91–2
Daily Express (Dublin) 10, 12, 25
Daily Independent 66
D'Alton, Louis 145, 146, 147, 149, 150

Dance Halls Act (1935) 134
Dash, S. 195
Davis, T. C. 18
Davis, Thomas 26
'The Day of the Rabblement' (Joyce) 7
De Blacam, Aodh 123, 124, 136
De Freyne, Lord French 38, 47
De Valera, Eamon 3, 84, 105, 114,
    115, 116, 191; relationship with
    Abbey Theatre 118–21, 129–30
'Deaf Mutes for Ireland' (Synge) 52–3
The Death of Humpty Dumpty (Reid)
    202
Deevy, Teresa 133–4
Delaney, Mairead 231
Derry 194, 196, 200, 201, 211
Derry Journal 167
Desart, Ellen, Countess of 17, 97, 225
Design for a Headstone (Byrne) 145,
    150–1, 153
Devitt, John 230
Devlin, Bernadette 193, 200
Diarmuid and Grania (Yeats and Hyde)
    31
Digges, Dudley 40
Dignan, Bishop 140–1
Dillon, John 28, 68
Dineen, Fr. 30
Diplock courts 195
Dixon, Roger 231
Donleavy, J. P. 158
Doolan, Lelia 194
Dooley, Ann 232
Dougherty, Sir James 62
Dowling, John 135–6
Doyle, B. 11
drama *see* literature/drama relationship
Drama at Inish (Robinson) 112–15,
    121, 132
The Drums of Father Ned (O'Casey)
    157
Dublin Castle 68
Dublin Chamber of Commerce 76
Dublin Corporation 76
Dublin Drama League 83
Dublin Horse Shows, the Royal 62, 97,
    128
Dublin Literary Society 77
Dublin Metropolitan Police 59
Dublin Municipal Gallery 228

Dublin Theatre Festival 154, 155,
    157–8, 161
Dufferin and Ava, Frederick Temple
    Hamilton, Marquess of 15
Dunphy, R. 117, 135, 141, 229
Dunraven, Earl of 2, 3, 54, 62
Dwyer, T. R. 116, 118, 119

Easter Rising (1916) 78–9, 95, 99
'Economic Movement in Ireland'
    (1898 lecture by Plunkett) 12
Edinburgh Festival 177
education 6, 47–9, 68–9, 88, 185
Education Act (1944) 185
Education, Ministers of 88, 172, 174
Edward VII 64
Edwards, Hilton 105
Edwards, Ruth Dudley 32
Eglinton, John 50
Éire-Ireland 150
Eliot, T. S. 169
Ellen, Countess of Desart *see* Desart,
    Ellen, Countess of
Ellis, James 179, 183, 184
Emigration 76, 72, 75, 104, 108, 141,
    147, 149, 162–5
Emmett, Robert 10, 106
Empire Theatre (Belfast) 179
The End House (Tomelty) 137–8, 167
The Enemy Within (Friel) 160–1
English, R. 221
English Stage Company 152
Ervine, St John 74–5; dismissed from
    Abbey Theatre 78–9; insensitivity to
    nationalists 77–8
Esmonde, Sir Thomas Grattan 96
Eucharist Congress (1932) 117
Evening Herald 127
Everson, I. G. 68
Evil Literature, Committee of Inquiry
    on (1926) 116

Fallon, Brian 114, 126
Fallon, Gabriel 135
Falsely True (Redmond) 67, 74
familism 104
Farrell, Michael (political analyst) 142,
    174, 192, 230
Farrell, Michael (writer for *The Bell*)
    125, 167, 170

INDEX

Murray, C. 22–3, 113, 160, 218
Murray, P. 174
Murray, T. C. 68, 71, 72, 73, 74, 80, 83, 102, 103, 123, 125, 136

National Council for the Federation of the Catholic Young Men's Societies 127
'National Drama – A Farce' (Synge) 53
National Dramatic Society 32
National League 13
National Library of Ireland 9, 10, 26
National Library Scheme 10
National Literary Society 78
'National Taste' (Abbey Theatre lecture, 1918) 81
National Theatre Act (1949) 143, 169
national theatre movement, aesthetic autonomy of 44; and constructive unionism 2–3, 21; and development of individuality 53; as different from English critical norm 43–4; differing views on 3–4; as educative/ prestigious 8–9, 27; flourishing of 160–5; Gregory's book on 68–71; and Irish nationalism 29–30, 44–50; literary component 10–12, 16–18, 27; as nationalist self-confidence vs national self-interrogation 37, 41, 44; political support for 8, 9–10, 21–2; post-war modernization process 144–65; as project of recuperation 18–19; as rehearsal for/anticipation of future political organization 37; struggle to determine ideological function of 38–41, 43–4; Yeats's views on 35–6
National Theatre Society, Limited (NTS) 2; anti-republicanism of 145–51; combative stance of 131–6; critical challenges to repertoire 123–6; cultural/social role 80–3, 191–2; and dangerousness of political militancy 73–5; decline in standards 139–40; educational role of 88; effect of Sinn Féin on 81; emergence of 3–5, 60; increase in subsidy for 129; as Irish institution 79–81, 138; maintains balance between unionists/Sinn Féin 83–5;

Monday night lectures 80–1; political dilemmas 194–5, 202; registered as limited 66; reinvigoration of repertoire 90–1; relationship with Fianna Fáil 114–21; rural plays 72–3; and theatre as only site of theatrical representation 95; theatrical support for government 107–11; Yeats/Gregory support for 60, 61–2, *see also* Irish National Theatre Society
'National Unionism' 14, 21
National Unity 185
National Vigilance Association 18, 82
nationalism, nationalists 33, 44; effect of Bloody Sunday on 195–6; and government rhetoric 193; imprisonment of 47; and individual conscience 28; irrelevance of 159–60; objections to Synge's plays 40; and political/social conciliation 13–15; support of Abbey Theatre policy 67–8; and support for ILT 19–21; and suppression of nationalist politics/culture 167–8, 169, 171–3; tactless speech concerning 77–8; theatrical representations of 102, 104–11, 205–9; views on Irish culture 122–6
The New Gossoon (Shiels) 102
New Ireland 81, 82
New Ireland Forum (1983–4) 220, 221
New Ireland Review 9, 14, 15
New Theatre Group 185
New Unionist Party 14
Newman Society (Queen's University, Belfast) 185
Ní Bheacháin, C. 143, 230
Nic Shiubhlaigh, M. 3, 32, 33–4
Noh plays 83
North (Heaney) 202
Northern Drama League 166
Northern Ireland, political crisis in 191–203; theatre/politics relationship in 166–90; theatrical representations 203–9, 210–23

257

politics, and advocates of conciliation
11–15; changed circumstance 66–7;
and crisis of legitimacy 141–3;
devolution proposed 54–5; and
economic liberalization policy 150,
154–5, 158–9; and individualism
12, 27, 50, 53; Irish problem 2–3;
and the landlord class 7, 13, 15, 16;
need for self-criticism/self-
examination 49; and places for
unionist minority in senate 96–7;
reasonable approach to 87; and
reforming agenda 12–14, 86–7;
republican sentiments 145–51; and
self-nationalization 13–15; widening
of consensus 76–7
Poor Law 140
Prisoners' Dependents' Fund 84
prisons, prisoners 141–2, 153, 209
'Prisons and Prisoners in Ireland'
(Labour Party pamphlet) 142
Protestants 48, 60, 69, 118; boycott of
businesses 155; and education 6;
plight of 44; theatrical
representations 131–2, 204–5, 208,
221–3
Public Order Act (1951) 174
Public Safety Act (1931) 109

Quadragesimo Anno encyclical 140
The Quare Fellow (Behan) 153–4
Queen's Royal Theatre (Dublin) 106
Queen's University (Belfast) 48, 172,
185
Quinn, John 61, 69

Radio Free Belfast 203–7
Radio Telefís Éireann (RTE) 142, 196
Ray, R. J. 73
Raymond, R. J. 141, 158, 159
Recess Committee (1896) 12
Reddin, G. N. 98
Redmond, Johanna 67, 74, 227
Redmond, John 3, 14, 49, 59, 66, 68,
76, 130, 225
Reform Act (1884–5) 13
'The Reform of the Theatre' (Yeats) 44
Regan, J. M. 89, 93, 95, 97, 98, 109
Reid, Graham 202
'Release the Prisoners' 142, 145

Report of the Tribunal (Widgery Report)
198
Republicanism, theatrical
representations 145–51
The Revolutionist (MacSwiney) 84, 85
Richtarik, M. 232
Riders to the Sea (Synge) 50–1
The Righteous are Bold (Carney) 149
The Rising of the Moon (Gregory) 18
Robinson, Lennox 71–2, 74, 75, 80,
88–9, 90, 98, 107, 108, 111, 121,
124, 125, 130, 131–2, 138, 145, *see
also* named plays
Rockett, K. 229
Roman Catholics 76, 114, 204–5; and
conflict with state 155; controversial
portrayal by Yeats 21–9; and debate
on culture/religion 35–6; and
education 6, 68; and government
legitimacy 141; interaction with
state institutions 185; literary
ignorance of 45; moral vigilante
powers given to 134; (non)theatrical
representations 125–9, 128–9,
150–1; in northern Ireland 184–5,
187–8; oppositions to 47–53, 54–5;
rise of populist 117; satirization of
104–5; and Synge's plays 53–4;
theatre controversies 157–8;
theatrical representations 21–9,
52–4, 104–5, 184–5, 221–3;
university for 47–9, 53
Roosevelt, Theodore 69, 70–1
Rose Tattoo Appeal Fund 156
The Rose Tattoo (Williams) 155–7
Ross, Sir John 47–8, 60, 66
Royal Court theatre (London) 152
Royal Dublin Horse Show 97
Royal Dublin Society 69, 96
Royal Ulster Constabulary (RUC) 204
Royal University 21, 23, 25–6, 36
The Rugged Path (Shiels) 69, 137, 150,
167
Ruskin, John 30
Russell, George 21, 58
Ryan, Fred 50

Salvation Army 18
Samhain 44
Saddlemyer, A. 38